Learn Unity for 2D Game Development

Alan Thorn

Apress·

Learn Unity For 2D Game Development

ISBN-13 (pbk): 978-1-4302-6229-9

ISBN-13 (electronic): 978-1-4302-6230-5

President and Publisher: Paul Manning
Lead Editor: Michelle Lowman
Developmental Editor: Kate Blackham
Technical Reviewer: Marc Schärer
Editorial Board: Steve Anglin, Mark Beckner, Ewan Buckingham, Gary Cornell, Louise Corrigan,
    Morgan Ertel, Jonathan Gennick, Jonathan Hassell, Robert Hutchinson, Michelle Lowman,
    James Markham, Matthew Moodie, Jeff Olson, Jeffrey Pepper, Douglas Pundick, Ben Renow-Clarke,
    Dominic Shakeshaft, Gwenan Spearing, Matt Wade, Tom Welsh
Coordinating Editor: Anamika Panchoo
Copy Editor: Linda Seifert
Compositor: SPi Global
Indexer: SPi Global
Artist: SPi Global
Cover Designer: Anna Ishchenko

Distributed to the book trade worldwide by Springer Science+Business Media New York, 233 Spring Street, 6th Floor, New York, NY 10013. Phone 1-800-SPRINGER, fax (201) 348-4505, e-mail orders-ny@springer-sbm.com, or visit www.springeronline.com. Apress Media, LLC is a California LLC and the sole member (owner) is Springer Science + Business Media Finance Inc (SSBM Finance Inc). SSBM Finance Inc is a Delaware corporation.

For information on translations, please e-mail rights@apress.com, or visit www.apress.com.

Apress and friends of ED books may be purchased in bulk for academic, corporate, or promotional use. eBook versions and licenses are also available for most titles. For more information, reference our Special Bulk Sales–eBook Licensing web page at www.apress.com/bulk-sales.

Any source code or other supplementary materials referenced by the author in this text is available to readers at www.apress.com. For detailed information about how to locate your book's source code, go to www.apress.com/source-code/.

Contents at a Glance

Contents

About the Author

Alan Thorn is a freelance game developer and author with over 12 years of industry experience. He is the founder of London-based game studio, Wax Lyrical Games, and is the creator of the award-winning adventure game Baron Wittard: Nemesis of Ragnarok. He has worked freelance on over 500 projects worldwide, including games, simulators, and kiosks and augmented reality software for game studios, museums, and theme parks. He has spoken on game development at universities throughout the UK, and is the author of ten books on game development, including *Teach Yourself Games Programming, Unity 4 Fundamentals* and the highly popular *UDK Game Development*. More information on Alan Thorn and his start-up Wax Lyrical Games can be found at: http://www.alanthorn.net and http://www.waxlyricalgames.com.

About the Technical Reviewer

Marc Schärer is an interactive media software engineer creating cutting edge interactive media experiences for training, education, and entertainment purposes on mobile, desktop, and web platforms for customers through his company Gayasoft (`http://www.gayasoft.net`) located in Switzerland.

His technology of choice is Unity, which he has been using since its early days (2007).

Marc Schärer has a strong background in the 3D graphics, network technology, software engineering, and interactive media field. Originally growing into it when starting to program at the age of 11, he built upon it later when studying Computer Science and Computational Science and Engineering at Swiss Federal Institute of Technology Zurich.

This knowledge found, among other projects, usage in Popper (`http://www.popper.org`), an interactive 3D behavioral research platform by Harvard developed by Gayasoft, powered by Unity, Mathlab, and the ExitGames Photon.

With the popularity of serious games, Marc's and Gayasoft's focus is on researching options and technologies for the next generation of interactive and immersive experiences, through state of the art AR and VR technologies (Vuforia, Metaio, Oculus Rift) and new innovative input technologies (Razer Hydra, STEM, Leap Motion, Emotive Insight).

Acknowledgments

This book would not have been possible without many people, connected in different ways. There are too many to list here individually. But special mention must go to the Apress team: Michelle Lowman, Anamika Panchoo, Kate Blackham, Linda Seifert, Kumar Dhaneesh, Jim Markham, and anybody else I've omitted here. In addition, I'd like to thank Marc Schärer for ensuring the technical correctness of my work.

Introduction

If you log on to any online or mobile marketplace for games and browse the titles offered today, it's likely that the majority of games you see will be 2D and not 3D. If you think back over the relatively short history of video games, or if you listen to industry veterans talking about their inspirations and favorite games, it's likely that the titles most mentioned are in the 2D style. Frequently listed titles in these video game reminiscences include: Pacman, Sonic the Hedgehog, Super Mario Brothers, Tetris, Lemmings, Arkanoid, Bejewelled, Angry Birds, Plants vs Zombies, Minesweeper, Civilization, Donkey Kong, and Sim City. Despite the manifold differences between all these landmark games both new and old, they all share the common ingredient of 2D-ness; of having their graphics presented in a very specific way that doesn't rely on three-dimensional space. In short, the 2D style represents some of the most well-known titles in video games history, and it is also a style that is alive and well today. 2D games are not simply stuck in history. They are not a thing of the past; a phenomena that has been and is no longer relevant to the demands of contemporary gamers. Rather, these games represent a significant and lucrative segment of the video game market. Often has been the occasion when this or that learned person has predicted the demise of 2D games, and yet despite all such predictions 2D games have not gone away. This resilience and strength is due primarily to their general popularity, charm, and stylistic simplicity. 2D imparts a classical and timeless feel to games that is technically difficult to replicate by alternative means. For this reason, gamers keep coming back to the 2D style and find within it new ways of enjoying games and experiencing richness. 2D games today play an especially prominent role in two large market areas, and for different reasons. These markets are the casual game market and the so-called "indie games market." In the casual games market, including games such as Mystery Case Files and Bejewelled, the 2D style is deployed to add an accessible "pick up and play" feel that does not require the user to learn any complex control systems or to concern themselves with moving a camera in 3D space. The Indie Games market, including games such as Retro City Rampage and Super Meat Boy, have used the 2D style to create a retro or old school feel that is popular to a general audience.

Whatever your reasons for wanting to make 2D games, 2D games offer a positive and promising future for game developers willing to embrace them with both hands and a with a can-do frame of mind. 2D provides a means of creating games that differ from the norm and from the mainstream, and for creating very distinctive flavors that all have a special kind of classical vibe. This book can help you get started with confidence on that road to making successful 2D games. There are many routes leading to that destination. Some are longer than others, and some are smoother than others.

Some involve the use of many tools and some involve the use of only a few. This book and the method presented here involve the use of the Unity Engine, and the pathway I discuss is intended to be a smooth and reliable one that will have relevance for most 2D games conceivable.

What Is This Book About?

This book is first and foremost a practical guide to making 2D games using the Unity Engine. That statement however, while informative, requires further clarification. First, the book is practical. This means most of the chapters are hands-on and project-based, as opposed to theoretical and abstract. They require you to be seated at the computer with the tools installed, and to follow along with me, step by step, as I do things. Practical does not mean however that I offer no explanations or detailed discussions about what is happening, and nor does it mean I simply expect you to repeat what I do verbatim in parrot-fashion. I do explore deeper theories, concepts, and ideas. But these are all presented around practical and real-world projects, which are the main focus, so that you can see how these ideas relate to game development in the field. The benefit of this is that you get to learn the theory and practice at the same time. You don't only understand what it is happening and why, but you can apply that understanding to your own games.

Second, this book is about 2D (two-dimensional) games. It is not about 3D or 2.5D games, or even about 4D games! But what does that really amount to in practice? What does it really mean to say 2D? After all, if every game is ultimately shown to the gamer on a flat, plane-like surface called a monitor, then isn't every game really 2D? Surely, the only truly 3D game is one shown as a holographic image or in some kind of virtual reality helmet as seen in cyberpunk movies? Well; that is true in the strictest sense possible. But 2D is used here in this book, and generally in the games industry, in only a conventional and relative sense. It refers to any video game whose graphics and gameplay mechanics do not use 3D space. It refers to games whose worlds exist on a mathematical plane with an X axis and a Y axis, but not a Z axis. In a 2D game, characters typically move up and down and left and right, but they do not move closer to and further from the camera. In a 2D game, the gamer cannot rotate the camera freely; they cannot look around in all dimensions to see objects and things from different angles and perspectives, as they can in a first person shooter game. What makes a game 2D is largely about the limitations and restrictions it places on gamers and developers: the third dimension of space (depth) is off limits so to speak. There are, as we shall see, exceptions and caveats to this general rule, but the basic idea holds that 2D games are called 2D because objects in those games live on a 2D plane.

Third, this book explains how to make 2D games using the Unity Engine specifically, as opposed to other viable tools such as GameMaker Studio or Construct 2 or Stencyl, among others. The latest version of Unity at the time of writing this book is version 4, but what is written here will most likely hold true for many later versions to come. The Unity Engine is sometimes informally named Unity 3D, and the "3D" part of the title reflects the main focus of the Unity Engine and the types of games it is typically used to make. Unity is primarily geared toward 3D games. It offers light-mapping tools, real-time lighting, particle systems, 3D coordinate spaces and more—all these are concepts associated with 3D and 3D games. For this reason, developing 2D games in Unity poses some challenges and hurdles that are not to be found when developing 2D games in many of the competing tools. This is because Unity was not designed primarily with 2D games in mind. But despite this, Unity is an attractive tool for 2D game development because it offers deployment to many popular gaming platforms and also the ability for developers to integrate many of its 3D features into their 2D games to make them look and feel even better.

In short, then this book details not only how to make 2D games, but how to make them in Unity while overcoming the hurdles we will face by trying to use a 3D engine to make 2D games. Further, it also explores how to optimize our games and assets so they can perform better on mobile devices. Not better in the sense of performing faster on mobiles than on desktop counterparts, but better in the sense of our games performing faster than they might do if we did not take certain precautions. In addition, this book also covers, as it inevitably must, a whole range of ideas, tips, techniques, and workflows that are useful life-skills generally and which are transferrable not only to non-2D games, but to practically any project-based work, whether game development or not.

Who Is This Book For?

Every technical book is apparently written with a target audience in mind. That is, it is written for a specific type of reader. Essentially, this means that when writing this book I, the author, must make certain assumptions about you, the reader. These assumptions are not about whether you might be male or female, or tall or short, or American or French, or like cheese or ice cream. Rather, the assumptions are about all the book-relevant topics that I think you will know about already, before even starting to read this title. The point of this is to help the reader get the best possible book they were hoping for. It is to ensure I write a book about only the subject-matter you are truly interested in, and also that I present it in a language that is both accessible and concise. Making assumptions and judgments about others is not something I like doing as a general rule, but it's something I must do here for the book to be possible. I'll write these assumptions in the form of five character profiles, as given here; though they don't represent real people. Three describe typical readers of this book. They're characters I've created to illustrate the skills and knowledge I think a reader of this book should have already. And the final two characters are people I think may not be suited to this book. I do recommend however that these profiles are not taken too seriously. If you happen not to match any of the profiles, or if you match to the latter two, then it certainly does not mean that you will inevitably not benefit from this book. These profiles are intended only as a guide and it is no part of my purpose to dissuade any person from reading this book who is keen to learn and succeed. Game development is infinitely knowable stuff, and nobody that has ever lived was born a game developer; everybody had to begin somewhere.

This book is probably for you if you match any of the following profiles:

- *Rosalind*—Rosalind is a second-year university student of game development. She has worked both in a team and alone making sample games in Unity. She knows the basics of the engine for 3D games. She can import meshes, arrange them in scenes, and create basic script files. She is looking to take her knowledge to the next level by creating 2D games with Unity.

- *Arnold*—Arnold is an independent game developer who has been working with the tools Unity, GIMP, and Blender for several years now. He's created a range of games for PC, Mac, and Mobiles, but all of them have been 3D games. He's tried creating 2D games by taking advice here and there, and following tutorials here and there, piecing together as much information as he can. But his 2D games never seem quite right: his textures look wrong and he doesn't feel in control of the process. He's looking for guidance about a solid workflow.

- *Roger*—Roger has been making 2D games for a long time in tools such as GameMaker Studio, Construct2, Stencyl, SDL, GameSalad, and others. He's looking to switch from these tools to the Unity engine for his next project. He's hasn't used Unity specifically before, but he is familiar with using other 3D engines and is familiar with the basic concepts of 3D, including meshes, vertices, edges, faces, and UV mapping. He is now keen to get started at continuing with this 2D game business in Unity.

This book may not be for you if you match any of the following profiles:

- *Caitlin*—Caitlin has no experience with game development, though she wants to get started because she thinks it'll be an easy career move. She has never even run Unity. She heard about it from a friend. She believes the best place to start is by learning how to use it for making 2D games.

- *Pierre*—Pierre is an experienced artist, game designer, and level designer but he really dislikes coding. He has recently decided to start up his own games company but wants to make 2D games in a visual way without having to code.

> **Note**   If you want to learn the basics of Unity before proceeding with this title, then I recommend any of the following resources: *Beginning 3D Game Development with Unity 4* by Sue Blackman, *Unity 4 Fundamentals* by Alan Thorn, or the *Complete Beginner's Guide to Unity for Game Development* by Alan Thorn (Online Video Course).
>
> In addition, if you'd rather avoid coding altogether (like Pierre in the preceding list), there are still development options for you in Unity. Specifically, you can use the Unity add-on PlayMaker (`http://www.hutonggames.com/`), which is a Visual Scripting tool. That being said, this book will make extensive use of traditional code-based scripting.

Why Is This Book Necessary?

If you're not already convinced about the value of this book, I anticipate this may be for one of two reasons. First, some might think this book unnecessary because there're so many engines and libraries already available and dedicated to 2D games that it's not really valuable to show how a 3D engine like Unity can be made to do the same thing. Why not just use the other engines instead and leave it there? There are two main lines of response to this that I want to present: one negative and one positive. The negative response is about existing users of Unity who do not want to switch away if possible: many game developers may have already invested in the Unity engine for making their 3D games, and while they have considered the possibility of purchasing alternative tools for 2D development, they would rather find a more cost-effective method for re-using the familiar Unity tools to create their 2D games as well. This book will demonstrate in each chapter how the familiar Unity tools can be used in new ways for a 2D workflow. The positive response is about non-Unity users looking around for new 2D development tools. Here, there are positive reasons to recommend Unity as a 2D game creator in its own right. Not only are 2D games possible in Unity, as this book will show, but Unity offers us the ability to mix and integrate its existing and powerful 3D functionality into the 2D games we create, such as mesh effects, particle effects, and 3D audio. These can all be put to creative use to further enhance and improve the quality of our 2D games. This book demonstrates how these techniques and workflows work in practice.

The second reason one may doubt the value of this book is as follows: there's nothing in this book that I cannot find out independently, and for free, by searching around the Internet; by looking on forums, searching on Google, watching videos on YouTube, and scanning blogs and tutorial sites. By doing this, I can gradually piece together everything I need to know without reading this book at all. Now in reply, it must be admitted that a reader probably can learn everything contained in this book by searching elsewhere, given enough time and effort and dedication. But this is not to be taken as a legitimate criticism of the book, just as it is not legitimate to criticize an encyclopedia for containing information that can be known elsewhere. This book is not supposed to contain secret, mystical or arcane knowledge that cannot be known through other means. On the contrary, it can be known from elsewhere. That should be a source of comfort, because it means everything I say here can be corroborated, technically reviewed, and verified. The purpose of this book is more modest but not unimportant. It is to bring together and synthesize valuable knowledge about how to make 2D games in Unity, and to structure it into a solid and complete course you can follow from start to finish. Consequently, pursuing this course saves you hours, days, and even weeks of time searching around and trying to piece together everything that is presented to you here in just one volume.

How Should This Book Be Read?

There are two main types of readers for technical books like this: the reference reader and the tutorial reader. The reference reader expects a book they read alongside their working practice. They expect something they can flick-through, visiting different sections in any order and finding the relevant material they need to continue with what they are doing. The tutorial reader expects a "classroom in a book"; a complete course they can read from start to finish, considering each chapter in sequence from left to right to gain a solid foundation and understanding of the relevant subject matter. This book has been written to be amenable to both types of readers. The chapters and materials are presented in a linear sequence allowing the book to be read as a complete course from start to finish. But the sections have also been divided in such a way as to be helpful and accessible to the reference reader. To get the most from this book, however, I recommend you read it through once completely as a tutorial reader, and then afterward to consider it as reference material that you can return to and read in any order as necessary.

Is This Book Out of Date Already?

Each and every technical book that is written has a lifetime or a shelf life. This is the amount of time for which the book still has relevance to its subject matter and to its audience. This time is related to the amount of change in the subject matter itself. Some books have potentially infinite lifetimes, such as books on the basics of arithmetic, because this knowledge is well established and does not change. Most books however, like this book, have finite lifetimes. The more frequently a subject changes, and the more dramatic the change, then the more the book becomes misaligned with its subject. As this misalignment increases, the book's lifetime reduces. A book might be considered dead when its pages have no practical relevance anymore to the subject it discusses. So what can be said about this book, concerned as it is with both 2D games and the Unity engine? The question of importance is not just whether this book is still in-date and relevant today, but whether it stands a chance of remaining relevant long enough in the future to make its reading worthwhile.

At first sight, the lifetime of this book might appear to be very short, because the Unity engine changes frequently. The Unity developers release software patches and updates frequently through the official website. In fact, it's likely that by the time this book is published and in your hands the Unity engine will have been updated even further to feature fixes and bugs and new features that I cannot possibly be aware of when writing this book. However, this frequency need not trouble us unduly because, despite the frequency of updates, the overall interface, tools, and workflow for the Unity engine for 2D games has remained intact for a long time, and there is no strong reason to suspect a radical departure in the near future. Subsequent releases of the engine maintain backward compatibility to some extent, and the overall mechanics and workflow of the engine is typically retained across releases to ensure usability for existing Unity users familiar with the tools. Even if the code samples of this book were invalidated by future versions for reasons of semantics and class renaming, the fundamental concepts, ideas, techniques, and workflows presented here would still hold relevance and have practical value. Consequently, it is reasonable to have confidence and to take comfort from the knowledge that the information presented here is likely to have value for the foreseeable future.

What Are the Companion Files?

As mentioned earlier, this book has a practical focus. That means it encourages you not just to read, but to do things. In each chapter, we'll be working in software, using the features of Unity and MonoDevelop, and other software, to create working 2D games. This book has been designed and configured so that you can follow along with each chapter without having to use any external files or dependencies at all. None of the chapters require you to have any files, except for the software itself. However, each chapter does have associated companion files if you want to use them. These are optional and can be downloaded from the Apress companion webpage. For each relevant chapter, the companion files are the result of all the work that I demonstrate, and using them will save you the trouble of having to repeat every step that I list. These files include Unity projects, assets, script files, scenes, and other data. Each chapter features notes and comments directing you to the relevant companion files when appropriate; so please keep a look-out for those as we progress. The Apress companion files for this book can be found at the following URL: http://www.apress.com/9781430262299.

What Is the General Structure of this Book?

This book features a total of 13 chapters grouped into three wider parts or sections. Chapters 1 to 3 together provide a recap over the basic Unity features relevant to 2D games, and offer background details about exporting and preparing 2D assets ready for importing into Unity. They offer advice also about how to get up and running quickly in Unity for creating 2D games. Together these chapters offer a foundation and starting point from which we'll delve deeper. Some of the topics in these chapters include:

- What are Scenes, GameObjects, Components and Assets?
- What is the optimal way to export texture files?
- How can I create textures with transparency?
- How do I create script files?
- How can I quickly create a 2D game in Unity?

Section 2 includes Chapters 4 to 9 and represents the core developmental work that we'll need to perform to achieve high quality and highly controllable results in our 2D games. Here, we'll look at the technical hurdles that Unity throws our way whenever we use its 3D tools for 2D purposes, and we'll also see issues that arise generally in a 2D workflow. This includes issues relating to resolution, aspect ratio, and pixel perfection. We'll also look at how to solve these issues in flexible ways that do not involve compromising our power as a developers or the quality of our game. Section 2 addresses the following questions:

- How can I achieve pixel-perfect 2D games?

- How can I configure my scene cameras for 2D games?

- How can I make the screen coordinates correspond to scene coordinates?

- How can I make my textures look sharp and crisp, and not blurry?

- How can I handle multiple resolutions and aspect ratios with my textures?

- What are Atlas Textures and how can I create them?

- How can I generate geometry for my 2D game?

- How can I animate 2D characters and objects?

- How can I control the game resolution?

Section 3 encompasses Chapters 10 to 13. In this section we'll move forward from our foundation, and from all the code we have created, and apply it to creating a complete 2D game. The game will be simple, but its purpose is to be a vehicle to demonstrate clearly the 2D workflow in action, and how the features and code we develop throughout this book can be used in practice. The final chapters close by consider possible ways forward and techniques for optimizing our 2D workflow even further. Section 3 addresses the following questions:

- How can I make a 2D game from start to finish?

- How can I apply our 2D tools to making a real 2D game?

- What runtime performance issues should I consider?

- How can I improve runtime performance on mobile devices?

Unity Basics for 2D Games

This book is about making 2D games using the Unity engine. It will focus not only on the central concepts critical to 2D games, such as 2D space and projections, but also on the practical workflow that can be followed in Unity for creating 2D games. I use the term 2D game (two-dimensional game) to mean any game that principally relies on only 2D coordinates. Famous 2D games include Tetris, Super Mario Brothers, Angry Birds, and many more.

In a 2D game, players typically cannot rotate or move the camera freely in 3D space to view objects from other angles and perspectives. The game objects themselves typically move in only two dimensions as well, such as along the X and Y axes (left/right and up/down) but not along the Z axis (forward/backward); like the characters in a side-scrolling platform game. There are, of course, some exceptions to these rules. But generally, 2D games are defined by the restrictions they put on the developer—they negate or remove the third dimension as a principle element in the game.

Necessarily, some might ask why bother creating 2D games at all? And the answer lies mainly in that 2D games have a charm and a simplicity that imparts a classical feel to them, and it is a feel that is popular with many gamers. This chapter represents the start of our journey toward 2D games. In keeping with its practical flavor, the chapter takes a summary look at the Unity engine as it pertains to 2D games only. This chapter acts as a refresher course in the basics for those already familiar with Unity, and as a crash-course for those who are not. The chapter's purpose is not simply to emphasize the engine basics in a general and standard way, but to depict them from a new angle; to look at them with a 2D mind-set as opposed to the 3D mind-set that usually introduces the Unity engine. For this reason, some features take on a new importance for us, and some features receive no coverage here at all. Some of the features not discussed in this chapter include light mapping, particle systems, and the animation system Mecanim. The reason is not because these features cannot be integrated into a 2D workflow, because they can. It's simply because we can make 2D games without them if we choose, and so they don't represent a core or a foundation in Unity for 2D games. So let's jump straight in and take a look at the Unity editor and tools from a 2D perspective.

Unity Projects, Assets, and Scenes

When you make a game in Unity, you'll come into contact with projects, assets, and scenes. These are high-level concepts that every developer needs to know about upfront.

Project Wizard and Project Panel

Let's start with projects: Unity is a project-based application. In practice this means every time you make a new game, you'll make a new project. In Unity, 1 project = 1 game. It doesn't matter whether your game is 2D or 3D, a project is simply a container for all your game files and data. It corresponds to a folder on your hard drive, and that folder houses all the files for your game project during its development. To create a new project in Unity, click the **File ➤ New Project** option from the application menu. This is the equivalent of saying "I want to make a new game." Do not however press the keyboard shortcut *Ctrl+N,* because this creates a new scene and not a new project. In Unity, a *scene* refers to a level. That is, a complete environment in the game.

> **Note** You can also open an existing project with **File ➤ Open Project**. Unity version 3.4 upward ships with a demo project known as AngryBots, as shown in Figure 1-2. This is a 3D game but is nonetheless worth examining in more depth if you're new to Unity.

The Project Wizard dialog appears (see Figure 1-1). This dialog allows you to specify the root location for the project. You can also choose to import a range of asset packages. These are pre-made files and data that can make your life easier, saving you from having to re-invent the wheel later on. But for 2D games we can usually leave all these asset packages unchecked—we won't need them here. Once you're happy with the settings, click the *Create* button to generate a new project.

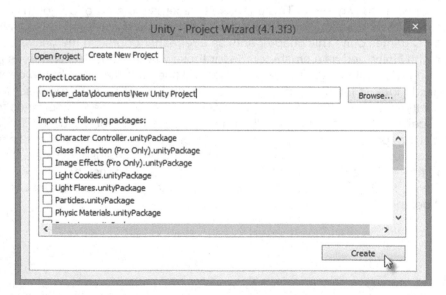

Figure 1-1. The Project Wizard dialog displays settings for creating a new project

Once the project is generated, Unity displays the default interface. This is where we'll spend a lot of time making games. Running along the bottom of the interface is the Project Panel (see C in Figure 1-2). This acts much like a folder view, showing the contents of the Project folder on the hard drive. For new projects, this panel typically begins completely empty. But as we add our own meshes, images, and other data, it populates with items. You can open the Project folder directly from the Project Panel in either Windows Explorer on Windows orFinder on Mac. To do that, right-click the mouse inside the Assets Panel (inside the Project Panel) and select *Show in Explorer* from the context menu.

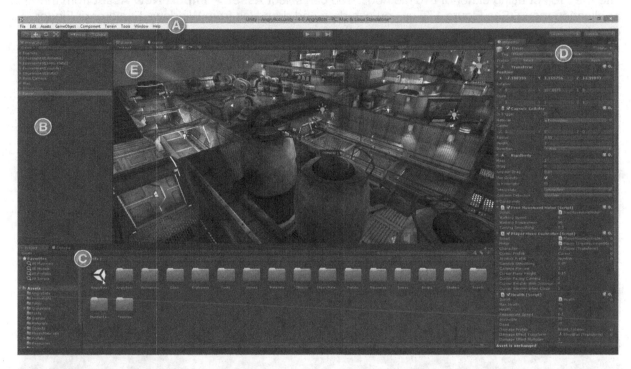

Figure 1-2. The Unity interface for Unity 4 in its default layout: A) The application menu B) The Scene Hierarchy C) Project Panel D) Object Inspector E) Scene Viewport

> **Note**   You can make the Project Panel, or any panel, larger by hovering the cursor over it and pressing the spacebar. This maximizes the panel to the size of the editor window. You can toggle the panel back to its original size by a second spacebar press.

The project folder typically contains four subfolders: *Library, Assets, ProjectSettings,* and *Temp.* The Project Panel in the Unity interface displays the contents of only the Assets folder, because this is where our game files will be stored when imported. The other three folders contain meta-data, and they should be managed by the Unity application exclusively. It is highly recommended never to manually remove or edit files from anywhere inside the Project folder or its subfolders. Doing so could lead to corrupted or damaged projects if the files are not copied in the proper way. I'm simply discussing the Project folder here so you know where it is, and its general structure.

Assets and Project Files

The project is the home of all your game files; all the files that make up your game. These may include meshes, textures, movies, animations, sounds, music, text data, and more. These files are together named *Assets* (plural) by the Unity engine. Each file is a unique *asset* (singular). When you want to put a mesh or object or file inside your game, you'll need to import it *first* as an asset of the project. Only assets in the Project Panel can be included in your game. You can import assets into the Project using either of two methods. You can select **Asset ➤ Import New Asset** from the application menu (See Figure 1-3) or, you can drag and drop files from Windows Explorer or Finder directly into the Project Panel. The former method allows you to import only one file at a time, while the latter allows multiple files to be imported together.

Figure 1-3. Importing asset files into Unity. Assets can be meshes, textures, audio files, movie files, animation data, text data, and more

Once the asset is imported, it appears in the Project Panel. Unity accepts many different file formats. See Table 1-1 for supported formats.

Table 1-1. *File Formats Accepted by Unity*

Meshes	Textures	Audio	Movies
.FBX	.PSD	.MP3	.MOV
.MA	.TIFF	.OGG	.AVI
.MB	.PNG	.MOD	.OGG
.MAX	.BMP	.IT	.ASF
.BLEND	.JPG	.XM	.MPG
.3DS	.TGA	.S3M	
.DXF	.DDS/PVR	.WAV	
.C4D			

Note   Any meshes not exported directly to FBX format (such as MA or BLEND) require the appropriate 3D modelling software to be installed on the system during import into Unity. Unity internally uses this software to export native formats to FBX.

Both 2D and 3D games typically make use of lots of assets—perhaps hundreds. 2D games rely especially on textures and materials. Sometimes the total size of these can reach into the gigabytes. The difference between textures and materials is considered in Chapter 2. Speaking about assets generally, it's good practice to organize your assets in the Project Panel into subfolders. This ensures you can find your assets quickly and when you need them. Textures are typically arranged in one folder, meshes in another, audio files in another, and so on. Avoid mixing together assets of different types. To create folders directly from the Project Panel, right-click in the Asset Panel and choose **Create ➤ Folder** from the context menu. Or, **Assets ➤ Create ➤ Folder** from the application menu. See Figure 1-4.

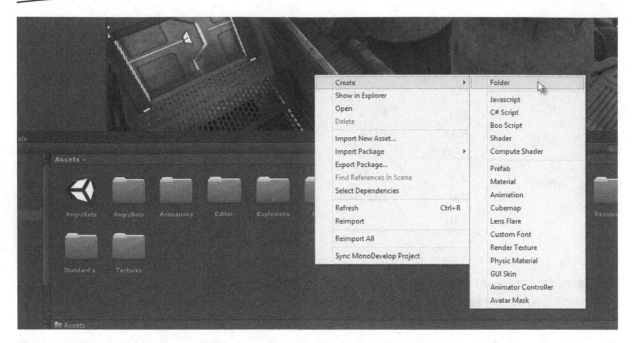

Figure 1-4. Create folders to organize the assets of your projects. This ensures you can find assets quickly and easily

Assets that are imported into Unity are automatically assigned a range of settings and properties by the Unity engine during the import process. These control how the assets work when included into your games. You can view these settings and change them easily. Just select your asset in the Project Panel and adjust its settings, which appear in the Object Inspector (D in Figure 1-2). Be sure to click the *Apply* button at the bottom of the Inspector when you're done to confirm and save the changes for the selected asset.

Scenes

When you've created a project and imported all your assets, it's usually time to start making the levels in your game. In Unity, a level (or an environment) is termed a scene. 1 scene = 1 level. Most games feature multiple levels, and so most projects feature multiple scenes. Unity is primarily a 3D engine, and this means that the *only* kinds of scenes available to us are 3D ones. A 3D scene features a 3D coordinate space, with an X and Y and Z axis. To create 2D levels in Unity, we simply create standard 3D scenes and then configure them to behave like 2D ones. The player will probably never know the difference—unless they're a Unity developer too! To create a new scene, select **File ➤ New Scene** from the application menu, or press the keyboard shortcut *Ctrl+N* (see Figure 1-5). After creating a scene, be sure to save it by selecting **File ➤ Save Scene**. Once saved, the scene will be added to the project as an asset. Scenes are assets too.

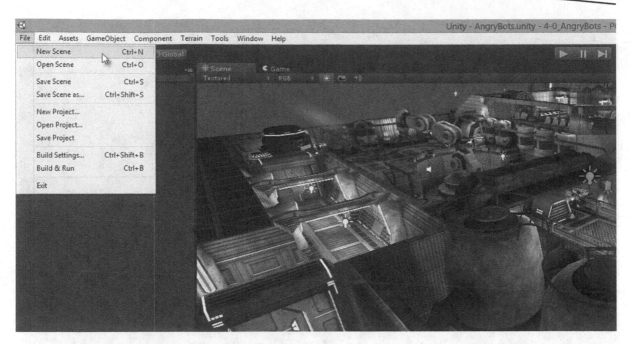

Figure 1-5. Scenes represent levels or environments. Unity offers only 3D scenes. There are special 2D scene types. 2D games are made by customizing how 3D scenes work

Navigating Scenes and Viewports

You can open up and examine any scene in your project by double-clicking it from the Project Panel. Every time you create a new scene, it will automatically be opened for you. When you open a scene in the Unity editor, you can build your levels and examine them. The Viewport component of the interface allows you to see inside your scene (see E in Figure 1-2). The Scene Hierarchy Panel (see B in Figure 1-2) also lists every object by name: all your lights, cameras, environments, creatures, power-ups, and other objects are listed here, even if the object is not actually visible to you or the player. The list is exhaustive; if an object lives within the active scene, then it is included in the Hierarchy Panel. By double-clicking an object in that list, you not only select the object in the scene but center the viewport on it for a better view. Further, the properties for the selected object are shown in the Object Inspector (see Figure 1-6).

Figure 1-6. *Selecting the player object from the Hierarchy Panel in the AngryBots sample project that ships with Unity. The Viewport centers on the selected object with a double-click, and the object's properties show in the Object Inspector*

> **Note** The Viewport area is divided across two tabs, named Scene and Game. The Scene tab is a director's eye view of the scene. We use this tab to build up our scenes and turn them into believable worlds. The Game tab displays the same scene but from the perspective of the player rather than the developer. It shows us how the scene will look when played. We'll work in both tabs for 2D games.

Even though we're making 2D games in this book, it's essential to know how to navigate around the viewport in 3D space. We need to see how our scenes are arranged and the positions of objects. For this reason, the navigation controls should become second nature to us. If you're a Maya user or a Blender user with the Maya pre-set active, then the Unity viewport controls will likely be familiar to you already. They use a combination of the mouse and keyboard. To start, try zooming the camera in and out of the Viewport. To do this, just scroll the mouse wheel: up zooms in and down zooms out. You can also center the Viewport camera on the object selected in the Hierarchy Panel by pressing the F key (F for Frame).

You can pan or slide around the Viewport by holding down the middle mouse button while moving the mouse around. You can rotate the camera around the selected object by holding down the *Alt* key on the keyboard and the left-button on the mouse while moving the mouse around. In addition, you can rotate the Viewport camera to look in any direction by holding down the right-mouse button and moving the mouse around. Together these controls allow us to move anywhere in the Viewport.

You can also simulate first-person perspective controls to move around. To achieve this, hold down the right-mouse button while using the WASD keys on the keyboard. Movement of the mouse controls the head movement, while A strafes left, D strafes right, W moves forward and S moves backward.

GameObjects, Transforms, and Components

Everything inside a scene is a GameObject. Characters, cameras, lights, ammo, weapons, particle systems, power-ups, sounds, music, spaceships, enemies; all of these are examples of GameObjects—each individual thing is a GameObject (singular). If you've imported a mesh asset into Unity, you can drag and drop it from the Project Panel into the Scene Viewport to instantiate an instance of it in the scene. That instance is a GameObject. You can drag and drop the object multiple times to create multiple instances in the scene, and thereby multiple game objects. In short, the Hierarchy Panel lists all GameObjects in the scene, and in order to create a game you'll need to work with lots of GameObjects.

Note   Unity allows you to create simple primitive objects in a scene, such as cubes and spheres, should you require them. To create these objects, choose **GameObject ➤ Create Other ➤ Cube**, or **GameObject ➤ Create Other ➤ Sphere**, or **GameObject ➤ Create Other ➤ Cylinder**. The Plane object can be useful for 2D games because it can easily display flat images aligned to the camera. We'll see more on this later.

The GameObject is not however the smallest thing or atom in the scene. Each GameObject is composed of smaller pieces or building blocks, called **components**. In fact, a GameObject is the sum of its components. The components for an object can be seen in the Object Inspector whenever the object is selected in the scene. The cube in Figure 1-7 is constructed from several components: a Transform Component, a Mesh Filter Component, a Box Collider Component, and a Mesh Renderer Component. Each of these components can be expanded and collapsed in the Object Inspector for easier viewing in the interface, just by clicking the twirl-arrow icon.

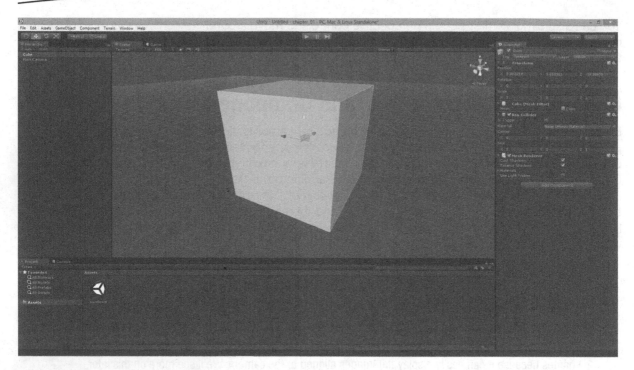

Figure 1-7. Even the simplest of cube primitive objects is composed from components

Now, you can duplicate that cube in Figure 1-8 in the scene in at least two ways. You *could* select the cube and press *Ctrl+D* on the keyboard. Or, you could create a completely new and empty game object from scratch and then replicate its component setup to reproduce a cube. The former method is easier, but the latter helps us to see the importance of components. If you want to try this "manual method" of GameObject creation, you can do so as follows: Select **GameObject ➤ Create Empty** (or press *Ctrl+Shift+N*) from the application menu to create an empty game object. Once created, ensure this object is selected in the Hierarchy Panel. Then add components to it by selecting *Component* from the application menu and choosing the appropriate components to add. For example, to add the *Mesh Filter* component, select **Component ➤ Mesh ➤ Mesh Filter** from the menu. Take a look a Figure 1-8 to see how I created a replicated mesh object with the *Mesh Filter, Box Collider,* and *Mesh Renderer* Components.

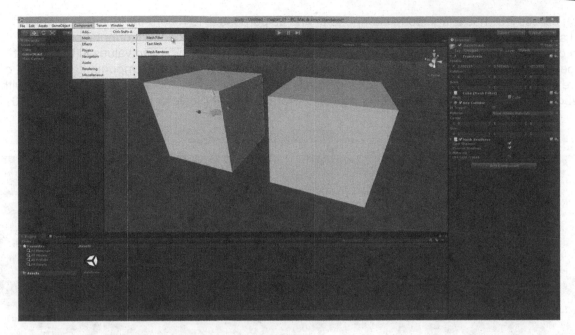

Figure 1-8. Creating a GameObject from scratch using components

In programming terms, each component is a unique class. A GameObject is made from multiple components and thus from multiple classes, all of which interact and define the behavior of that object. Because objects in the scene will naturally differ (players do not act like enemies, and guns do not act like volcanoes, and so on) then each GameObject will be composed from different components with different settings. Despite the differences between objects, every GameObject in a scene has one component in common. That is the **Transform** Component (see Figure 1-9).

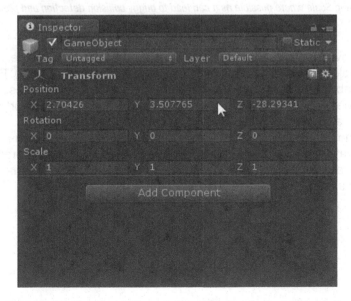

Figure 1-9. The Transform Component defines the position, rotation, and scale of a GameObject in the scene coordinate space

Each GameObject has a Transform Component, and its purpose is to record the position, rotation, and scale of the object. You can change these settings to adjust the location, orientation, and size of object respectively. This can be achieved in several ways: by typing in values in the Object Inspector, or by using script files to adjust the properties of the Transform Component as a class, or more simply by using the Transform tools on the Editor toolbar. These tools are also accessible with keyboard shortcut keys W (Translate or move), E (Rotate), and R (Scale or resize). See Figure 1-10.

Figure 1-10. The transformation tools. Translate moves an object, Rotate can turn or revolve an object, and Scale will enlarge or shrink an object. Avoid using Scale where possible as it can lead to buggy collision detection and problems with third-party plugins

Translation is about moving objects in any axis: X, Y, or Z. Typically, in 2D games, all objects exist on a plane, meaning all objects have the same value on one axis (often the Z axis). But as developers we still need to know about translation in 3D space. To translate an object, press the W key on the keyboard, select the object to move, and then use the gizmo in the Viewport (see Figure 1-11). The gizmo is a colored axis-primitive that centers on the object when selected. Just click and drag on any of its axes to move the object on that axis—in that direction. Avoid translating objects in a freeform (every axis) way, because perspective distortion makes it difficult to precision-place objects in the Viewport when translated on all three axes simultaneously. Instead translate objects on a per axis basis, one axis at a time.

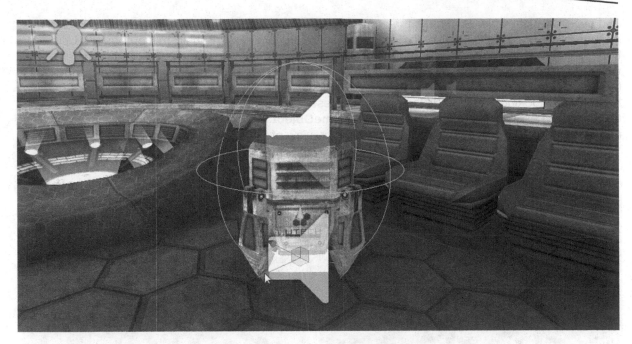

Figure 1-11. Use the Translate tool to move objects interactively in the Viewport using the Translate Gizmo

> **Tip**   Remember, by holding the V key while translating you can snap an object to vertices, which is great for fast, precision aligning. Also, you can lock translating to planar axes (XY, XZ, and YZ) by clicking the colored rects between the axis arrows on the gizmo.

You can rotate objects with the E key in conjunction with the Rotate Gizmo, and you can scale objects with the R key in conjunction with the Scale Gizmo. Beware of scaling as a general rule, and use it only where essential. Scaling can corrupt our understanding of size if caution is not exercised. If a texture of 512×512 pixels is imported into Unity and is scaled upward by a factor of 2 to appear on-screen at 1024×1024, the texture internally is still of a 512×512 size and Unity recognizes it as such. This has implications when reading and referring to texture sizes in script using the width and height properties of the *Texture2D* class. It's important to recognize that a texture or a mesh that has been scaled to appear at one size can really be at a different size as far as its internal representation goes. Only a scale factor of 1 corresponds to the true size of an object or texture.

Cameras

By default every Unity scene is created empty except for one GameObject, the **camera**. This object is typically named *Main Camera*. The camera is an important object for games, and especially so for 2D games, as we'll see. It represents the eye-point or viewpoint in the scene from which all game events are viewed and shown to the gamer on the monitor. A Unity scene *can* have more than one camera, if necessary. And this offers us a lot of potential. We can switch between cameras during gameplay, and even show the view from more than one camera at the same time in a split screen mode or in a picture-in-picture style. Like all other GameObjects, the camera has a Transform Component. Using this, you can set the position and rotation of the camera in 3D space. For 2D games, the camera will not typically rotate during gameplay, and its position will normally only change in one plane (on two axes rather than three). However, these are simply limitations we choose to put on the camera to create 2D-looking games, and they do not represent any limitations that the Unity engine puts on us. To add a new camera to the scene, select **GameObject ➤ Create Other ➤ Camera** from the application menu. When selected in the scene, a preview of the camera's view will show in the Scene Viewport (see Figure 1-12).

Figure 1-12. *Selecting a camera object in the scene displays a render preview in the Scene Viewport. This can be helpful to position and orient the camera to get the best looking view and angles of your scene at runtime. Remember, the camera is a GameObject and can be controlled and accessed like any other object*

Each camera has a Projection property, which is accessible in the *Camera Component* in the Object Inspector. It's also accessible in script via the *Projection* property of the Camera class. This property can be one of two values: Perspective (*Default*) or Orthographic (see Figure 1-13).This value controls how the camera renders or converts a 3D scene to the flat monitor or display. Typically 3D games will have the Projection property set to *Perspective*, because this mode ensures the scene is rendered according to the laws of perspective: lines and angles converge toward the horizon line, objects get smaller with distance, and distortion occurs to objects the further they move from the center of the view due to the curvature of the lens at its extremities. For 2D games however, *Perspective* projection can be problematic, and often we'll use *Orthographic* instead to create a Side View or Top View, or Front View. More on this topic is discussed in Chapters 3, 8, and 10.

Figure 1-13. The camera object has two Projection types: Perspective and Orthographic. This plays a key role in creating truly 2D games. Many 2D games use the Orthographic Projection type. This type usually requires further tweaking and configuration to display 2D scenes correctly

Each newly created camera features an active AudioListener Component by default. This component acts like a virtual ear. In a scene without an AudioListener Component you cannot hear anything: no sound or music is played to the speakers. When an AudioListener Component is attached to an object, you hear the scene as though you were standing in the position of that object—sounds nearer to you are louder than those further away. Typically, a game will have only one AudioListener Component active at one time during gameplay. This ensures the player hears a sensible range of sounds, and not a chaotic cacophony of sounds from different parts of the scene. If you add more than one camera, it's likely they'll both come with an AudioListener Component, and these will clash when you try to run the game because Unity will not know which Listener to choose. Be sure to configure the AudioListener Components, if you have multiples, so that only one is active at any one time.

Meshes and Geometry

In Unity, a **mesh** is an asset. It's perhaps one of the most common assets in a video game. Each model or object or "tangible thing" in your scene will be a mesh. Enemy creatures, the player character, the walls and floors, the terrain and sky, and more—these are all examples of meshes. Meshes are made from three main ingredients: geometry, mapping, and animation. The geometry features vertices, edges, and faces. Together these three constructs form a complete model and its surface data. Meshes are especially prominent in 3D games, but they also have a place in 2D games. 2D games rely on a special type of mesh known as a *quad* or *billboard* or *plane*. This is a rectangular surface formed from four corner points. In reality, this surface is made from two right-angled triangles aligned together at the hypotenuse. This surface is useful because, when aligned to the camera, it acts like a sheet of paper that can show images and textures. Typically, 2D games feature many camera-aligned quads: one for each object in the scene. Unity comes with a Plane object that can behave like this. It can be added to the scene by selecting **GameObject ➤ Create Other ➤ Plane** (see Figure 1-14). However, the Unity Plane is highly tessellated with vertices and edges running in rows and columns across the plane surface. This makes it an unsuitable choice for games that need a lot of quads and graphical objects, because more edges and more vertices lead to greater complexity and performance intensiveness, especially on mobile devices.

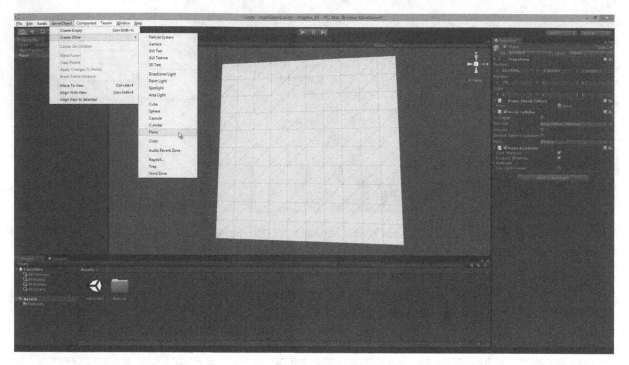

Figure 1-14. Quads can be generated into the scene through Unity's Plane object. Quads are like sheets of paper, aligned to the camera and are used to display textures

> **Note**   Many 2D games also utilize skeleton animation, rigging, and bones straight from 3D applications, to handle a lot of their animation needs. This is especially true for animations involving translation, rotation, and scaling.

A more effective alternative to using the Unity Plane is to generate your own quad mesh from script, using the properties and methods of the Mesh class. Chapter 5 shows you how to do this in-depth. With this method, you can build a tailor-made quad with the minimal number of vertices needed, and also have fine control over the mapping to control how a texture is painted across its surface.

Most games feature a lot of so-called "static geometry." This typically refers to walls, floors, ceilings, most furniture (such as tables and chairs and statues and bookcases), and also most terrain elements (such as hills and mountains). If the object is part of the scenery and doesn't move or change or deform during gameplay, then it qualifies as a static element of the scene. This applies to both 3D and 2D games. Static elements such as these provide us with an opportunity for optimizing our games and improving their runtime performance. In short, if your scene has static objects, then be sure to select those objects and enable their *Static* check box from the Object Inspector, as select those objects and enable their *Static* check box from the Object Inspector, as shown in Figure 1-15. Doing this allows Unity to batch those objects together and render them as a single batch with the minimum of computational overhead. Though ticking a check box in the editor is a very simple thing to do, do not underestimate the significant performance benefits this can have on your game. I recommend investing extra time and effort, checking through your scene and objects, ensuring that no static element is left unmarked.

Figure 1-15. Be sure to always enable the Static check box for meshes that don't move or change or deform during gameplay. This helps Unity batch together meshes and optimize the geometry of your scene, improving its runtime performance

Note   Unity ships as two separate versions: Free and Pro. Static batching is a Pro Only feature.

Scripting and the Unity API

To get the most from Unity, it's usually necessary to be confident with scripting. It gives us high-level control and power over the behavior of our games. Scripting is offered via three prominent languages: C#, JavaScript, and Boo. Although your project can potentially feature many different source files written in any of the three languages, some in one language and some in another, it's recommended you choose only one of the three and apply it consistently through all source files in your project.

This helps avoid confusion and having to jump between different mind-sets and coding paradigms. So select only one language to use for your project. The code samples in this book use C# exclusively. This should not to be taken as a comment or reflection on any of the other languages—all are capable in their own ways of achieving results. I've selected C# partly because of its popularity and partly because of my own background and experience. To create a new script file for your project from the application menu, select **Assets ➤ Create ➤ C# Script**, *or* **Assets ➤ Create ➤ Javascript**, *or* **Assets ➤ Create ➤ Boo Script**.

Note   You can also add existing script files to your project. Just drag and drop them into the Project Panel like any other asset.

MonoDevelop

You can edit your source files using any third-party code editor, including Microsoft Visual Studio and Notepad++. Unity however ships with a code editor and IDE named MonoDevelop that is associated with C# source files by default (see Figure 1-16). To open your files, simply double-click your source files in the Project Panel. When you've made code changes that you want to compile, save your source file and return to the Unity Editor. When the Unity Editor window becomes focused and activated, it will automatically detect file changes and recompile your code. Errors and warnings found, if any, will be listed in the Unity console. Warnings are printed in yellow and errors in red.

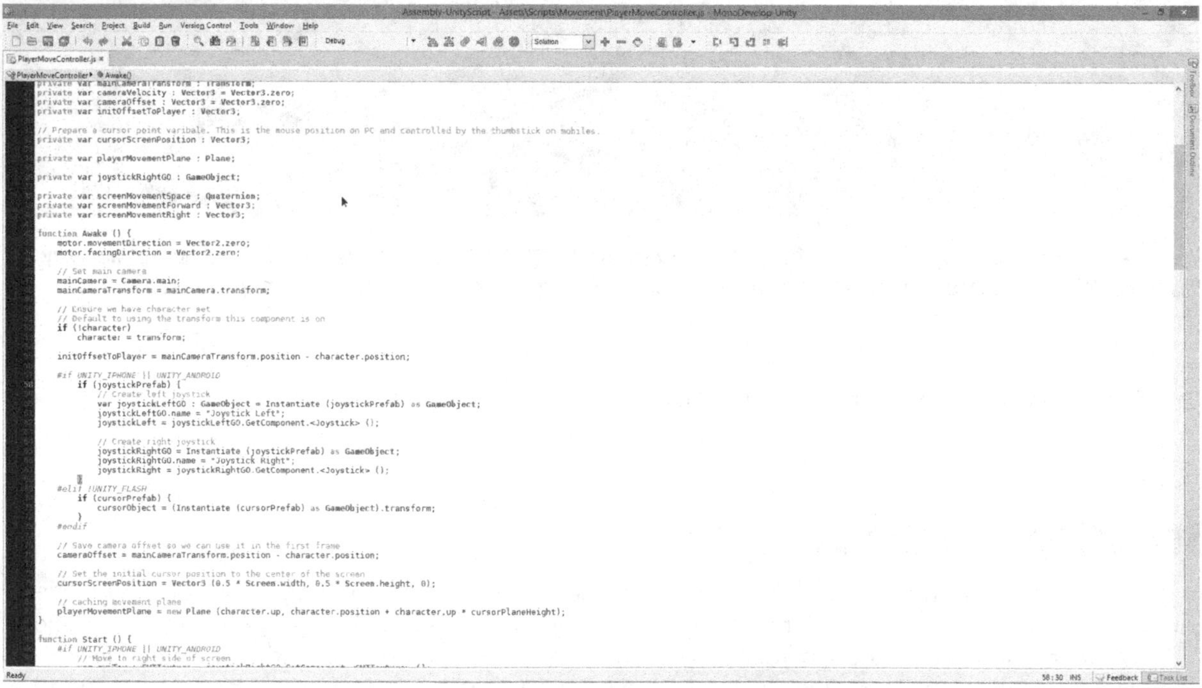

Figure 1-16. MonoDevelop is a cross-platform and open source IDE that ships with Unity. It can be used for editing Javascript, C#, and Boo source files. It features syntax highlighting, code-completion, and collapsible code-blocks

Every new script file in C# is typically generated with template code inside of it to reflect the most common usage of scripts. Normally, scripts are object oriented and each defines a class. The template class descends from MonoBehaviour, and that is a premade class in the Unity API—along with a range of other useful classes. MonoBehaviour is the base class for almost all components. This means that C# scripts are, by default, configured to be a component. It's the kind of thing that can be dragged and dropped from the Project Panel and onto GameObjects in the scene. Once attached to a GameObject, the script acts as a component that is instantiated on the object, and it shows up in the Object Inspector. One really useful feature of Unity is that it shows all public properties of a class in the Object Inspector, where they can be viewed and edited, both at design time and runtime (see Figure 1-17).

Figure 1-17. Scripts can be attached to objects as components. Public properties of a class can be edited and shown in the Object Inspector at design time and runtime

Tip   Public properties set from the Object Inspector override the default values assigned to them in code.

Components

Components exist on GameObjects. All components on an object can receive and handle a number of common events *for that object*. These are functions inherited from the MonoBehaviour class and can be overridden in the descendant classes to perform custom behaviour on key events. Two common events that a Component can handle are Start and Update. More details on these are given later in this book, in chapters 3, 4, 10 and 11. In short, the Start function is called on a script when the GameObject (*to which it is attached*) is created in the scene. For objects that are created in the editor and are always present, this event is called when the scene begins. The Update function in contrast is called once per frame (not once per second). This means Update is typically called many times per second: for a 25 frames per second game, it'll be called 25 times per second. The Update function is useful for coding behaviour that moves or animates objects over time. More information on the MonoBehaviour class can be found at: http://docs.unity3d.com/Documentation/ScriptReference/MonoBehaviour.html.

The Unity API (Application Programming Interface) is a library of classes that developers can use to make their scripting life a lot easier for game development. The API reference documentation can be found at the following URL: http://docs.unity3d.com/Documentation/ScriptReference/. This library features more classes and properties than can possibly be documented here comprehensively. But it is enough here to simply say that many of the key classes and structures of the API that apply to 2D games will be explored and detailed as this book progresses. For now, some of the key classes can be listed as: Vector2, Vector3, Mathf, Screen, Texture2D, MonoBehaviour, ScriptableWizard, GameObject, Transform, Mesh, Input, MeshFilter, and MeshRenderer.

Performance, Profiling, and the Stats Panel

How well a game performs is a relative rather than an absolute matter. A game that runs well on one computer, at one time, can run poorly on another computer (or the same computer) at a different time. One symptom of poor performance is lag and freezing. If a game runs with random stops, freezes, or with continual jitter and erratic frame rates, then this is usually a sign that everything is not well with performance. Sometimes these symptoms can be the result of software conflicts, old drivers, buggy hardware, and other faults or failures external to the game. In these cases, the situation can sometimes be remedied by steps the user can take, such as updating drivers or uninstalling software. But, other times, the source of the problem can be traced to the game itself and to its architecture—the way it is put together and constructed. To diagnose these kinds of problems, and to trace the possible source of problems, Unity provides us with some tools for measuring and gauging the runtime performance of a game in more systematic and quantitative way. These tools are the Profiler window (see Figure 1-18) and the Stats Panel (see Figure 1-19). These do not *solve* the problems themselves—they are not debugging miracles. They are *diagnostic* tools. They can help us identify problems in our code more quickly and accurately so we can set about finding educated and careful solutions. The solutions themselves still have to come from us, the developer.

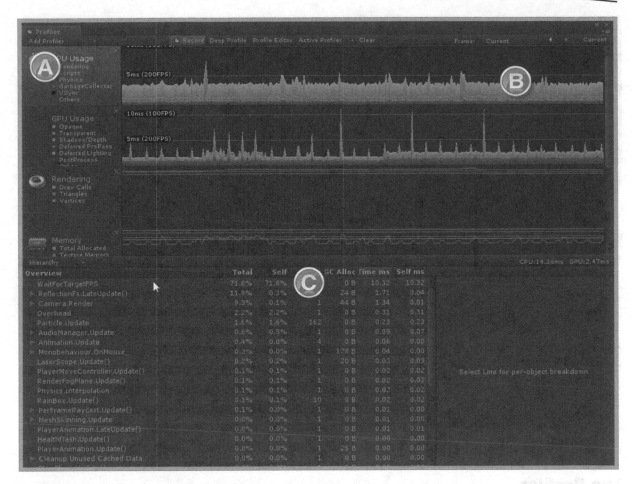

Figure 1-18. *The Profiler window offers a statistical overview of runtime performance. Using this tool you can get an illustration for how much GPU and CPU time is dedicated to specific tasks on a frame by frame basis. This helps us identify the most computationally intensive processes*

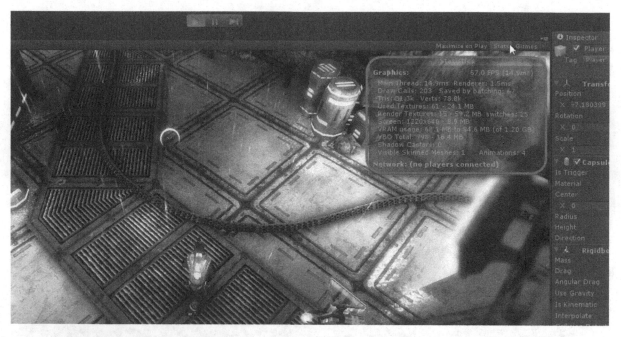

Figure 1-19. *The Stats Panel can be a helpful tool, especially during early and mid-development, to help you keep your game on-track and to tailor its performance and demands to your target hardware*

Note   The Profiler is a Pro Only feature.

The Profiler

The Profiler window can be accessed from the application menu by selecting **Window ➤ Profiler**, or by pressing *Ctrl + 7* on the keyboard. This tool is only effective and informative if it is viewed while the game is running in *Play* mode. While running, the Profiler takes snapshots or regular measurements of the game on a per frame basis and plots them onto its graphs so developers can visualize the game's performance over time, seeing potential trends and trouble spots. The Profiler window is divided into two main sections: the upper half of the window (Areas A and B in Figure 1-18) and the lower half (Area C in Figure 1-18). Areas A and B together represent a collection of vertically aligned graphs displaying a graphical overview of the runtime performance for your game. The horizontal axis charts *Frames* in relation to the vertical axis, which charts *Performance Time*. The CPU and GPU graphs, as listed in Area A, for example, demonstrate *how much time on each frame* your game spent in milliseconds dedicated to a specific runtime task. These tasks are color coded on the graph. For the CPU graph, Rendering is green, Script execution is blue, and Physics calculations are orange.

An important trend to watch for in the Profiler graphs is spiking. If you see sudden mountains or spikes in the graph that are much higher than the surrounding data, and if these spikes correspond to lag and performance issues in game, then you *may* have identified a trouble spot. If so, note the color of the spike in the graph to determine the kind of processing task that is the cause. Once you have identified trouble-spots, you can then use Area Cof the Profiler to investigate deeper. This panel breaks down the tasks into even smaller categories, telling you how long each function takes to complete, or how intensive a specific GameObject is. In short, the Profiler can be a handy feature when used appropriately. But it is of most value when you are only dimly aware of a performance problem in your game but have little or no clue as to its whereabouts.

> **Note**   The Profiler can also be connected to standalone builds of your game to give you an insight to its runtime performance. This can be useful for mobile development. More information can be found online here: http://docs.unity3d.com/Documentation/Manual/Profiler.html.

The Stats Panel

The Stats Panel is another useful diagnostic tool. It can be accessed from the Game tab: press the toggle-button *Stats* in the top-right corner of the *Game* Viewport. During gameplay this panel offers a live-update summary of your game's performance and its overall statistics concerning frame rate, memory footprint, texture usage, and more *for the target hardware*. That is, the Stats Panel applies to the computer on which you are running the game. So, when assessing performance, be sure to test your game and measure it on your target hardware (your *minimum specification*). Testing on other hardware can lead to different statistics and cause confusion about your performance metrics. Key properties to watch for on the Stats Panel include: FPS (frames per second), Draw Calls, Saved by Batching, Tris, VRAM Usage, and Shadow Casters. Let's consider these in turn, as follows:

- **FPS** (frames per second). This records the number of frames that your game is actually sustaining per second. There is no right or wrong or magic number for this field per se. Two ingredients are important: first, the FPS should almost never be below 15 FPS, because the human eye begins to perceive lag and stutter at frame rates below this value; and ideally the frame rate will be above 25. Second, the FPS should generally be consistent. It will likely fluctuate up and down between values depending on the processing overhead on the computer—that is to be expected and is normal behaviour. But, generally speaking, consistency is good.

- **Draw Calls**. This value will become especially important for us later when developing 2D games, as we'll see. It refers to the total number of times per frame that the Unity engine calls on the lower-level rendering functionality to render your scene to the screen. The higher this value, the more complex and expensive your scene is to render. For this reason, lower values are generally to be preferred. There are some steps and methods available to us for reducing the number of draw calls per frame, and we'll explore what those are throughout this book.

- **Saved by Batching** indicates the number of batching operations Unity managed to perform on your objects to reduce the number of draw calls. Typically, each *Saved by Batching* operation saves us at least one additional call. In most cases, the higher this value, the better.

- **Tris** lists the total number of triangles currently being rendered to the screen in the current frame (not the total number of triangles in the scene). Most contemporary graphics hardware on desktop computers and consoles is adept at processing triangles quickly, meaning very high tri-counts can in principle be achieved. The same cannot always be said of mobile devices however. For this reason, the lower this value is the better it will be for performance across devices. That advice should, of course, be taken within reasonable limits: reduce the tri-count to a level that is consistent with your artistic vision and which respects your target hardware.

- **VRAM Usage.** Again, the lower this value is the better for performance—keeping within reasonable limits. It tells us how much of the video memory on the graphics hardware is being used for processing and texture storage.

- **Shadow Casters.** This lists the total number of *real-time* shadow casters in the scene: it does not include shadow-casters during light-mapping operations and baked lighting. Real-time shadow casters are computationally expensive and should be reduced to a minimum or eliminated entirely, if possible. These can be among the most significant performance hits a game can take. For many 2D games, real-time shadow casters will not be necessary.

Note   Be sure to check whether your version of Unity supports the shadow types you need.

Editor Add-Ons

The Unity Editor is featured-filled especially in the context of 3D games, but that doesn't mean it is necessarily comprehensive or all-encompassing. The extent to which the Editor meets all the requirements of a project depends on the project and your needs. In the case of most 2D games, the Unity Editor lacks some valuable GUI features—specifically the ability interactively generate meshes, such as quads. In addition, it lacks the ability to control the UV mapping coordinates for vertices, and also the ability to generate 2D textures in an optimized and clean way, as we'll see. These hurdles can all be addressed however, and in different ways. One helpful way is to use the Unity Editor classes in scripting to extend the Unity interface and develop our own custom add-ins and GUI tools to provide the missing features. Specifically, we can develop our own custom editors for 2D games that work as seamlessly with the Editor interface as if they'd been part of the native Unity package all along. This kind of behaviour is achievable through Editor classes like `ScriptableWizard`, and later chapters (4, 5, 6, and 7) will show you how.

Unity Interface Configuration

The last issue to consider in this chapter is that of interface configuration. When you first run Unity, the interface appears in its default layout on screen, and for Unity 4 that amounts to the Hierarchy Panel being aligned to the left, the Viewports aligned to the center, the Project Panel aligned to the bottom, and the Object Inspector aligned to the right side. While there's nothing inherently wrong with any interface arrangement (I recommend working with the arrangement you like best), I want to share with you a layout I find very helpful for developing 2D games. This layout can be seen in Figure 1-20. The key difference between the default layout and this one is that the *Scene* and *Game* tabs are aligned side by side in a split-screen view.

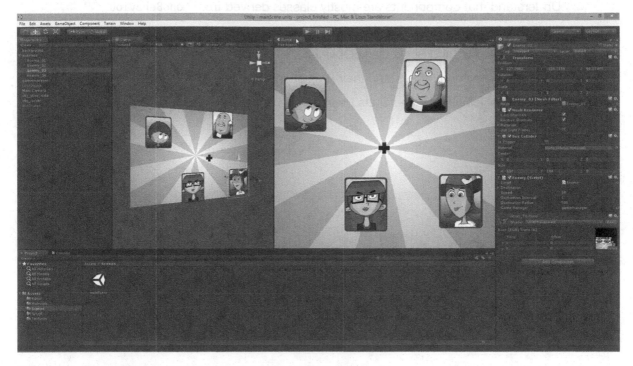

Figure 1-20. Unity Interface layout that can be helpful for 2D game development

The reason for this arrangement stems from the fact that 2D graphics tend to be measured and sized in pixels, as opposed to 3D meshes, which are measured and sized in world units (often in meters). This difference often means we need to precisely place and arrange our 2D graphics not just in world space, as we do in the Scene tab, but also in screen space, which is measured in pixels and is rendered from the scene camera (in the Game tab). For this reason, much of our work will have us constantly switching between the Scene tab and the Game tab where we can preview the results of our work. We could, of course, jump between the tabs, as we do in the Default layout, if we wanted. But personally, I find it more convenient to have the two tabs aligned side by side.

Summary

This chapter outlined some of the concepts fundamental to creating 2D games in Unity, and I'll assume you're familiar with them as we proceed. By now you should be able to:

- Create Unity projects and scenes

- Import assets into a project, including meshes, textures, and audio

- Instantiate assets into scenes as GameObjects

- Navigate the Scene Viewport
- Understand that GameObjects are built from components
- Understand that components are defined in script
- Understand that components are mostly classes derived from `MonoBehaviour`
- Edit and view class properties from the Object Inspector
- Translate, Rotate, and Scale GameObjects
- Create cameras and understand their Projection Type
- Use the Profiler window and Stats Panel

Chapter 2

Materials and Textures

Materials and textures are the raw materials for 2D games. They are to 2D games what 3D meshes are for 3D games. Practically, all your game graphics, from characters and backgrounds to special effects and in-game menus, will be implemented in the form of materials and textures. If you can see *it* on-screen, then it's due to materials and textures. There's simply no getting around them, so it's important to have a solid understanding of them—and not just for 2D games either but for games more generally. This chapter aims to provide that understanding. It'll explain the crucial difference and relationship between materials and textures. It'll also discuss how you can create both of them, as well as many other relevant considerations to keep in mind when working with Unity. So fire up your PC and let's get started.

Using Materials and Textures

By now you've probably created some scenes and gameplay in Unity. In doing this you've likely made use of materials and the Material Editor to change the surface appearance of objects in the scene. If you haven't, however, then don't worry. Here we'll take a closer look at the Material Editor and its features to see how to use it, and also what the difference is between materials and textures. Both are related and both have the power to fundamentally alter how the surface of a 3D model looks in the scene. In Unity, whenever you want to change how an object looks, you'll need to *either* create a new material, *or* use an existing material, if you have one. If you want a plane object to look like a brick wall, or a sphere to look like a marble, or a cube to look like a crate, or any similar case to this, then materials have an important role to play.

Getting Started with Materials

To start using materials and textures, I recommend opening the sample project associated with this chapter from the book's companion files (this can be found in `Project_Files/Chapter02/Start`). Alternatively, you can create a completely new Unity project, with a Sphere object in the scene, and a Directional Light pointing at it, as seen in Figure 2-1. Either way is fine.

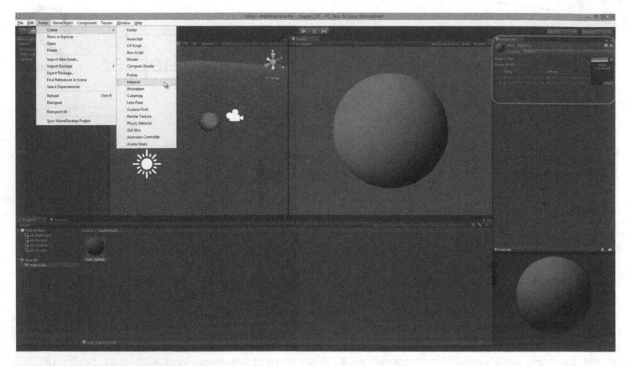

Figure 2-1. *Starting a new project to explore materials. The Material Editor is used to change the properties of materials: this includes material colors, textures, and other properties such as Specularity, Bumpiness, and Transparency*

Let's make the Sphere surface red instead of leaving it at its default gray colour. To do this, we'll create a material asset: so select Assets ➤ Create ➤ Material from the application menu, or right-click inside the Project Panel and select Create ➤ Material from the context menu. This creates a new material in the Asset view of the Project Panel. Name the material *mat_sphere* and then select it to show its properties in the Object Inspector. Together these properties form the Material Editor. From the Editor, left-click inside the Main Color swatch, changing the material color from white to red. Then assign the material to the Sphere object by simply dragging and dropping the material from the Project Panel onto the Sphere object in the Viewport. The Sphere surface then changes to red, because its surface information is now being defined by the material. You can even change the color of the material from red to, say, green and the Sphere will automatically update to the new color.

> **Note**   Notice the prefix convention used for the material name when creating a material for the sphere: mat_sphere. The name begins with *mat_* to indicate the asset is a material, as opposed to a texture or mesh or audio clip. This convention is not compulsory—you can name materials whatever you want. I do recommend applying some similar convention to your own materials and assets, however, to help organize them and make them easier to work with.

Mesh Renderers

Now select the Sphere object in the Viewport. In the Object Inspector, expand the `Materials` property of the `MeshRenderer` component to see the material assigned to the object. You can click the name of the material to locate and select it quickly in the Project Panel, if required. The `Materials` property of the `MeshRenderer` is important because it defines the material assigned to the mesh. You can change a mesh's material by changing the materials property, even in script. In addition, it's possible for two or more meshes to *share* the same material: you can drag and drop the material onto multiple meshes. When you do this, all the assigned meshes will reference the *same* material; meaning that changes to the material (such as changes in color) will be propagated and applied to *all* associated meshes. See Figure 2-2.

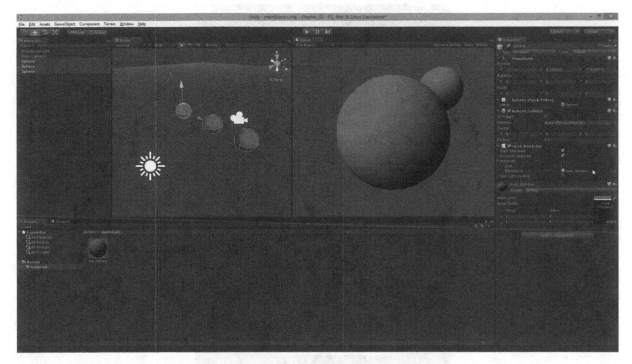

Figure 2-2. The material for a mesh is defined by the Materials property in its MeshRenderer component. Materials can be shared among multiple meshes and GameObjects—see three spheres with a single red material. If materials should differ between objects, you can either create a completely new material, or duplicate an existing material (with Ctrl+D) and then tweak the duplicate's settings as required

Shaders

Materials are not just about specifying an object's color. There's more to them. The material is essentially an algorithm or formula defining how the surface of an object should look. Different appearances and looks often require us to use different types of materials. These types are known as **Shaders**. The default Shader is the Diffuse Shader. But if we wanted to add a shiny highlight to the red sphere, for example, to make it look metallic or smooth as opposed to rough or cloth-like, then we can use a Bumped Specular Shader. To do this, click the Shader drop-down list from the Object Inspector and select Bumped Specular. This adds a shine to the sphere, which can be seen in the Viewport. You can control the size and power of the shine using the Specular Color and Shininess properties in the Material Editor. See Figure 2-3.

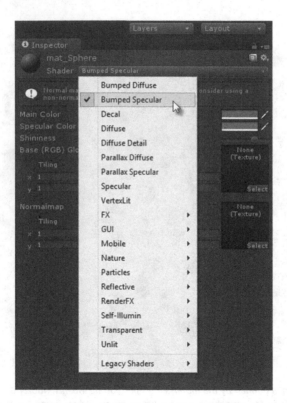

Figure 2-3. Changing the Shader type for a material controls its method of shading an object's surface

Note   The majority of Shader types will not apply to most 2D games, as we'll see soon. After playing around with Shaders, you can just switch back to Diffuse.

Working with Textures

Materials define not just shader types and other properties like shininess and bumpiness, but also how the surface color normally looks to the eye when illuminated- and not simply in terms of bold colors like red or blue. To define color more completely, materials use **textures**. A material may *contain* none, one or more textures. A texture is a pixel-based image (like a BMP, JPEG, or PNG file) that can be loaded into a material to color an object's surface. The UV mapping of a mesh controls how the texture of a material is wrapped around its surface. The details on how to import and load-in textures optimally is discussed later in this chapter. For now, let's make the sphere appear to have a grassy/earthy surface. To do this, we'll load in some textures from the Unity standard terrain assets. Select Assets ➤ Import Package ➤ Terrain Assets from the application menu, and then import the package. Doing this imports a range of texture assets into the project, and these can be viewed in the Project Panel at Standard Assets ➤ Terrain Assets ➤ Terrain Textures. See Figure 2-4.

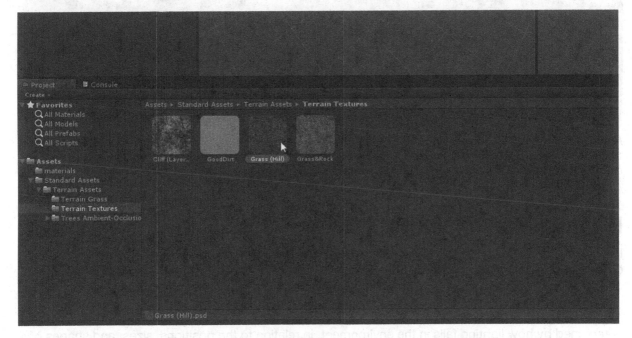

Figure 2-4. *Import textures from an Asset Package into your project. You can also import textures like any other asset, by dragging and dropping them from the file explorer into the Unity Editor's Project Panel. Take care when importing textures (and all assets), as guidelines and techniques apply that can help you optimize them and achieve the best quality possible. Details for importing textures optimally are considered later in this chapter*

For a material using the default Diffuse shader type, we can plug in a texture by clicking on the Base RGB texture swatch, beneath Main Color in the material editor, and then we select a texture from the Asset Picker dialog. Once a texture is added to the Base RGB slot, the sphere meshes in the Viewport update to show the texture on their surface. If you still have a red color (or a different color) applied to the Main Color slot, then the grassy texture will be tinted or shaded by that color. If you want your texture to appear as it does in the image file, independent of any colored shading, then set the Main Color to pure white RGB(255, 255, 255) as shown in Figure 2-5.

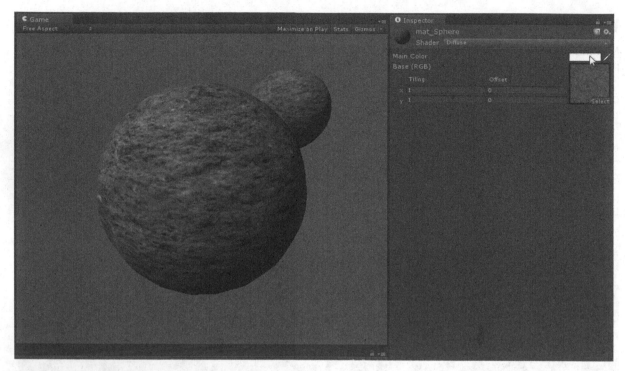

Figure 2-5. Plug textures into materials to display them on the mesh surface according to its UV mapping. For the Diffuse Shader, the texture specified in the Base RGB slot is multiplied by the color in the Main Color slot. Thus, a black color results in a black output, and a white color leaves all the texture pixels intact since white (represented as 1) is mathematical identity

Materials for 2D Games

In practice, almost all materials and shader types provided with Unity are designed to work with 3D objects in 3D space. This means most materials are configured to shade the surfaces of objects in combination with scene lights. The bumpiness, normal, and specularity effects common to materials in games rely heavily on meshes being illuminated by lights in a 3D environment. Similarly, the brightest regions of a mesh in the scene (the highlights) and its darkest regions (the shadows) are determined by how lighting falls in the environment, in relation to the positions, sizes, and shapes of objects. Meshes obscured from lighting by other intervening objects will appear darker because they are in shadow, and objects standing close to lights will appear brighter in the areas most exposed to light. Both the lights in the scene and the material shader types make these kinds of effects possible. Now while this behaviour and mechanic can produce highly believable results for many 3D games, it can stand in the way of 2D games. It can act as an obstacle and a hindrance rather than a help and a benefit. This is because most 2D textures and graphics are created with lighting and shading baked into them by the artist, and they are not supposed to be shaded or illuminated any further by the engine. Backgrounds for adventure games and hidden-object games, and tile sets for RPG games, are all prominent examples of these kinds of graphics. With these, you usually just want to show them on screen without any further illumination or shading, as shown in Figure 2-6.

Figure 2-6. This screenshot from adventure game Baron Wittard: Nemesis of Ragnarok shows a dilapidated environment, complete with lighting and atmospheric effects. This should be shown in-game without any further lighting and illumination added

Unity does not ship with a "2D Game" material or shader type that we can simply select and apply. Rather, we must resort to a range of tricks and techniques to achieve the result we need. The result is that we want to have multiple objects in a scene, with a material applied, and for those objects to show their materials and textures on-screen as they appear in the image file. We don't want the shading of objects to be affected by scene lighting, appearing darker in some areas and lighter in others. This result of creating "lighting-immunity" can be achieved in Unity through many different methods. Here are two of them that'll be used throughout this book.

Method 1: Use White Ambient Light

If you delete *all* lights from a scene and then view that scene in the Game Viewport, or even in the Scene Viewport, you'll see that it's not completely black as it should be. If the scene were truly devoid of lights, then nothing should be visible—darkness should pervade everywhere. Instead, every object in the scene appears illuminated by a uniform and consistently dull-illumination—by a global light whose color and intensity is close to black but is still not quite black, and this allows objects to be visible. This light is known as the Ambient Light. It can be helpful in making 2D games. In short, if you know that your 2D game is never going to need any lighting in 3D, then you can remove all lights from your scenes and change the Ambient Light to white, allowing all materials and textures to be shown at their full, default brightness. To control the ambient light, ensure your scene is open and active in the Editor, and select Edit ➤ Render Settings from the application menu. Then in the Object Inspector, change the Ambient Light color swatch to white. See Figure 2-7.

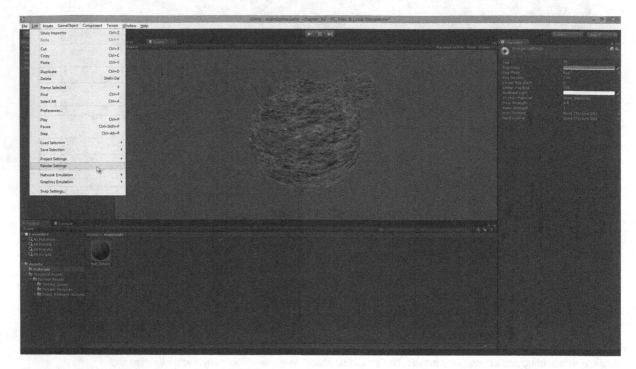

Figure 2-7. You can display 2D textures at full brightness on-screen, as defined in the image file, by removing all scene lights and setting the Ambient Light to white

---

Note The project files (`Project_Files/Chapter02/ambient_light_disable`) demonstrate a project with Ambient Light set to white.

The main drawback of the Ambient Light method is its all-pervasiveness. For objects to appear correctly in your game with white ambient light, your scenes should have no lights at all. This is often fine for many 2D games, but there might be times when you want to mix and match 2D and 3D elements in a game, or put the scene lighting to creative uses. In these cases, you want to keep scene lighting and be able to selectively disable lighting on specific objects in the scene. Method 2 shows you how to achieve this.

Note You can also change the Ambient Light to black to remove all Ambient Light in a scene; meaning that illumination is provided entirely by scene lighting and nothing else.

Method 2: Use Light-Immune Shaders

If you want to keep the benefits of scene lighting but be able to *pick and choose* specific objects in the scene to be immune from lighting entirely, then you'll need a specific shader and workflow. This involves a two-step process. First, select the material you want to be immune from lighting and set its Shader type to Self-Illumination / Diffuse. This is shown in Figure 2-8.

Figure 2-8. *Self-illuminated materials remain unaffected by the darkening that can result from scene lighting or shadows. It's still possible however to brighten self-illuminated shaders by using other lights, and also to colorize them using colored lights*

Note   You can also use the Unlit or Mobile Unlit shader types to make a material immune from regular scene lighting.

Setting a material to a self-illuminated shader is not enough however to secure complete light-immunity for an object in the scene. Even though a self-illuminated object cannot be darkened, it's still possible for it to be brightened or colorized by surrounding lights. To protect against this, a second step is required. You need to create a new Scene Layer to which all light-immune objects are attached, and then exclude the layer from scene lights by using their Culling Mask property. To do this, create a new layer by selecting Layers ➤ Edit Layers... from the Layers drop-down list at the top-right side of the Editor interface. Then type the layer name into the next available slot. Here, I've named the layer IgnoreLights. See Figure 2-9.

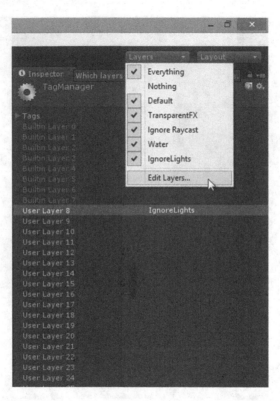

Figure 2-9. Creating a new layer in the scene to contain all light-immune objects. Remember to assign objects to the layer after it has been created!

Once the IgnoreLights layer is created, be sure to add all light-immune objects to it. Select the relevant objects in the scene and assign them to the layer by clicking in their Layer drop-down list from the Object Inspector and choose the IgnoreLights layer. Then select all lights in the scene, and use the Culling Mask property in the Object Inspector to remove a check mark from the IgnoreLights layer. This excludes objects on this layer from lighting, but keeps them illuminated (through the self-illuminated material). See Figure 2-10.

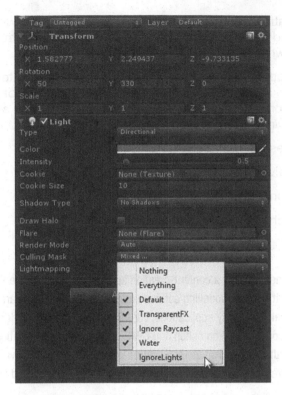

Figure 2-10. Use the Culling Mask property for lights to selectively remove objects from scene lighting while keeping them illuminated

Note   The setup for Method 2 can be found in the book's companion files
(Project_Files/Chapter02/lighting_selective_disable).

Creating Textures

Textures are image files. If you can create files in the format of JPG, BMP, TIFF, TGA, PSD, PNG, or others (as listed in Table 1-1 in Chapter 1), then you can create textures for your games. Provided you keep to these Unity-accepted formats, then it really doesn't matter in the larger scheme of things which software you use to create them, or any graphics. The key rule for creating graphics is: if it *looks* right, then it *is* right. Consequently, a wide range of options and software are available to you for creating textures, some commercial and some free. Some of the famous "industry standard" applications include Adobe Photoshop (http://www.adobe.com/uk/products/photoshop.html) and Adobe Illustrator (http://www.adobe.com/uk/products/illustrator.html), and also 3D software such as Autodesk 3DS Max (http://www.autodesk.com/products/autodesk-3ds-max/) and Autodesk Maya (www.autodesk.com/products/autodesk-maya/). However, these are certainly not the only options available to you. Many successful games, both 2D and 3D, have been created using only freely available content-creation tools. These tools include: GIMP (http://www.gimp.org/), Inkscape (http://inkscape.org/), and Blender (http://www.blender.org/). I recommend taking a look at all the tools listed here to see what works best for your project.

For the remainder of this chapter, I'll restrict my discussion to creating 2D textures for Unity using the software Photoshop CS6 and GIMP. Specifically, I'll go through many of the requirements Unity makes about textures and consider ways of optimizing textures for import at the best quality. In short, there are three rules to keep in mind for creating textures:

- Make your textures a power-2 size (in almost all cases).

- Work nondestructively at the highest quality settings.

- Expand alpha channels for transparent textures.

- Let's examine each of these rules in more detail.

> **Note**   Remember, Unity is not typically a content-creation application. It's possible to download add-ons
> from the Asset Store to turn it into 3D modelling software and image editing software. But normally game
> assets are created in external third-party applications. For this reason, the remainder of this chapter will
> consider the image editing software of Photoshop and GIMP. Though these applications are not a part of Unity,
> and thus might not strictly fall within the scope of a Unity-based book, the workflow in those applications is
> highly relevant to how textures look and perform in Unity. Thus, they are addressed here.

Rule #1: Power-2 Dimensions

Every pixel-based image has a width and height measured in pixels, and each pixel is a block of color. The image is essentially a grid of juxtaposed pixels: the content of the image (the picture itself) emerges from the collection of pixels. The width and height of the image in pixels is known as the **pixel dimensions** of the image. It is also commonly referred to as the **resolution** of the image. Whenever you create a new image inside either Photoshop or GIMP, you get the choice to set the dimensions, specifying the width and height in pixels. Though Unity imports textures of practically any size from 4096x4096 downwards, this does not mean that all textures will look and work equally well when imported. This is because resolution matters. Due to limitations in graphics hardware and real-time rendering, most textures should be of a power-2 resolution. That is, their width and height should be a power-2 size. What does that mean? In short, it means the dimensions can be any value such as: 4, 8, 16, 32, 64, 128, 256, 512, 1024, 2048 and 4096. These values are termed a power of 2 size because: $2^2=4$, $2^3=8$, $2^4=16$, $2^5=32$, $2^6=128$, and so on. The textures do not need to be square, of course. The width and height can differ, such as: 128x64, 2048x512 and 128x4096. But, whatever the dimensions and aspect ratio, your textures should generally be of a power-2 size. If you import a nonpower-2 texture into Unity, Unity will (by default) scale and stretch that texture to the nearest power-2 size. That is not generally desirable because it involves unnecessary image resampling and can adversely affect how your textures appear in your scene.

Note   Later in this book, we'll see a sneaky way around the power-2 limitation by using Atlas Textures. Using this technique we'll be able to create our textures at practically any size we want and still have them display correctly. Further, this technique will work regardless of which image software you use. Take a look a Figure 2-11 to see the image creation settings for Photoshop and GIMP.

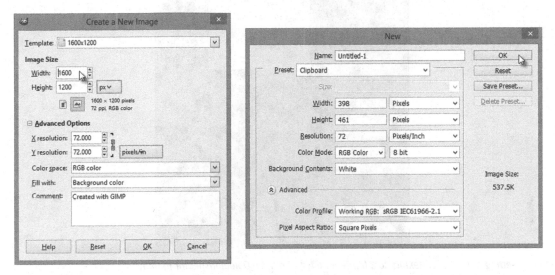

Figure 2-11. Creating a new image with Ctrl+N, and specifying pixel dimensions in GIMP (left) and Photoshop (right)

There is an exception to the power-2 rule in Unity and it relates to **GUI Textures**. If you select any valid texture in the Unity Project Panel and examine its import properties in the Object Inspector, you'll see a Type drop-down list. From this list you can choose the option GUI Texture and then click Apply. Doing this converts your texture into a GUI Texture, which is used *exclusively* for images drawn in 2D screen space. This refers to elements for user interfaces: such as buttons, menus, drop-down lists, icons, power-up bars, heads-up displays, and more. These textures cannot be assigned to models and meshes in 3D space. Textures used for these purposes can be of any dimension (though ideally with an even-numbered dimension). This works because of the way Unity internally handles these sorts of textures. See Figure 2-12. We will not have reason to use these kinds of textures in this book, however.

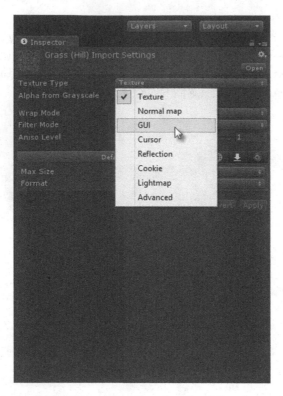

Figure 2-12. Setting the selected texture to a GUI Texture type from the Object Inspector in Unity

Note   You might wonder whether we couldn't just use the GUI Textures for making 2D games? After all, if Unity already allows us to draw GUIs in 2D screen-space using textures of non-power 2 sizes, then why can't this system be adapted for 2D games? The answer is: Yes, it can be adapted in the way suggested. That's one way of making 2D games. But that method involves complications we can avoid by using the method described in this book. The GUI Texture method involves performance issues for games with many textures and objects, and those issues are especially prominent on mobile devices.

Rule #2: Retain Quality

In the world of pixel-based images, such as PNGs and TGAs, the term *quality* typically refers to data integrity. If you save an image to a file and import that into Unity, you typically want that image to appear on-screen with all the pixels and information intact. You want to know that what you see in-game from Unity's real-time renderer is an accurate representation of the texture images you actually imported. On this understanding, there are two main enemies to retaining quality in pixel images. These are: **Image Resampling** and **Lossy Compression**. These two processes (which occur along the path of image creation and importing) each take an image as input and give out another image as output, but the output is of reduced quality: the pixels are changed in some undesirable way. If you feel your images are looking grainy, jagged, rough-edged, blurry or distorted; or if you detect that something is wrong with the image but cannot quite see what it is, then it's likely your image has become a victim to one or both of these enemies. The question of retaining quality is about how to either completely avoid these enemies, or (at least) encounter them as few times as possible. Thankfully, there are steps we can take to protect our images from most degrading processes.

The first sub-rule here is to save your image files in a **lossless** format. In practice this means: save your images in the PNG, TGA, TIFF, or PSD format, and *not* JPG. Both Photoshop and GIMP support all these formats. For **lossy** formats like JPG, image quality is lost on each file-save operation: JPG only saves an approximation of the original image. This means that more and more data from the original is compromised on each successive save. To retain the quality without data loss, a Lossless format is needed. I recommend either PNG for standard textures and PSD or TGA for textures with transparency. Take a look at Figure 2-13 to see image export options for Photoshop and GIMP.

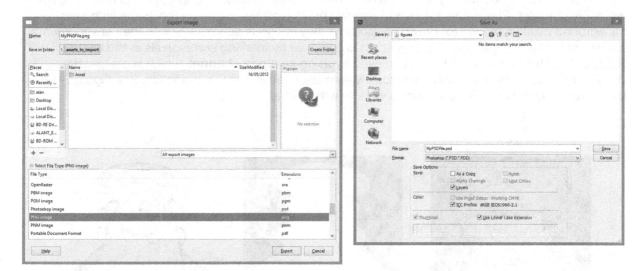

Figure 2-13. Save your images to lossless formats to preserve quality. In GIMP Choose File ➤ Export (Left) and In Photoshop choose File ➤ Save or File ➤ Save As . . . (right)

The second sub-rule relates to resampling (or *Image Filtering*). This process determines how the pixels in a texture are mapped to objects and shown on-screen in perspective as Texels (Texture Pixels). The settings for this are controlled not by adjusting anything in your image editing software, but by adjusting settings in the Unity editor. You control Image Filtering from the Object Inspector, through the Filter setting that appears in the Import Settings for the texture when selected. Simply select a texture in the Project Panel, and set the Filter mode from the Object Inspector. The Filter value can be one of the following: Point, Bilinear, or Trilinear. These range in quality from left to right, with Point being the lowest quality and Trilinear being the highest. Typically Bilinear produces "good enough" results for most games and situations. But sometimes Trilinear is used to further increase quality, especially if textures are highly skewed in perspective. In short, there is no wrong or right setting to use here: try them all and see what works best for your textures and game.

Finally, the third sub-rule relates to image size. Always import your textures into Unity either at their largest sizes, or at the size you need for your game. The Unity Editor can downsize textures, if required. Do not, however, upsize textures ever! Unless, of course, there's simply no alternative. Upsizing a texture (that is, scaling them up from smaller to larger sizes) is a recipe for blurriness, poor quality, and shoddy looking textures. The maximum texture size in Unity is 4096 pixels in any one dimension, and I recommend sizing your textures to this maximum in both dimensions (width and height) wherever possible. That way, you can always downsize your textures through the complete range of sizes, if needed.

Rule #3: Expand Alpha Channels for Transparency

Unity gives the name *alpha texture* to any texture that contains transparency information. In most games, there'll be times when you need to display only parts of a texture as opposed to a complete rectangle of pixels. Player characters and enemy sprites typically appear in the scene with their background pixels removed (or drawn invisible) so they integrate seamlessly with their environments and seem part of the game world. This effect is achieved by marking some pixels in the texture transparent. This marking process is achieved by using an **alpha channel**, which is a separate channel of pixel information using grayscale values encoded inside the image file. See Figure 2-14 for an illustration of how alpha channels work to achieve transparency.

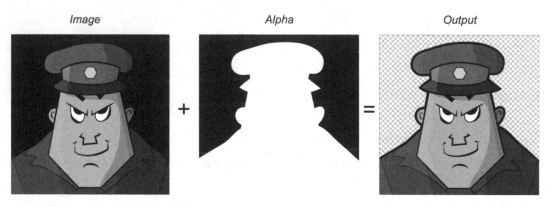

Figure 2-14. Alpha channel encoded inside the file to achieve transparency. Pixel values in the alpha channel are mapped to pixels in the RGB channels and are used to control its degree of transparency. Black = 100% transparent, white = fully opaque, and values between express opacity (strength of transparency)

To create an alpha channel in Adobe Photoshop, switch to the Channels Palette and click the New Channel button on the bottommost toolbar, as shown in Figure 2-15. This adds a new channel to the image for storing alpha values. You can also generate an alpha channel from a selection in your image: create a pixel selection using the selection tools (such as the Marquee Select tool or the Magic Wand tool) and then click the Channel From Selection button on the bottom toolbar of the Channels Palette.

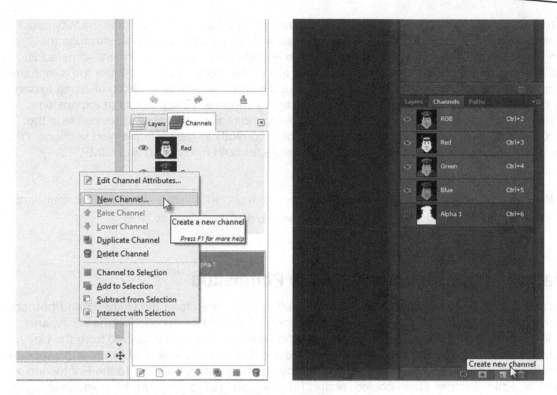

Figure 2-15. *Creating an alpha channel in GIMP (left) and Photoshop (right)*

To create an alpha channel in GIMP, switch to the Channels Palette, then right-click and choose New Channel from the context menu, as shown in Figure 2-15. This adds a new channel to the image for storing alpha values. You can also generate an alpha channel from a selection in your image. First create an empty channel, and then create a pixel selection using the selection tools (such as the Marquee Select tool or the Magic Wand tool). Finally, right-click the alpha channel in the Channels Palette, choosing the option Add to Selection from the context menu, and then flood fill the selection with white using the Paint Bucket tool.

Note   Remember, white pixels in the alpha channel create visible pixels in the texture, and black pixels in the alpha channel create invisible pixels (100% transparent) in the texture. Intervening values (grayscale) reflect in-between degrees of transparency. For performance reasons, use transparency only when essential in your game. If transparency is required, ascertain whether you need only visible and non-visible (black and white) values, or whether you need a full range of transparency in terms of grayscale values between white and black. If possible, choose the simpler (black/white) duo-color scheme. This is because, as we'll see, Unity ships with optimized Cut-Out shaders that typically outperform fully alpha blended shaders.

Creating an alpha channel in an image achieves transparency effects for textures in Unity, provided the file is imported and configured appropriately, as we'll see shortly. However, although the presence of an alpha channel *is* enough in itself to encode transparency, there are some additional steps and precautions to be taken when creating alpha channels. This is to ensure the transparency appears correctly and as intended in Unity, without distortion and error. In short, all alpha textures must have their alpha channels expanded before being imported. The process of expansion effectively creates a thin buffer of additional pixels around regions that should be visible in the image. Doing this ensures alpha transparency shows correctly in-game. In the next sections, I'll show you step by step how to create an alpha texture for both Photoshop and GIMP.

> **Note** Further information online on alpha channel expansion can be found here at the Unity Documentation: `http://docs.unity3d.com/Documentation/Manual/HOWTO-alphamaps.html`.

Creating Alpha Textures in Adobe Photoshop

If you're creating alpha textures in Photoshop, you'll need to download the Unity-made Photoshop add-on, which will help in the texture creation process. This add-on is called *Alpha Utility,* and it's a Photoshop Action that automates much of the work. It can be downloaded from the Unity Documentation webpage here: `http://docs.unity3d.com/Documentation/Manual/HOWTO-alphamaps.html`. Download this add-on and install it into Unity, copying and-pasting the file into the Photoshop ➤ Presets ➤ Actions folder. Once copied, restart Photoshop (see Figure 2-16). Now you're ready to create an alpha texture.

Figure 2-16. Photoshop with the Alpha Utility installed to the Actions Palette

Step 1. Separate Foreground From Background

Begin with an image where your character's or sprite's pixels are separated onto a completely new layer on top of a transparent background, as seen in Figure 2-17. This starting image does *not* need to contain any alpha channel. If your sprite is baked or merged into a nontransparent background, then you'll need to use a combination of the selection tools (Marquee Select, Quick Select, Magic Wand, and Magnetic Lasso tools) to separate it first.

Figure 2-17. A sprite layer created in Photoshop. Note the checked-pattern background to indicate transparency

> **Note** If you want to follow along with these steps, working on the same image used in this example, you can find it in the Chapter 2 companion files at: `Project_Files/Chapter02/Images/texture_trans_start.psd`. The completed project is saved to: `Project_Files/Chapter02/Images/texture_trans_end.psd`.

Step 2. Duplicate and Defringe

Duplicate the sprite layer by dragging and dropping it onto the New Layer option at the bottom of the layer palette, and rename the duplicate to Expanded. Do not delete the original, but leave it at the bottom of the layer stack for reference later. Ensure the Expanded layer is selected in the Layer Palette but that no pixels on the layer are selected (deselect all with Ctrl+D, or choose Select ➤ Deselect from the menu). Then choose Layer ➤ Matting ➤ Defringe from the application menu, as shown in Figure 2-18. This command removes any halos or aberrant edge pixels from the layer that can be difficult to spot and remove manually—it helps to create a clean and crisp edge around the pixel border.

Figure 2-18. Remove aberrant edge pixels from a transparent layer with Defringe

Step 3. Expand Edges

Expand the border pixels of the Expanded layer using the Unity Alpha Utility action. To do this, select the Expanded layer in the Layers Palette, and either run the action Dilate (but run this several times), or run the action Dilate many times once. Doing this will produce a succession of new layers based on the Expanded layer. You'll see the pixels around the border of the layer have expanded outwards, creating a thicker or wider edge buffer. See Figure 2-19.

Figure 2-19. Duplicated layers created using the Alpha Utility have expanded the border pixels of the original Expanded layer

Step 4. Merging and Alpha Channels

Now merge the Expanded layer together with all its derivatives from the Alpha Utility, leaving the file with only two layers: the Expanded layer and the original layer. Then select the original layer in the Layers Palette (not the Expanded layer) and select all its nontransparent pixels to create a "marching ants" selection around them. From this selection, create an alpha channel in the image. To do this, switch to the Channels Palette, and select the Save Selection as Channel button, as shown in Figure 2-20. Finally, save the file. Congratulations you've just created an alpha texture that is Unity ready!

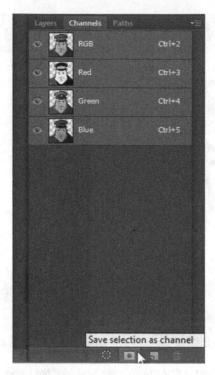

Figure 2-20. Complete the alpha texture by creating a new alpha channel from the pixel selection in the original layer

Creating Alpha Textures in GIMP

Creating Unity compatible alpha textures in GIMP is typically an easy process. First, load up your image where the character's or sprite's pixels are separated onto a completely new layer on top of a transparent background, as featured in Figure 2-21.

Figure 2-21. Preparing to export a Unity-compatible alpha texture from GIMP

Note   If you want to follow along with these steps, working on the same image used in this example, you can find it in the Chapter 2 companion files at: `Project_Files/Chapter02/Images/texture_trans_start.xcf`.

Then, select File ➤ Export from the application menu. Finally, save your image in either the Targa format, or the PNG format. If you choose PNG, be sure to disable the export option Save Background Color. Congratulations you've just created an alpha texture that is Unity ready! See Figure 2-22.

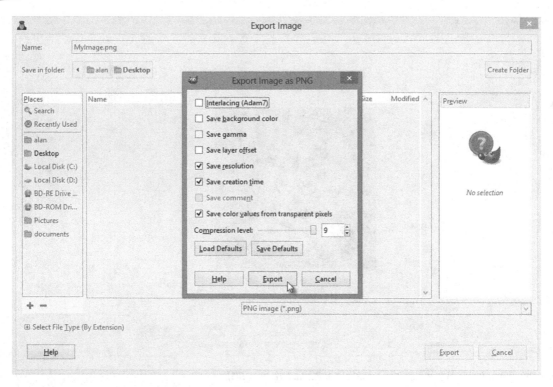

Figure 2-22. Exporting an alpha texture from GIMP to the PNG file format

Importing Textures into Unity

Once you've created one or more textures, with or without transparency, it's time to import them into your Unity Project for configuring with your materials. Importing them into Unity works much like importing any other asset: you drag and drop the files from Windows Explorer or OSX Finder into the Project Panel of the Unity editor. On import, Unity applies default settings to all your textures, and often these settings will be acceptable. But sometimes they require further tweaking to make them look sharper, crisper, or more vibrant. This section considers these settings further. Consider Figure 2-23 to see the settings, editable from the Object Inspector.

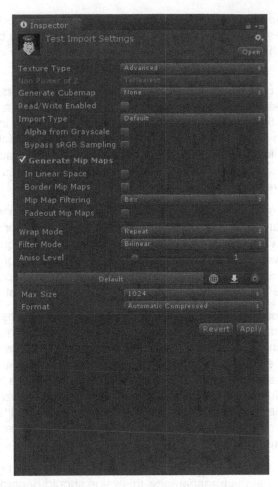

Figure 2-23. *Default Texture Import Settings are applied to every newly imported texture. Sometimes the settings will work fine; other times not, depending on your project and needs*

- *Texture Type*: This specifies the texture type for the selected texture. A range of types are available, and each controls how Unity handles and manages that texture in-game. For 2D games, this value will typically be Advanced, although a value of Texture (for standard texture) is also possible. Textures of type Texture, should be sized to a power-2 size and non-power-2 textures will be scaled to the nearest power-2 size. The Advanced mode offers the greatest control over texture import settings. We'll return to this mode later in the book.

- *Generate Cubemap*: This allows a texture to be used as a plane image inside an environment cube. Generally, this should be set to false for nearly every kind of texture for a 2D Game.

- *Import Type*: The Import Type setting can be left at its default value of Default. We'll not have cause to change this value here for 2D games.

- *Generate Mip Maps*: Likewise, this setting should be unchecked for all Advanced textures for 2D games. This setting can vary texture quality based on Z-distance from the camera, but because this kind of distance is meaningless for truly 2D games, we'll have no need to change this value.

- *Wrap Mode*: This controls how the texture will appear on surfaces that tile their textures and repeat them in a pattern, like checkered floors. If a value of Repeat is specified, then the texture can tile horizontally and vertically in a pattern, if required. If Clamp is specified, then the texture will not tile and the edge pixels of the texture will instead be stretched indefinitely to fill the space. Generally, I make a habit of specifying Clamp as the default for all textures, except for those I know will repeat.

- *Aniso Level*: This specifies how clearly and crisply your texture will look on a surface that is dramatically skewed in perspective, like the floor or ceiling in a 3D game, which typically runs perpendicular away from the camera. For most 2D games, however, textures will not appear in perspective. For this reason, the Aniso Level will not be a consideration of the same magnitude as it is for 3D games. This value will therefore almost always be the default of 1.

- *Max Size*: Specifies the maximum size in pixels at which your texture will show. For 2D games textures, will almost always show at their Maximum Size or their Default size, whichever is smaller. If you set the Maximum below the texture's default size (as specified in the image file), and then click the Apply button, the texture will be resampled down to the specified Maximum Size. Unity however always keeps an internal copy of the original. So if you downsize and then upsize again to the original settings, Unity refers to the original texture at its default size, rather than upsize the shrunken version it generated previously. This helps retain texture quality.

- *Format*: This further controls texture quality and performance. For Advanced textures containing alpha transparency, this value should generally be ARGB 32 Bit, or RGBA 32 Bit.

Importing an Alpha Texture into Unity

Everything said about importing textures in the previous section applies here to alpha textures. But alpha textures come with additional requirements. Specifically, once imported, alpha textures must be assigned in specific ways to materials for their transparency to display correctly during gameplay.

By default, alpha textures assigned to the default diffuse material will not appear transparent in the scene at all. This is because only certain kinds of materials display transparency from alpha textures—all other materials, like the Diffuse material—ignore transparency and show textures as though they had no transparency.

In this section I'll walk you through importing the sample alpha texture character.tga, found in the book's companion files in the folder Project_Files/Chapter02/Images/. Of course, this import workflow applies not only to this specific alpha texture, but to any alpha texture you choose. Once imported, we'll then configure a material to show the texture with transparency on a Plane object in a sample scene.

Step 1. Import Alpha Texture

Begin from a new and empty Unity project, with a new scene open and active in the Viewport. Drag and drop the alpha texture character.tga from Windows Explorer or OSX Finder into the Project Panel in the Unity Editor to import the texture into the project. You don't have to use this file; you can use your own alpha texture, if you want. Whichever file you use, Unity will import the texture and apply default settings to it. These can be viewed by selecting the texture in the Project Panel and seeing its settings in the Object Inspector. Leave the settings at their defaults. See Figure 2-24.

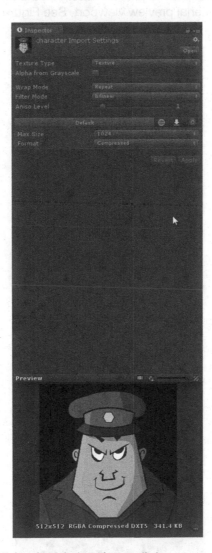

Figure 2-24. Alpha texture imported into Unity with default settings applied. . .

Step 2. Create Alpha Compliant Material

Create a new material and assign it a Unlit ➤ Transparent CutOut Shader. This shader is lightweight and optimized for alpha textures that use only white and black colors in the alpha channel to indicate fully transparent or fully opaque regions in the image. If your texture uses intermediary values between white and black to indicate degrees of transparency, then you can use the most expensive Unlit ➤ Transparent shader instead (that is, *most expensive on desktop platforms*, such as Windows and OSX. For mobile devices, however, it's often preferred to CutOut shaders). Once created, click on the Base RGB texture swatch for the material and assign it the alpha texture. You'll see the transparency take effect in the material preview viewport. See Figure 2-25.

Figure 2-25. Configuring an Unlit Transparent CutOut Shader for showing an alpha texture. Note: this shader belongs to the Unlit group. This means it is not affected by scene lighting- this can be helpful for 2D games

Step 3. Create a Textured Quad

Create a Plane object in the scene, aligning it to the camera, and then drag and drop the newly created material onto the plane to see it textured in the Viewport, complete with alpha transparency. This allows you to see right-through the geometry in the transparent areas, showing the contents of the scene behind. See Figure 2-26. Congratulations, you've just configured an alpha texture in Unity.

Figure 2-26. A Plane object with an alpha texture applied to the material Base RGB. The transparency allows you to see the scene behind the transparent regions

Summary

This chapter outlined the fundamentals of using textures and materials in Unity, complete with a summary about how to get up and running with transparency in both Photoshop and GIMP. In short, you should now:

- Understand the difference between materials and textures
- Know how to work with materials and textures in Unity
- Understand the import settings for textures

- Understand the three rules for importing optimized textures

- Be able to save textures at the highest quality settings

- Be able to create textures in both Photoshop and GIMP

- Understand how alpha channels work to create transparency

- Be able to create alpha channels in Photoshop and GIMP

- Understand how to generate an alpha channel, expand colors, and save transparency

- Be able to import alpha textures into Unity

- Be able to create materials to work with alpha textures

Chapter 3

Quick 2D Workflow

In this chapter we'll put together a simple 2D game in Unity using only the standard tools and editor features. This game is a space-invaders style clone featuring a player-controlled spaceship at the bottom of the screen (see Figure 3-1). In this game, the player can move horizontally, left and right, and must shoot invading aliens at the top of the window. The purpose of this exercise is not to show you how to make space-invader style games (though it will do that!) but to show you the more abstract principles and workflows for making "simple" 2D games quickly without having to code any additional features or editor plug-ins. This workflow shows that it's entirely possible to make 2D games straight away in Unity by using only the 3D-oriented tools. But it also shows the limitations of this approach, as well as its far-reaching performance implications for making games that'll perform well across all types of devices, especially mobiles. Once we concretely identify these challenges and issues, we'll proceed to tackle them one by one throughout subsequent chapters. So now, follow along with me as we create our first 2D game.

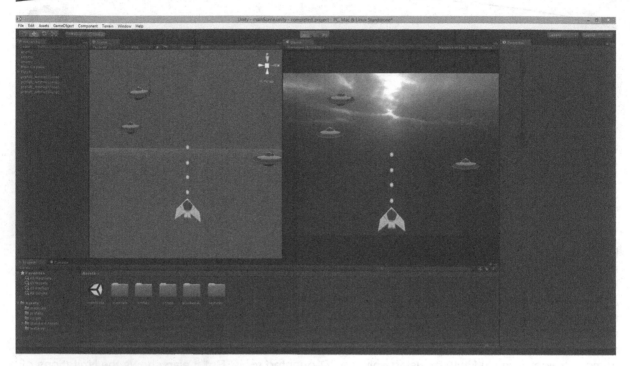

Figure 3-1. The "2D Alien Invasion" completed project in action

Getting Started at Making "2D Alien Invasion"

The first steps in making any Unity game are to create a new project, and then to create a new scene, and finally to import assets. For this project, there are three texture assets to import, all in the PSD format complete with alpha channels. These are: the player spaceship (spaceship.psd), the enemy spaceship (enemy.psd), and the ammo graphic (ammo.psd). These files can be found in the book's companion files, in the folder Project_Files/Chapter03/source_assets/. Go ahead and import all these files into a new project and set the texture sizes to their maximum of 4096, which matches the dimensions of the texture files. Be sure to click the *Apply* button on the Object Inspector after making the changes, to confirm the settings and have them take effect (see Figure 3-2).

> **Note**   Each texture file for this project is square and is of a power-2 size (4096×4096 pixels). Further, there is a separate texture file for each game element: the spaceship, the enemy, and the ammo. This project will not use Atlas Textures (considered later in this book).

Tip Organize the assets in your project as soon as possible to keep things tidy: copy imported textures to a *textures* folder, create materials inside a *materials* folder, create scripts inside a *scripts* folder, and so on. Doing this is not essential, but it can make your life a lot easier.

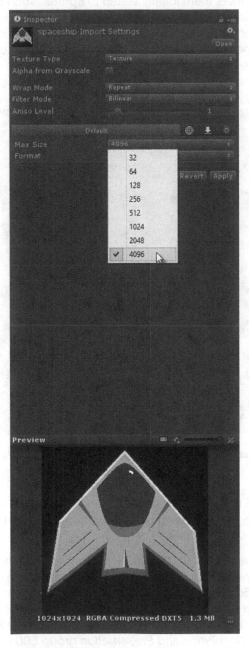

Figure 3-2. Configuring imported textures to show at their maximum sizes

Now let's create three "transparent cut-out" materials, one for each of the newly imported textures. To do this, create three new materials in the Project Panel using the application menu option **Assets ➤ Create Material**, and name each material appropriately. I've named mine: mat_Player, mat_Enemy, and mat_Ammo. Each material should have the shader type **Unlit ➤ Transparent Cutout** selected. More information on this shader type can be found in Chapter 2. In short, this shader is optimized for textures with only fully opaque and fully transparent pixels, as opposed to semitransparent pixels. This makes them ideally suited to sprites, such as the player spaceship and the enemies for our game, which all have transparent backgrounds. Take this opportunity to load the textures into the *Diffuse* slot for each material, and from the Preview Window in the Object Inspector you'll see the alpha transparency has taken effect. This means our materials are now ready to be assigned to objects in the scene (see Figure 3-3).

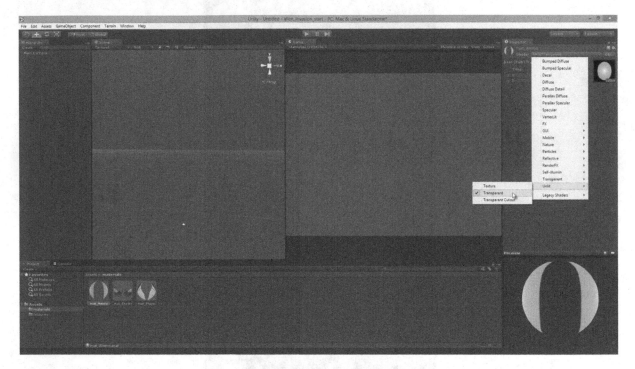

Figure 3-3. *Three materials now created from three textures, using the Transparent Cutout Shader type for optimized sprite transparency*

The materials in Figure 3-3 are immune from scene lighting. Notice the Editor GUI is arranged with the Scene and Game tabs side by side, using the "2D games interface layout" recommended in Chapter 2.

Before constructing our 2D scene, let's set the Ambient Light to white and also set the Game Resolution (the size of the game window). For this game, the resolution will be 800×600 pixels. To set the Ambient Light, select **Edit ➤ Render Settings** from the application menu, and change the *Ambient Light* swatch to White (*R:255, G:255, B:255, A:255*) in the Object Inspector. To set the game resolution, open the Player Settings dialog by selecting **Edit ➤ Project Settings ➤ Player** from the application menu. Unwind the *Resolution and Presentation* group 600 in the Object Inspector, and set the *Default Resolution* width and height to 800×600, as in Figure 3-4.

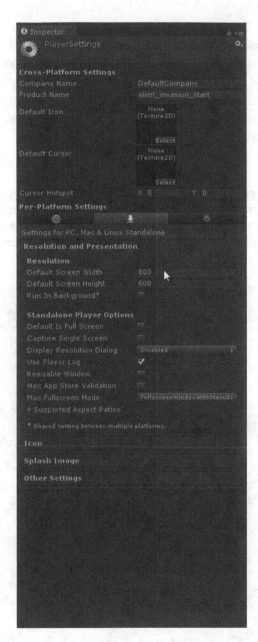

Figure 3-4. Setting the default resolution of the game to 800×600 pixels. This fixes the size of the game window

> **Note**   Setting the default resolution to 800×600 still allows the player the possibility of customizing the game to display at other resolutions, if he wants. A player could do this either through the default Unity Resolution dialog that shows at application start-up, or through any custom-made game option screens. To disable the ability to change resolutions, ensure the option *Display Resolution Dialog* is set to *Disabled* in the Resolution and Presentation group. You can also remove check marks from all non *4:3* Aspect Ratio groups in the *Supported Aspect Ratios* setting.

Once the default resolution is set to 800×600, you will want to see the game shown at this resolution while testing in the Game tab from the Unity editor, to get an accurate representation of how the final game will look to the user. To configure this, move over to the Game Viewport, and from the Aspect Ratio drop-down box in its toolbar (which is probably set to *Free Aspect*), select the Resolution 800×600. See Figure 3-5.

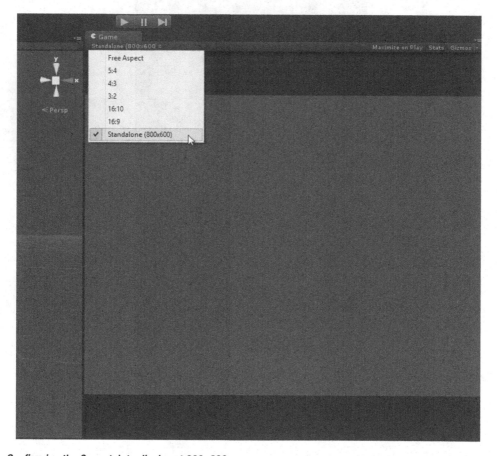

Figure 3-5. Configuring the Game tab to display at 800×600

Note   In Unity version 4.2 or above you can set the game resolution directly from the Aspect drop-down in the Game tab. Click the aspect drop-down list on the Game toolbar, and click the + icon at the bottom of the context menu to add your own custom resolution.

Adding the Player and Enemies to the Scene

The scene we have so far in our project is completely empty and devoid of functionality, apart from the default `MainCamera` object. So let's add a player in the form of a spaceship object. There are multiple ways to do this that would be appropriate here, but for this project we'll create a flat, camera-aligned plane using the standard Unity Primitives. This plane will be assigned our spaceship material. Select **GameObject ➤ Create Other ➤ Plane** from the application menu. Doing this creates a tessellated plane in the scene, as shown in Figure 3-6. Ensure the plane is positioned at the world origin of (0, 0, 0) and you may also need to rotate it to stand upright in the scene, parallel to the camera (use discreet rotation by holding down the *Ctrl* key to rotate the plane neatly in specified increments). Feel free to drag and drop the spaceship material onto the `Plane` object also. You'll notice from the wireframe view that the plane is more highly tessellated than we really require: it has more vertices and edges than is needed. We could optimize this by creating a flattened cube instead or by importing our own custom-made quad plane (with only four corner vertices) from 3D modelling software, but this project will simply use the Unity generated plane.

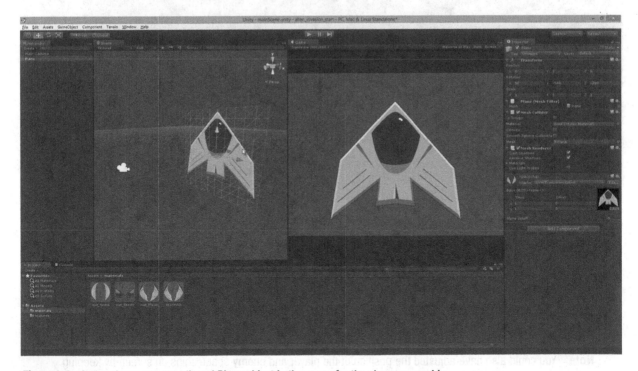

Figure 3-6. *Generating a camera-aligned Plane object in the scene for the player spaceship*

To be 'camera-aligned' the Plane object should be facing the camera head-on so the camera has a clear and direct view of the plane surface and its material.

Things are looking great so far. However, the spaceship appears too large for our purposes, covering most of the screen in the Game tab. This is certainly not what we want. To fix this, select the camera in the scene and translate it backward, away from the spaceship to decrease its size on-screen (Notice: The spaceship decreases in size as it moves further from the camera. By default, objects are rendered in perspective—more on this later). Also raise up the camera on the Y axis to lower the spaceship to the bottom of the screen where it should appear. If you're using the Scene/Game tab split view that I recommended earlier, then you can translate objects in the Scene tab while keeping your eye on the Game tab to see the results easily. Now add one Enemy object, using the same, general procedure for creating the player character. Position the enemy at the origin, assign it the mat_enemy material, and raise it upward, above the player, so it appears at the top of the screen in the Game tab as seen in Figure 3-7.

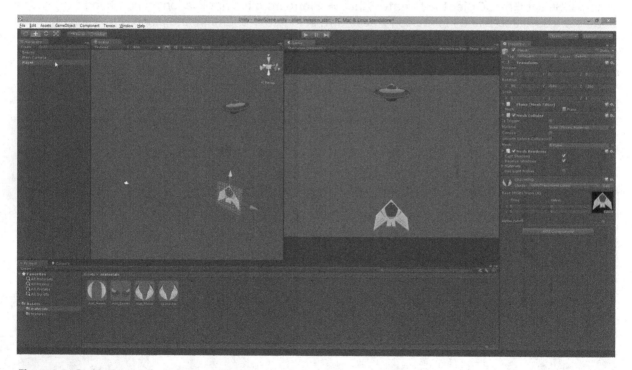

Figure 3-7. Positioning the Enemy object in the scene

Tip   Give your scene objects meaningful names (preferably as you create them) so you can easily select them from the hierarchy panel if necessary.

Note   You could also have adjusted the position of the player and enemy space ships on screen by keeping the camera in position and adjusting its *Field of View* property to control its perspective.

If you select either the player or the enemy in the scene, you'll see from the Object Inspector that both feature `Mesh Collider` Components to approximate their volumes for physics and collision detection. While it's important for objects to have `Collider` Components (we'll need them), the `Mesh Collider` specifically is computationally expensive—especially for mobile devices. So remove it from *both* objects and replace it with a simpler `Box Collider` (one for *each* object). Size it to encompass its `Plane` object. Components are removed by choosing the cog-icon at the top-right side of the component, and by selecting *Remove Component* from the context menu. See Figure 3-8.

Figure 3-8. Removing the Mesh Collider Components from the player and Enemy Plane objects

Note   Colliders need to have a minimum thickness (non-zero), even for flat objects such as textured quads. Completely flat colliders do not always detect collisions.

Once the `Mesh Collider` component is removed, replace it with a `Box Collider` component. To do this, ensure your object is first selected in the scene, and then choose **Component ➤ Physics ➤ Box Collider** from the application menu. Use the *Size X, Y,* and *Z* fields in the Object Inspector to size the Collider Volume to encompass or enclose the `Plane` object reasonably tightly, but leave a thin margin of space in each dimension. Be sure to give the collider some depth or volume too, even though the plane mesh is perfectly flat. This will improve collision detection later. The Collider Volume appears in the Scene Viewport by default as a green bounding-box wireframe. You can also show the Collider Volume wireframe in the Game tab, by enabling the *Gizmos* toggle-button on the toolbar, see Figure 3-9.

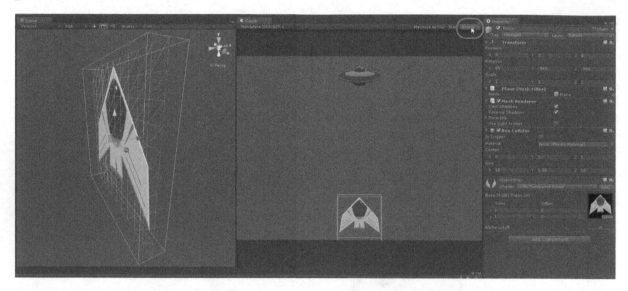

Figure 3-9. Sizing a Box Collider to a Plane object

> **Note**   An alternative to the two-step process of adding a collider, as given previously, is to simply add a Box
> Collider to an object, even if it already has a collider attached. If you do this, Unity will automatically ask
> you if you want to replace the existing colliders on the object with the latest addition.

The Collider Volume guides can be seen in the Scene tab and Game tab. To enable collider viewing
in the Game tab, enable the Gizmos toggle button on the toolbar. Be sure to apply this process to
both the Enemy and Player objects.

Implementing Player Movement

The scene now features a Player and Enemy object. However, if you click *Play* on the application
toolbar to run the project, nothing in the scene moves or responds in any way. The scene is
completely static and dead. To fix this, we'll code the player spaceship. Specifically the spaceship
will react to player input, sliding left and right horizontally across the bottom of the screen according
to button clicks, allowing the player to both target and avoid enemies above. Let's create a new C#
script file PlayerController.cs and attach it to the Player object. The class is shown in Listing 3-1.

Listing 3-1. PlayerController.cs

```
using UnityEngine;
using System.Collections;

public class PlayerController : MonoBehaviour
{
    //Player move speed in units per second
    public float Speed = 10.0f;
```

```
    //Player min and max X position in world space (to keep player in screen)
    public Vector2 MinMaxX = Vector2.zero;

    // Update is called once per frame
    void Update ()
    {
        transform.position = new Vector3(Mathf.Clamp(transform.position.x + Input.
GetAxis("Horizontal") * Speed * Time.deltaTime, MinMaxX.x, MinMaxX.y), transform.position.y,
transform.position.z);
    }

}
```

> **Tip**   This code could be optimized further by using object caching for the `Transform` Component.
> The basic idea is that on each `Update` call, the code relies on the `transform` property, such as
> `transform.position.x`, and so on. Each mention of this property, in that way, entails a further call internally
> to `GetComponent<Transform>()`. To avoid this overhead we can use the `Start` event to get or cache a
> reference to the `Transform` Component with a one-off call to `Transform MyTransform = transform`.
> Then in all subsequent calls to the `Transform` Component, we use the cached version `MyTransform`, as
> opposed to `transform`. In the code samples here, however, I use `transform` for simplicity and brevity.

The code in Listing 3-1 allows us to control movement of the player by the left and right arrow keys
on the keyboard, clamping his position between a minimum and maximum horizontal value, to
ensure he stays on-screen. His *Speed* and his Min and Max X values can be customized from the
Object Inspector, since they are public variables of the class. For this project, I've set the Speed to
50, the Min X to -30, and the Max X to 30. Speed is specified in World Units Per Second, and the
Min and Max position values are specified in World Units and not Pixels (see Figure 3-10). This is
significant and will be mentioned again later.

Figure 3-10.   Setting the speed and X Positional Range for the spaceship using the Object Inspector and the C# PlayerController class

Implementing Player Weapons with Prefabs

We've now coded the PlayerController class to allow horizontal player movement across the bottom of the screen. We can further fine-tune that movement by controlling speed and position-clamping directly from the Object Inspector. But still, the player cannot attack enemies, and enemies cannot attack him. We'll take care of that here, by creating an ammo prefab object. This prefab will be instantiated by the PlayerController every time the player presses Fire (by default Fire is either left-control on the keyboard or the left mouse button).

Creating an Ammo Prefab Object

To get started, create an Ammo object in the scene using the earlier Plane workflow used for creating the Player and Enemy objects. Specifically: create a plane, assign that plane the mat_Ammo material, and then replace the Mesh Collider with a Box Collider (and don't forget to give the object a meaningful name in the scene, such as Ammo or objAmmo). See Figure 3-11. You may also want to scale down the Ammo object from its default size to be consistent with both the Player and Enemy objects. It needs to look like something the player spaceship could really fire from its cannons.

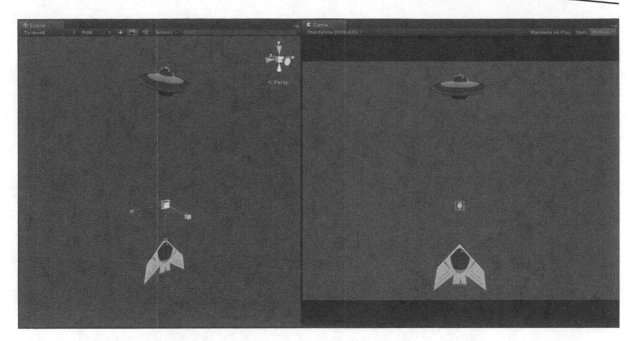

Figure 3-11. Creating an Ammo object and setting its scale to harmonize with the Player and Enemy

Note   Although you could *in theory* change the size of the ammo (on-screen) without scaling, such as by translating it away from the camera and further into the distance than either the player or the enemies, this would raise a problem for collision. If the Player object fires instances of the ammo upward on the Y axis, those instances will never actually collide or intersect with the enemy above, because the ammo is positioned deeper into the scene. The only way this could work would be if either the Enemy or Ammo colliders were extended radically, but this feels counterintuitive. In short, try to avoid linking an object's depth position to its size on-screen for 2D games. An object's depth can be used for all kinds of other things, as we'll see.

Implementing the Ammo Trajectory

The Ammo object needs motion too. When it's fired from the spaceship's cannons it needs to travel along its trajectory at a specified speed. For this project, its trajectory will always be up, and it'll continue traveling that path until it's either destroyed by colliding with an enemy or deleted because it has left the screen without hitting anything at all. After all, we don't want to waste valuable processing resources keeping track of ammo that has left the screen. To create this motion, a new C# script file is required called Ammo.cs. This file should be attached to the ammo object. Consider Listing 3-2.

Listing 3-2. Ammo.cs

```
using UnityEngine;
using System.Collections;

public class Ammo : MonoBehaviour
{
    //Direction to travel
    public Vector3 Direction = Vector3.up;

    //Speed to travel
    public float Speed = 20.0f;

    //Lifetime in seconds
    public float Lifetime = 10.0f;

    // Use this for initialization
    void Start ()
    {
        //Destroys ammo in lifetime
        Invoke("DestroyMe", Lifetime);
    }

    // Update is called once per frame
    void Update ()
    {
        //Update travel in direction at speed
        transform.position += Direction * Speed * Time.deltaTime;
    }

    //Function to destroy ammo
    void DestroyMe()
    {
        //Remove ammo from scene - has expired
        Destroy(gameObject);
    }
}
```

If you attach this script to your Ammo object in the scene and click *Play* on the application toolbar to run the project, it should shoot upward along its path and off-screen, where it's destroyed after an interval of ten seconds (the Lifetime). The Direction variable controls the trajectory of the ammo and is initialized to an up vector. Notice also that all its properties are editable from the Object Inspector. The issue to address now is the player firing ability. Specifically, we must instantiate instances of this class every time the player presses Fire. To get started with this, we'll convert the Ammo object *as it is right now* into a Prefab. Prefabs are a handy Unity feature–they allow you to select any object of any complexity in the scene, to create a snapshot or template from it (recording all the settings of all components), and then to create further independent instances or clones of it in the scene as though it were a regular asset like a mesh or light or primitive. This ability is important here to instantiate instances of the ammo object from script when the player fires the spaceship's weapons.

Creating the Prefab Ammo Object

So to create the Prefab object, select **Assets ➤ Create Prefab** from the application menu, and assign it the name prefab_Ammo. All newly created Prefabs begin as empty containers, waiting to receive a designated object in the scene. To assign the ammo to the Prefab, drag and drop the Ammo object from the scene onto the Prefab object in the Project Panel. And that's all there is to creating a Prefab! See Figure 3-12.

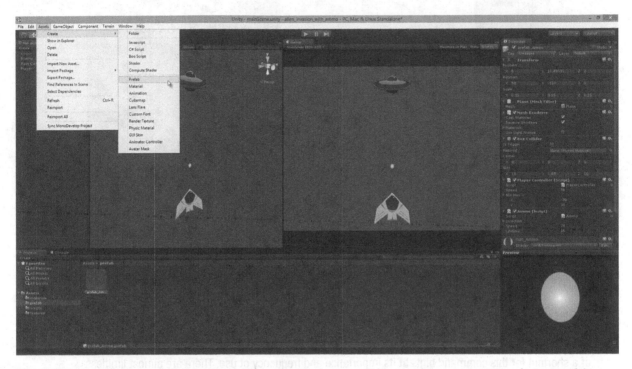

Figure 3-12. Creating an ammo Prefab from an Ammo object in the scene. This makes it easy to create new instances of the Prefab from script, just like instantiation regular objects

Defining the Cannon Point

Creating a Prefab is the first step toward a spaceship that fires ammo. But it's not the final step. In addition to reworking the PlayerController script file (we'll see that shortly), we also need to mark a point on the spaceship's body where new instances of the ammo will begin their life when the weapons are fired. This point corresponds to the tips or heads of the cannons. We can mark it in different ways, but here we'll use a *dummy* GameObject. To create this, start by choosing **GameObject ➤ Create Empty** (or press *Ctrl+Shift+N* on the keyboard). This creates an object in the scene that features nothing but a Transform component to describe its position, rotation, and scale. When this object is selected, you see it represented in the Viewport by the familiar Transform Gizmo widget. When it's not selected, however, you cannot see it at all and have to select it by name from the Hierarchy Panel. See Figure 3-13.

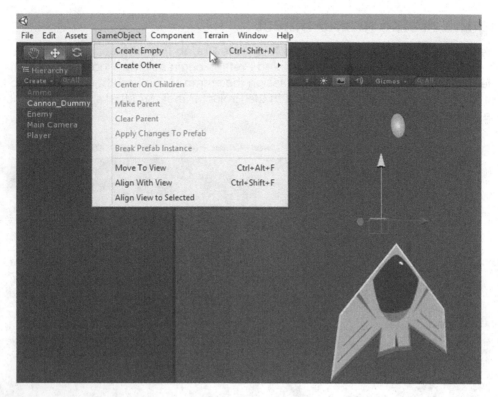

Figure 3-13. Empty GameObjects can act as dummy objects, and more. They are created using the keyboard shortcut Ctrl+Shift+N

Note   The Create Empty command has an associated keyboard shortcut of *Ctrl+Shift+N*. The existence of a shortcut for this command hints at its importance and frequency of use. There are almost limitless possibilities with empty GameObjects. You can use them to achieve different behaviors: pivot points, rotation centers, place holders, spawning locations, teleportation points, and more.

I've said it many times: never underestimate the lessons to be learned from trees: programmers use trees all the time, and we'll use them here. Add the newly created dummy object (which I've named cannon_dummy) as a child object of the spaceship. This establishes a hierarchical (or tree-like) relationship between the objects, ensuring the child (the cannon point) will move relative to its parent (the spaceship). We want the cannon point to follow the player as it moves left and right from player input. To achieve this connection, simply drag and drop the dummy object onto the spaceship in the Hierarchy Panel. Once the connection is established, use the Move tool to translate the dummy to the tip of the spaceship, approximating the position of its cannons (see Figure 3-14).

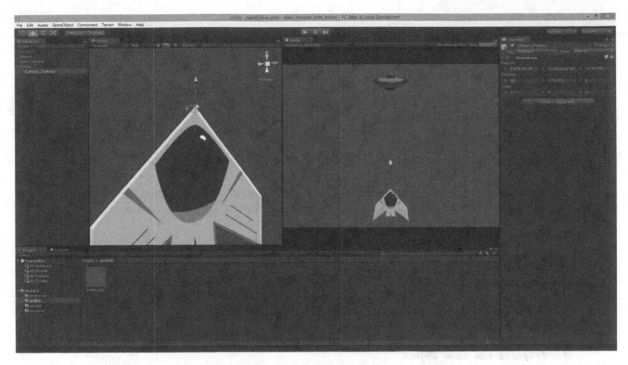

Figure 3-14. Positioning the cannon dummy object to the tip of the spaceship to mark the birth point for new instances of ammo

Coding the Firing of Ammo

Now we've marked the location of new cannon fire, we'll return to the PlayerController script file and code the functionality for firing weapons. Specifically, when the player presses the Fire button, we'll instantiate new instances of the ammo Prefab at the cannon point. Consider Listing 3-3 for the reworked PlayerController class.

Listing 3-3. PlayerController.cs

```
using UnityEngine;
using System.Collections;

public class PlayerController : MonoBehaviour
{
    //Player health
    public int Health = 100;

    //Player move speed in units per second
    public float Speed = 10.0f;

    //Player reload delay in seconds
    public float ReloadDelay = 0.2f;

    //Player min and max X position in world space (to keep player in screen)
    public Vector2 MinMaxX = Vector2.zero;
```

```
    //Prefab to instantiate
    public GameObject PrefabAmmo = null;

    //Gun position
    public GameObject GunPosition = null;

    //Can fire ammo
    private bool WeaponsActivated = true;

    // Update is called once per frame
    void Update ()
    {
        transform.position = new Vector3(Mathf.Clamp(transform.position.x + Input.
GetAxis("Horizontal") * Speed * Time.deltaTime, MinMaxX.x, MinMaxX.y), transform.position.y,
transform.position.z);
    }

    //Check input
    void LateUpdate()
    {
        //If fire button press, then shoot ammo
        if(Input.GetButton("Fire1") && WeaponsActivated)
        {
            //Create new ammo object
            Instantiate(PrefabAmmo, GunPosition.transform.position, PrefabAmmo.transform.rotation);

            //Deactivate weapons
            WeaponsActivated = false;

            Invoke("ActivateWeapons", ReloadDelay);
        }
    }

    //Enable fire
    void ActivateWeapons()
    {
        WeaponsActivated = true;
    }
}
```

The reworked PlayerController script as shown in Listing 3-3 adds a lot of extra functionality for working with the ammo Prefab and the cannon dummy object. The public variable PrefabAmmo should be assigned in the Object Inspector to the ammo Prefab object in the Project Panel—it indicates to Unity the Prefab object that should be instantiated for ammo. The GunPosition variable should be assigned the dummy cannon object—it specifies the location of the cannons. Assign these variables now in the Object Inspector. Drag and drop the ammo Prefab from the Project Panel onto the *Prefab Ammo* field, and drag and drop the cannon_dummy object into the *Gun Position* field (see Figure 3-15). This sets their default values, which will remain unchanged.

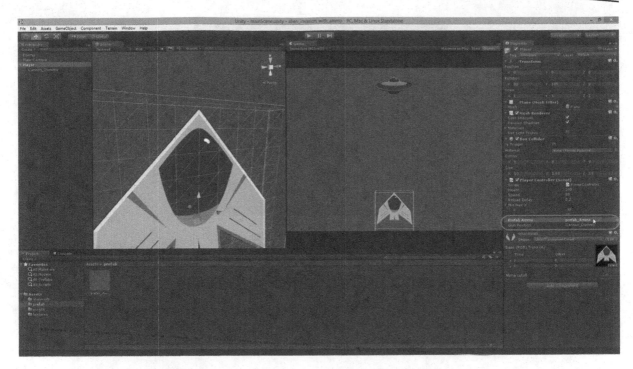

Figure 3-15. Assigning the Prefab Ammo and the Gun Position fields in the Object Inspector for the PlayerController class

Note   As shown in Listing 3-3, objects and Prefabs are spawned in the scene with the `Instantiate` method. They are removed using the `Destroy` method, as shown in Listing 3-2. These methods are dynamic ways of creating and removing objects. In the interest of performance it's often good practice to spawn all needed objects at scene start-up and remove them at scene termination, changing only their visibility at other times to make them *appear* to be created or removed. This is especially applicable in mobile development and legacy hardware.

Now we're almost ready to test this project. Before doing so, remove any and all manually created instances of the Ammo object in the scene. The scene should contain no Ammo objects, because the PlayerController class will create them automatically when the weapon is fired. With that done, click Play on the toolbar and enjoy your work so far! The space ship can now fire ammo (see Figure 3-16).

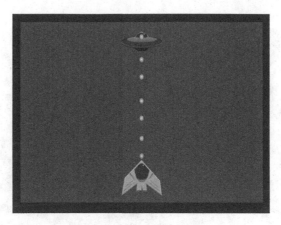

Figure 3-16. The 2D Alien Invasion game so far: a spaceship can fire at enemies

Implementing Moving Enemies and Collision

It's important to have Enemy objects respond to the player's ammo and fire events, otherwise there'd be no point in the player firing their weapons at all. For our project, we'll make sure that enemies are destroyed whenever they collide with player ammo.

The EnemyController.cs Script

To get started, let's create a new C# script file for the Enemy object (EnemyController.cs), as shown in Listing 3-4.

Listing 3-4. EnemyController.cs

```
using UnityEngine;
using System.Collections;

public class EnemyController : MonoBehaviour
{
    //Enemy health
    public int Health = 100;

    //Enemy move speed in units per second
    public float Speed = 1.0f;

    //Enemy min and max X position in world space (to keep Enemy in screen)
    public Vector2 MinMaxX = Vector2.zero;

    // Update is called once per frame
    void Update ()
    {
        //Ping pong enemy position
        transform.position = new Vector3(MinMaxX.x + Mathf.PingPong(Time.time * Speed, 1.0f) *
(MinMaxX.y - MinMaxX.x), transform.position.y, transform.position.z);
    }
```

```
    //Trigger enter
     void OnTriggerEnter(Collider other)
    {
        Destroy (gameObject);
        Destroy (other.gameObject);
    }
}
```

The EnemyController script file is coded on a similar principle to the PlayerController. Both offer customisation over object speed and position clamping, except the PlayerController allows player input to affect the motion of the spaceship while the EnemyController bases enemy motion on a ping-pong value generated on each frame. This functionality has the effect of moving the enemy back and forth in a patrol. Notice the addition of the OnTriggerEnter function. This function should be called when another physical body in the scene, like the ammo, enters or intersects the Enemy Collider. It represents the moment at which the enemy is hit by ammo and should be destroyed, along with the Ammo object itself. At this stage, drag and drop the EnemyController script onto the Enemy object in the scene, and then click *Play* on the toolbar (see Figure 3-17). Test the game by firing your weapons at the enemy, but notice that the enemy is not destroyed on a collision event. Right now, this is because the OnTriggerEnter function is never called.

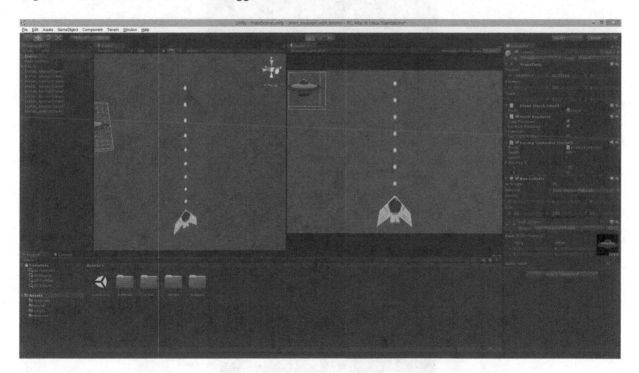

Figure 3-17. Assign the EnemyController to the enemy object in the scene and take the game for a test run…

The OnTriggerEnter function is never called because of two main reasons. First, the enemy BoxCollider Component should be marked explicitly as a *trigger volume*. This ensures the Enemy object is ignored by the standard Unity physics system and only receives notifications when objects enter its volume. Second, the Ammo object must have a RigidBody Component. This component is required because OnTriggerEnter events are generated only when RigidBodies enter the trigger volume.

Setting the BoxCollider as a Trigger Volume

To get started at fixing these issues, select the Enemy object in the scene, and in the Object Inspector enable the Is Trigger check box, which is available inside the BoxCollider Component (see Figure 3-18).

Figure 3-18. Marking the enemy collider as a trigger volume to receive OnTriggerEnter notifications in script

The notifications in Figure 3-18 will be generated when the Ammo object intersects the enemy.

Adding a RigidBody Component

Next, we need to add a `RigidBody` Component o the `Ammo` object. We made a Prefab of this object earlier, and one of the great qualities of Prefabs is their editable power. We can simply select the `Prefab` object in the Project Panel and change any of its properties, like a regular game object, and have all of its changes propagated to all associated instantiations, if there are any. Select the ammo Prefab, and then choose **Component ➤ Physics ➤ RigidBody** from the application menu (see Figure 3-19).

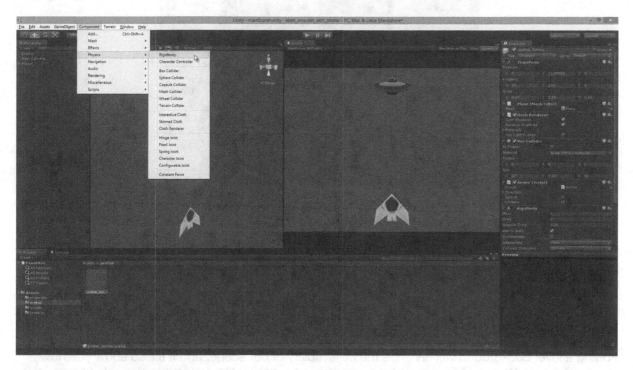

Figure 3-19. Adding a RigidBody Component to a Prefab object in the Project Panel. Prefabs can be edited after their creation!

Doing this adds a `RigidBody` Component to the ammo and makes the object compliant to the Newtonian laws of physics. This means that if you test run your game now with the `RigidBody` at its default settings, and fire your weapons, the ammo will fall to the ground under the effects of gravity instead of shooting upward toward the enemies as they should do. This behavior totally transforms the appearance of our ammo, from looking like fiery balls of energy to orange tokens and innocuous confetti. To complete the configuration for the `RigidBody` we must enable the *Is Kinematic* check box. Doing this allows our object to keep many of the benefits and qualities of a `RigidBody` (including the ability to invoke `OnTriggerEnter` events) but makes it immune from the normal physical laws: from gravity, friction, inertia, and more (see Figure 3-20).

Figure 3-20. Enabling Is Kinematic for a RigidBody makes it immune from most aspects of the Unity Physics System. It indicates that developers will animate and move the object manually

Now, finally, with these settings in place go ahead and run your game. You can now control the player spaceship, as well as fire ammo and shoot down moving enemies. Excellent work! Let's go one step further and add a backdrop to the level.

Adding a Level Background

Adding a level background will enhance the believability of our scene, and it'll also show you how to use a skybox. We could import a background image from any file, but in this example I'll import a premade Unity package that ships with the software and it includes a range of special cube-texture backgrounds, known as *skyboxes*. This package is named Skyboxes, and it can be imported into the existing project using the **Assets ➤ Import Package ➤ Skyboxes** command from the application menu. Once selected, the Import dialog appears. From here, accept the defaults and the skybox textures are then added to the project (see Figure 3-21).

Note   The imported skybox textures are imported into the Project to the folder Standard Assets/Skyboxes.

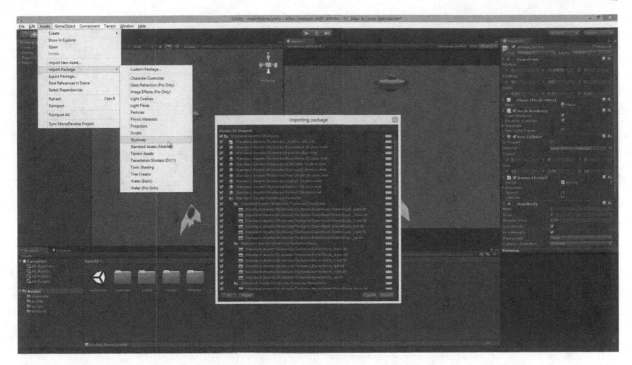

Figure 3-21. *Skyboxes are cube-like textures that wrap around the extents of your scenes to appear as an all-surrounding and ever-distant background*

The skybox refers to six seamless textures (*top*, *left*, *right*, *front*, *back*, and *down*) intended to be mapped onto the interior faces of a cube that surrounds the level to give the appearance of an ever-distant background. They make it really easy to add clouds and distant mountains and terrain to a scene. To add a skybox to your scene camera, just select the camera in the scene and then add a Skybox Renderer component to it. Choose **Component ➤ Rendering ➤ Skybox** from the application menu. This adds a skybox rendering component to the camera. Now assign the skybox to the camera using the Object Inspector. Click the Custom Skybox material swatch and select the skybox you want to add. I've chosen the skybox *Eerie Skybox*. Once selected, see the skybox take effect in the Game tab, and also when the game is run (see Figure 3-22.)

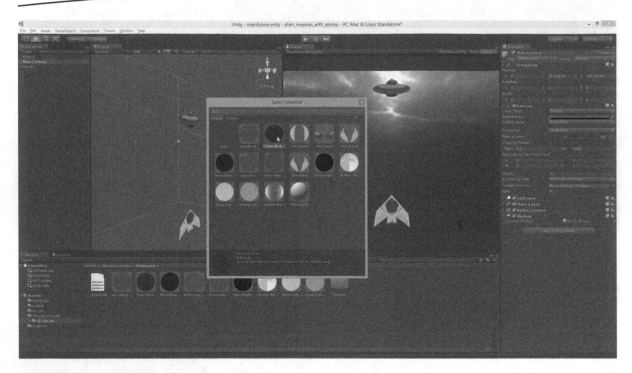

Figure 3-22. Adding a skybox material to the selected camera adds a background to the scene

Moving Forward and Project Limitations

Congratulations! You've now created a 2D game in Unity using only the native and standard tools. No editor plugins were required, no tweaking of the interface, and no major scripting operations either. Of course, the game is limited in many respects and there's much more room for improvement. You could proceed to apply all the principles discussed to customize enemies so they can retaliate, explode, and even change attack types and weapons. You could implement health bars, power ups, shields, new boss enemies, as well as background music, and if you're feeling really energized: multiplayer functionality. Of course, if you do create these features (and I hope you do), remember not to lose sight of our main objective–to create 2D games in Unity. And now that we've coded one, let's also take stock and appraise our work to see what problems and limitations we faced in this project. Some of them were significant.

- **Perspective Distortion:** One problem we encountered relates to perspective distortion. By default, all cameras in Unity are configured for 3D games. These cameras are known as *perspective* cameras because they render objects in perspective. This means nearer objects are drawn larger than distant ones, parallel lines converge at a single vanishing point, and objects are foreshortened based on their orientation in the scene and their distance relative to the horizon line. This is often problematic for truly 2D games, such as card games, Tetris-style games, hidden objects, isometric games, and others. In these games, objects are not subjected to perspective distortions in this way. Rather, they are drawn orthographically. In old-school isometric games like *Sim City 2000*, parallel lines remain parallel and do not really converge: this is a characteristic feature of isometric perspective. But it runs against the grain of perspective cameras. For our space-shooter game too, our objects were made smaller or larger based on their distance from the camera, but this is something we often want to avoid for 2D.

- **World Unit and Pixel Correspondence:** During development you may have wondered about pixel placement. Perhaps you asked: what's the pixel position of that space ship on screen? Or how can I position that space ship at an exact pixel location, measured from the top-left corner of the screen? Or perhaps you asked questions about a potential 2D game you have in mind, such as "I have this Photoshop file with all the graphics looking great and positioned just where I need them, not a pixel of inaccuracy. Now how I can set up my game so everything appears in exactly the same places?" These questions arise because of confusion about how Unity's world space relates to pixels on-screen. When you select an object in the scene and examine its world position in the Object Inspector, the numbers you see correspond to world units and not pixels. But, in 2D games we often do want to specify object locations and sizes and movement in terms of pixels.

- **Pixel Perfect Textures:** One problem that follows from the previous is that we can never know whether our game objects are showing textures on screen at a 1:1 ratio. If a texture is 512×512 pixels in the file, how can we be sure it's being shown on-screen at 512×512 pixels when our objects appear in perspective and are measured in Unity units? We could use the Unity GUI framework to overcome this problem, but in doing this we lose all the benefits that attach to game objects and scenes. Further, setting the size or scale of an object to 512×512×512 world units will not solve the issue on its own either, because the appearance of objects depends critically on the camera position, its field of view and its projection type. The problem this raises is that of pixel perfection. In 2D games we often need to guarantee that textures will be shown on-screen exactly as they are defined in the image files, without drastic resampling, without distortion, and without resizing.

- **Non-Power-2 Textures:** Square textures are all well and good for texturing 3D objects where textures can be tiled, flipped, mirrored, overlapped, and UV edited. But in the world of 2D we often have many sprites and objects of different shapes and sizes, and we want to maintain these sizes without the constraints of power-2 textures. We've seen already how we can overcome this restriction by using GUI textures, but again these types are not intended for 3D objects in the scene. For those, we typically use regular textures and these will always scale non-power-2 textures to the nearest power-2 size, and this resampling and scaling is not what we want. There are exceptions to this rule: it is possible to configure textures in Unity to avoid this scaling, even non GUI textures. But as a general principle we'll want to keep the textures a power-2 size, but find a way to overcome the limitations this brings. We'll see how to do this later.

- **Draw Calls and Textures**: If you run the Alien Invasion game right now and check the Stats panel in the Game tab, you'll see an interesting statistic under the Draw Calls field. The number of draw calls relates to the number of *different* materials being used in the scene. If we have a scene with one player space ship and ten enemies, there will be a total of two draw calls because all these objects together rely on only two different materials–one for the player and one for the enemy. If we add an ammo material and show an ammo object on screen, then we add a further draw call, and so on for each separate material. If all the sprites and graphics for a 2D game are divided up into separate and multiple files like this, then we incur a greater performance penalty for each new object or sprite we add to the game. Better is to paste all the sprites and textures into one larger texture sheet (known as an *Atlas Texture*), and then assign the appropriate pixel regions to the geometry in our scene through customized UV mapping. Doing this achieves *draw call batching*. See here for more information: `http://docs.unity3d.com/Documentation/Manual/DrawCallBatching.html`. It allows us to reduce the number of draw calls in the scene and thereby to improve the performance of our game.

Together these problems pose significant challenges for larger and more elaborate 2D projects. Nevertheless, these are challenges we must meet to optimize the performance of our 2D games and to increase their quality. Throughout the subsequent chapters of this book we'll see how to tackle all these issues directly.

Summary

This chapter outlined some of the concepts and techniques involved in creating a 2D game quickly using the existing Unity tools. It represents only one approach that could be taken, admittedly. But in taking that approach we encounter a set of important problems that present themselves to all 2D games, in Unity and beyond. Overall, after completing this chapter you should be able to:

- Create basic 2D games in Unity

- Create `Prefab` objects

- Import and configure materials and textures

- Understand the basics of perspective cameras

- Understand how perspective cameras conflict with 2D games

- Use skyboxes

- Understand the basics of physics and collision

- Appreciate the problems concerning pixel perfection

- Understand the need to reduce draw calls and optimize

- Understand the purpose of Atlas Textures

- Understand the need for pixel-precise placement

Chapter 4

Customizing the Editor with Editor Classes

In the previous chapter we created a 2D space-invaders style game with Unity. Although this game proved functional and "fit for purpose," we nonetheless foresaw a range of problems or limitations that could arise when creating more complex 2D games- such as a top-down RPG game. These problems arise largely because we're using a 3D engine and toolset to make 2D games. We were left with the following questions: How can I position game objects in the scene to align on the screen at specific pixel positions? How can I make textures pixel-perfect? How can I make them render as sharply and cleanly as they appear in Photoshop or GIMP? How can I create hundreds of sprites and tiles without increasing the draw count for each unique texture? Throughout this book we'll answer all these questions. To get started at doing this however, we'll need to explore Editor Classes. So let's look at those here and see how they work.

> **Note** Unity lacks many of the 2D Game features natively (such as screen-space, tile-sets, animated sprites etc.), but we can add them using Editor Classes.

Editor Classes

Before Unity and other similar tools appeared on the market, if you were a small-sized game developer and didn't have access to a proprietary in-house engine from a larger company, then you typically made games the hard way. You sat at a code editor, typing in hundreds of lines of code, and editing verbose configuration files. You probably didn't have comprehensive level editors, property inspectors, real-time viewports, and asset managers (unless you coded them all yourself). So the introduction of tools such as GameMaker Studio (see Figure 4-1) and Unity makes game development easier and more enjoyable for many of us. It gives us a GUI experience as opposed to a command line experience. The editors and tools ultimately help us visualize our game more clearly so we can concentrate on creating content rather than on creating infrastructure. Chapter 1 demonstrated many of the GUI features available for making games, but notice that almost all these features implicitly assume we'll be making a 3D and not a 2D game. For example: with Unity, we can drag and drop 3D models into the Project Panel to add them as mesh assets. We can use the Beast Lightmapper to precalculate the lighting of a 3D scene into its textures. We can measure distance and express size within a 3D coordinate space and with Unity Units. And we can even use navigation meshes to give 3D path-finding abilities to the enemies and agents in our scene. However, despite this extensive feature set, Unity has no obvious out of the box support for 2D specific features. This includes: animated sprites, 2D layering systems, parallax scrolling, tile-sets and tile maps, 2D brushes, pixel painting tools, or tools for customizing the render depth of objects in orthogonal viewports. These are all features common to many 2D engines, but they are lacking in Unity.

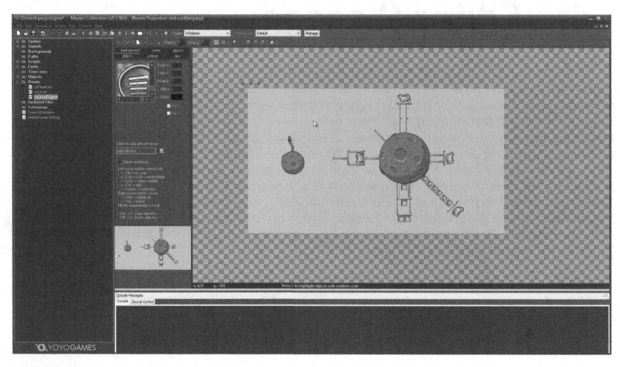

Figure 4-1. GameMaker Studio is an engine tailored to 2D game development. It features a tile-map editor and other tools for managing layers, animated sprites, 2D physics, and more

> **Note**   It's certainly possible to get around lots of these limitations. They are not insurmountable. If they were, this book would not be possible. First, there are many assets and add-ons already available from the Unity Asset Store offering 2D functionality. There are packages such as: NGUI, 2D Toolkit, UniTile, Sprite Manager 2, Tidy Tile, and RotorZ Tile System. Second, there's always the option to ignore most of the Unity editor tools and add-ons, and instead rely solely on scripting to code a completely new 2D superstructure or sub-engine for your games, on top of the existing Unity API. However, it's important to acknowledge the risks and issues these solutions can introduce if care is not taken. The former method involves additional expense and (sometimes) compatibility issues, especially if the add-on developers don't update their packages to work with the latest version of Unity. And the second method creates a strong disconnection between the native Unity toolset and your code, and this disconnection seems wasteful because you're reinventing the wheel. Your code just doesn't integrate tightly enough with the existing Unity tools.

Given these issues, it might seem that Unity should be discarded as a viable 2D engine. But this discarding would be premature. Why? Because by using the Unity Editor Classes (a collection of special classes in the API) we can customize and extend how the Unity editor looks and works. We can add our own GUI tools and add-ons that integrate seamlessly with the existing interface, making them operate as though they were part of the native package. The Editor Classes permit us to add menu items, windows, dockable editors, and inspectors and panels. This means we can add as much or as little of the 2D functionality as we need to the editor, and in doing this we tweak and tailor the tools to our needs. Creating editor classes for a 2D workflow has an additional benefit too: it allows us *to keep using the existing Unity* toolset and functionality, but to build on it and extend it for 2D games. We don't have to give up on the 3D features already present; rather, we can use them to enhance our 2D games. Rather than seeing the existing toolset as an obstacle or hindrance, we can see it as a starting point from which to improve.

> **Note**   More information on the Unity Editor Classes can be found at: `http://docs.unity3d.com/Documentation/ScriptReference/20_class_hierarchy.Editor_Classes.html`

In this chapter we'll take our first steps into creating an Editor Class that extends the Unity Interface. Specifically, we'll make a *Batch Rename* tool. This tool allows us to select multiple objects in the Scene Viewport and then rename them all automatically according to a custom naming and numbering convention that we specify upfront. Now, you may be thinking that our Batch Renaming tool has nothing to do with 2D games. In some senses that is true. But still, it is a useful feature for game development generally, both 2D and 3D, especially if you're dealing with lots of objects in a scene. More crucially however, it'll provide us with the basic grounding and workflow for making Editor Classes. And this is something we'll call on in later chapters where we'll build more extensive and feature-filled tools that are directly related to 2D.

Getting Started with Batch Rename

In the world of Unity scripting there are two fundamental types of scripts. The most common are the standard scripts–those which run *in-game* at runtime. The classes created in these scripts typically derive from MonoBehaviour and handle common events, such as Awake, Start, OnGUI, Update, FixedUpdate, and LateUpdate. The other type of script file is the Editor Script. These don't run in-game at all, and nor are they part of any game per se. They just run *in the Unity Editor,* and they customize the way the interface and tools work. These classes are not related to MonoBehaviour. They are typically derived from EditorWindow, EditorUtility, or ScriptableWizard. Here, we'll derive from ScriptableWizard to create a Batch Rename feature that'll integrate into the Unity Interface.

BatchRename.cs

So to get started with that, let's create a new C# script file–just like any regular script file. Choose **Assets ➤ Create ➤ C# Script** from the application menu and name this file BatchRename.cs (see Figure 4-2).

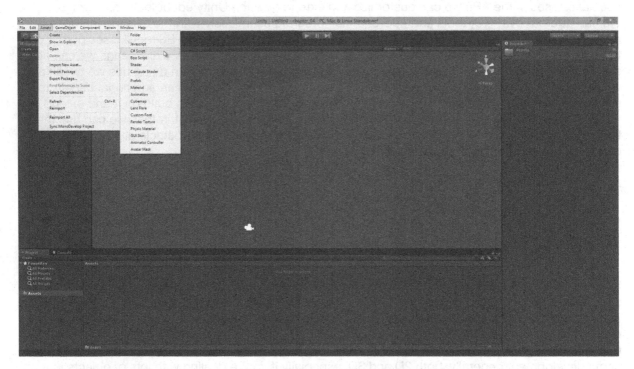

Figure 4-2. Editor Classes are created in script files using any of the Unity supported languages: C#, JavaScript, or Boo. They typically derive from EditorWindow, EditorUtility, or ScriptableWizard

Because most classes are designed to run in-game rather than as Editor Classes, Unity automatically derives the auto-generated class from MonoBehaviour. This is Unity's default behaviour. But it's not what we want here, so let's now amend the class to derive from ScriptableWizard. Also, be sure to append the directive using UnityEditor to the top of the script, because the class ScriptableWizard is defined within that namespace (see Listing 4-1).

Listing 4-1. BatchRename.cs

```
using UnityEngine;
using UnityEditor;
using System.Collections;
public class BatchRename : ScriptableWizard
{
}
```

In Listing 4-1 I've removed the Start and Update functions to the class too. These were autogenerated with the MonoBehaviour class.

Creating a Folder for Editor Extensions

Now we've created the beginnings of our first Editor Class. However, there's an additional step to perform for Unity to truly recognize this class as an Editor Class. We must store the script file inside a folder named Editor. It doesn't matter if the Editor folder is a top-level folder in the Asset hierarchy, or if the folder is nested and embedded inside others of a different name (such as MyData/Scripts/Editor). All that matters is for our file (BatchRename.cs) to be inside a folder named Editor. The presence of this folder in our project means Unity treats all script files inside as editor extensions. Create this folder by choosing **Assets ➤ Create ➤ Folder** from the application menu, and drag and drop the script file inside (see Figure 4-3).

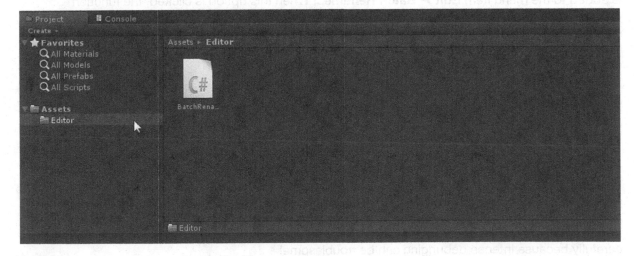

Figure 4-3. Editor Classes must be kept inside a folder named Editor

Adding Batch Rename to the Application Menu

The *Batch Rename* functionality must be easily accessible to us so we can rename multiple objects quickly and smoothly. For this reason, it's important to integrate it appropriately into the Unity Editor, to make it feel like it belongs in the interface. One way to do this is to add *Batch Rename* to the application menu as a selectable option, just like the regular options of *Undo* and *Redo*. To achieve this, we add the CreateWizard function to our class, using a specific syntax and structure.

The CreateWizard Function

Consider the code in Listing 4-2.

Listing 4-2. BatchRename.cs–CreateWizard Function Added

```
using UnityEngine;
using UnityEditor;
using System.Collections;

public class BatchRename : ScriptableWizard
{
    [MenuItem("Edit/Batch Rename...")]
    static void CreateWizard()
    {
        ScriptableWizard.DisplayWizard("Batch Rename",typeof(BatchRename),"Rename");
    }
}
```

The MenuItem statement inserts an entry into the application menu of the Unity Editor (not MonoDevelop), allowing access to our Batch Rename feature. For this specific example, the feature is added to the menu item **Edit ➤ Batch Rename...** When this option is clicked, the function CreateWizard is executed. The CreateWizard function is a static member of the ScriptableWizard class. It's used to instantiate instances of our custom made BatchRename class. Because the CreateWizard function is static, you cannot use it to initialize instance specific variables. To perform class initialization, you use the OnEnable function, considered later.

Testing the Batch Rename Menu Option

Now save and compile this code as it is, making sure it's saved inside an Editor folder. Then click the *Edit* option from the application menu to show the *Edit* menu, and see your newly added option for *Batch Rename* at the bottom (see Figure 4-4). Note that after compilation, the Editor Classes take effect immediately in the Editor–you don't have to click the *Run* button from the toolbar to experience your code changes. Remember: Editor Classes run in Edit mode. This can be a blessing and a curse–it means you see your code changes right away from the editor. But, runtime errors and infinite loops can cause freezes and even editor lock-ups. So take care to write your Editor Classes carefully because intense debugging can be troublesome!

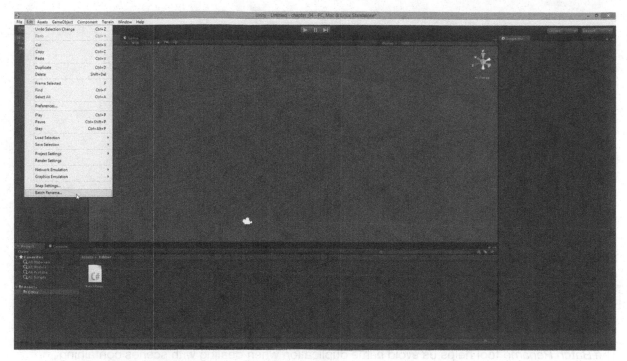

Figure 4-4. Adding the Batch Rename option to the application menu

Note   You can add an Editor Class as an option to any menu, and even create new menus that don't already exist, such as [MenuItem("MyNewMenu/MyNewFeature")].

If you click the *Batch Rename* option from the application menu, a window appears with the title "Batch Rename," matching the "Batch Rename" string argument passed to the DisplayWizard function of ScriptableWizard. It also has a Rename button listed in the bottom-right side of the window (see Figure 4-5). Clicking this button right now invokes an error. This error is printed to the console in red, like most errors. It occurs because our class doesn't yet implement the expected OnWizardCreate function. This function is discussed later in this chapter.

Figure 4-5. The Batch Rename window features a confirmation button Rename to complete the rename operation. By default this button is not implemented because the BatchRename class does not include an OnWizardCreate event. Adding this event will handle the On-Click event for this button

Reading Object Selections in the Scene

The *Batch Rename* tool helps us avoid name duplication when dealing with scenes containing many objects–such as hordes of enemies or architectural elements. It means each unique object can easily have its own descriptive name. To work effectively, *Batch Rename* requires one or more objects to be selected in the scene–if nothing is selected, then *Batch Rename* won't work. So let's start implementing the *Batch Rename* window by displaying a help string, indicating the number of objects currently selected in the scene, if any. This gives the user an indication about how many objects will be affected by the rename operation. To ascertain the current selection in the scene, we use the Selection class–part of the Unity API. More information on Selection is found here: http://docs.unity3d.com/Documentation/ScriptReference/Selection.html.

Making Use of Selection in BatchRename.cs

Take a look at Listing 4-3 to see how to amend the BatchRename class.

Listing 4-3. BatchRename.cs–Working with Editor Selections

```
using UnityEngine;
using UnityEditor;
using System.Collections;

public class BatchRename : ScriptableWizard
{
    [MenuItem("Edit/Batch Rename...")]
    static void CreateWizard()
    {
        ScriptableWizard.DisplayWizard("Batch Rename",typeof(BatchRename),"Rename");
    }
```

```
//Called when the window first appears
void OnEnable()
{
    UpdateSelectionHelper();
}

//Function called when selection changes in scene
void OnSelectionChange()
{
    UpdateSelectionHelper();
}

//Update selection counter
void UpdateSelectionHelper()
{
    helpString = "";

    if (Selection.objects != null)
        helpString = "Number of objects selected: " + Selection.objects.Length;
}
}
```

There are three additions to BatchRename in Listing 4.3:

1. UpdateSelectionHelper builds a helpString variable to show the number of objects currently selected in the scene. We retrieve the selection count using the Selection.objects.length variable of the Selection class. The helpString variable is inherited from the ScriptableWizard class and is automatically printed to the top of the Wizard window.

2. The inherited OnEnable method has been added. This event is invoked whenever the *Batch Rename* window is shown–that is, whenever the *Batch Rename* option is selected from the *Edit* menu.

3. The inherited OnSelectionChange method has been added. This updates the selection count every time the selection changes.

Testing Object Selections in Scene

If you run this code now by selecting **Edit ➤ Batch Rename** from the application menu, you'll see the Wizard window now shows a selection count. This count is visible as soon as the window is shown, due to the OnEnable event. Plus, the count also updates every time you change the selection in the scene with the window open–thanks to the OnSelectionChange event (see Figure 4-6).

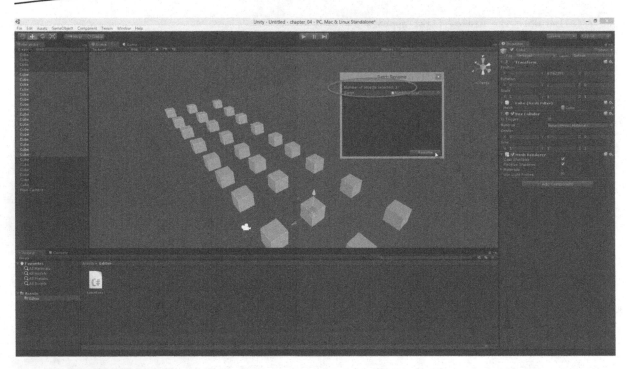

Figure 4-6. *Updating the selection count in the Batch Rename window. This tells you how many objects are currently selected in the active scene. Notice this scene is a prime candidate for the Batch Rename tool. It features lots of cubes, all named Cube*

Adding User Input to the Batch Rename Window

With *Batch Rename*, the user must specify the naming convention applied to the selected objects. Specifically, they'll want to choose a **base name**, such as ("MyObject_"), and a starting *suffix* to be appended to the base, which tells Batch Rename where numbering should begin, such as ("MyObject_01"). Finally, we'll also have an Increment property, for offering control over how the suffix numbering is incremented for each file in the selection, meaning that numbering can work in multiples if required, such as "MyObject_05", "MyObject_10", "MyObject_15", etc. If the user is to provide these values at all however, we must give them input fields in the Batch Rename window. Often, when working with Editor Classes, we'll have to use the EditorGUI class to create the inputs and widgets manually. This class works like GUI, but applies to windows in the Unity Editor as opposed to in-game GUIs. However, for ScriptableWizard, we just need to add public properties to the class! ScriptableWizard automatically detects those properties and generates the relevant input fields for us in the *Batch Rename* window. I really love that feature. Let's see it in action. Add the following properties to the BatchRename class, as shown in Listing 4-4. Then take a look at Figure 4-7 to see the effect this has in the editor.

Listing 4-4. BatchRename.cs–Adding Public Properties

```csharp
using UnityEngine;
using UnityEditor;
using System.Collections;

public classBatchRename: ScriptableWizard
{
    //Base name
    public string BaseName = "MyObject_";

    //Start Count
    public int StartNumber = 0;

    //Increment
    public int Increment = 1;

    [MenuItem("Edit/Batch Rename...")]
    static void CreateWizard()
    {
        ScriptableWizard.DisplayWizard("Batch Rename",typeof(BatchRename),"Rename");
    }

    void OnEnable()
    {
        UpdateSelectionHelper();
    }

    //Function called when window is updated
    void OnSelectionChange()
    {
        UpdateSelectionHelper();
    }

    //Update selection counter
    void UpdateSelectionHelper()
    {
        helpString = "";

        if (Selection.objects != null)
            helpString = "Number of objects selected: " + Selection.objects.Length;
    }
}
```

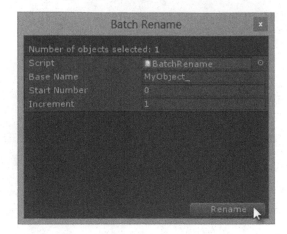

Figure 4-7. ScriptableWizard autogenerates associated input fields in the window for selected public properties. Editing these values in the window updates the linked properties of the class

---

Note   The ScriptableWizard class autogenerates input fields for only serializable public properties, and not simply any public properties. Why not? Have you ever created your own custom class and found you cannot view its members in the Object Inspector as you can with some other Unity-based classes, such as Vector2 and Vector3? That's because your class is probably not marked as serializable.

Both the Object Inspector and `ScriptableWizard` can only show GUI inputs for serializable classes. This typically includes many standard data types, including: `string`, `int`, `float`, `color`, `vector3`, `rect`, `texture2d`, `material`, `mesh,` and more. In short, if a class or object shows in the Object Inspector, then it'll show in the `ScriptableWizard` window when added as a public property of the class. We'll return to the issue of `Serializable` later when creating our own custom object that'll show in the Objet Inspector.

Note   Some examples of non-serialized classes include: `Dictionary` and `Queue`. These will not display in the Object Inspector, even when declared as public members of your class. Of course, that doesn't mean those members aren't genuine members or won't work properly at runtime. It means only that their values won't *show* in the Object Inspector. For more information visit:
`http://docs.unity3d.com/Documentation/ScriptReference/Serializable.html`

Completing the Batch Rename Feature

We've now added all properties and methods necessary for our BatchRename class. The user can select objects in the scene for renaming and can also provide information about the convention to be applied. Now it's time to create the nuts and bolts functionality of the rename operation itself. This happens whenever the user clicks the *Rename* button at the bottom-right side of the window. The code in Listing 4-5 features the complete BatchRename class, including the newly added OnWizardCreate method.

Listing 4-5. BatchRename.cs–Adding Rename Functionality

```
using UnityEngine;
using UnityEditor;
using System.Collections;

public class BatchRename : ScriptableWizard
{
    //Base name
    public string BaseName = "MyObject_";

    //Start Count
    public int StartNumber = 0;

    //Increment
    public int Increment = 1;


    [MenuItem("Edit/Batch Rename...")]
    static void CreateWizard()
    {
        ScriptableWizard.DisplayWizard("Batch Rename",typeof(BatchRename),"Rename");
    }

    //Called when the window first appears
    void OnEnable()
    {
        UpdateSelectionHelper();
    }

    //Function called when selection changes in scene
    void OnSelectionChange()
    {
        UpdateSelectionHelper();
    }
```

```
//Update selection counter
void UpdateSelectionHelper()
{
    helpString = "";

    if (Selection.objects != null)
        helpString = "Number of objects selected: " + Selection.objects.Length;
}

//Rename
void OnWizardCreate()
{
    //If selection empty, then exit
    if (Selection.objects == null)
        return;

    //Current Increment
    int PostFix = StartNumber;

    //Cycle and rename
    foreach(Object oin Selection.objects)
    {
        o.name = BaseName + PostFix;
        PostFix += Increment;
    }

}
}
```

Give this code a test-run and see it in action–try renaming as many and as few objects as possible (see Figure 4-8). Congratulations, you've just created your first productive Editor Class. Sure, Batch Rename is a "simple" feature, but its implementation was far from being just an exercise for flexing our coding muscles. Batch Rename is powerful. It comes in handy in scenes with lots of objects. Further, Unity doesn't really have any native Batch Rename tool. This means you've just added a valuable new feature to your install of Unity.

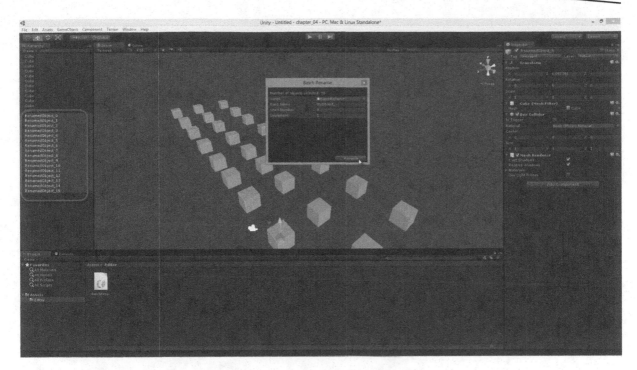

Figure 4-8. The Batch Rename Editor Class at work, renaming the multiple cube objects in a scene

Summary

This chapter described how to extend the Unity editor with a Batch Renaming tool. However, despite its usefulness, there is a more critical core of knowledge to take with you. You now know how to create `ScriptableWizards`, as well as the basic workflow for creating Editor Extensions generally. This is an important foundation that we'll take with us and build on throughout subsequent chapters, as we create more and more editor extensions for creating 2D games. Hopefully, by the end of this book, you'll be dreaming in Editor Classes and about how to create new ones to make 2D development even easier. Overall, after completing this chapter you should be able to:

- Understand the difference between standard script files and editor classes

- Understand that Editor Classes derive from `ScriptableWizard`, `EditorWindow`, and `EditorUtility`

- Understand that Editor Classes should be stored in the `Editor` folder

- Create `ScriptableWizard` classes

- Use the `Selection` object to get the selection in the active scene

- Understand the `OnEnable`, `OnSelectionChange`, and `OnWizardCreate` methods

- Add features to the application menu with the `MenuItem` command

- Understand the purpose of `Serializable` classes

- Add GUI inputs to the `ScriptableWizard` window

Chapter 5

Procedural Geometry and Textured Quads

Nearly every 2D game uses *sprites* and *tilesets*, in one form or another. Games such as Phantasy Star, Zelda, Final Fantasy, Dizzy, Contra, Donkey Kong, Mario, Sonic, and others, have all used sprites and tiles. Some games use them in a conventional and obvious way while some less so. But the very fact that jargon terms exist for these two concepts is testament to their prevalence in games. The sprite is to 2D games what a mesh is to 3D games; and tilesets find their closest 3D equivalent in the static and modular geometry of the scene.

If your game has a player character that runs around the level, killing enemies and opening doors, and jumping from platform to platform, then your game needs a sprite: the player sprite. This is an image asset featuring all pixel data for the player character, including all its fully-drawn frames of animation. Sometimes, each frame is separated out into different image files, one frame per file, or sometimes the frames are stacked together neatly inside a single image, in equally sized rows and columns. Similarly, if your game has enemy characters, doors, waterfalls, or other dynamic and active objects, then you'll need sprites for these things too.

Tilesets, in contrast, are used for scenery and background. They are drawn behind sprites in the scene. Tiles are used for all nonsentient things: that is, the things that don't move and don't "act:" walls, floors, mountains, terrain, water, trees, and more. Think of these as representing static geometry. All these elements are typically loaded from only a single image file: one in which all tiles have been copied and pasted together in rows and columns—the tileset. The term tileset also is used in games to convey how the artist has created the image; specifically they paint each tile so its edge pixels align seamlessly with the edges of other related tiles. This means that level designers working with the engine can fit the tiles together and repeat them throughout the scene to create more expansive and reusable environments. However, I'm guessing you probably don't need me to tell you in detail what sprites and tiles are—you probably already know. Instead, the question of critical importance is: how do you create sprite and tile functionality in Unity when it offers no native or out of the box support for them? This chapter begins to answer that question.

> **Note**   Want to see examples of tilesets and animated sprites? Simply search Google Images for "animated sprite" or "tile sets," and see just how plentiful these kinds of images really are!

If you want to show any graphic on-screen with Unity (including sprites and tiles), then you have to use geometry. The Unity renderer is ultimately a sophisticated system for drawing geometry to the Viewport in the form of shaded polygons. So, to render sprite and tile textures to the screen, we'll need to assign them to polygons. In Chapter 3 you saw how to do this by assigning spaceship textures to a native Unity *Plane* object that was camera aligned. The *Plane* object is created in the scene by selecting **GameObject ➤ Create Other ➤ Plane** from the application menu. But the plane proved highly tessellated for our purpose. It had lots of unnecessary vertices and edges. We needed only four corner vertices for a rectangle or quad. Using the tessellated plane might not be a problem for only a few sprites or tiles, but when these objects are multiplied, we quickly run into performance penalties. Also, the Plane object gave us no easy way to adjust its UV mapping. This meant we couldn't really choose specific tiles or regions within the texture and its UV space to show on the Plane's surface. The Plane simply showed a *complete* texture, from its top-left corner to its bottom-right corner.

> **Note**   We could, of course, solve the issue of plane tessellation by simply modelling our own basic quad plane from 3D-modelling software (such as *Blender, Max, Maya,* etc.). However, this solution lacks flexibility because Unity offers no easy or convenient method for editing the UVs of imported meshes.

To fix these issues of tessellation and UVs, we'll make our own quad from code in Unity. Meshes generated in this way are known as procedural meshes or procedural geometry. Specifically, we'll create an interactive editor plugin, derived from `ScriptableWizard`. It'll allow us to generate quad meshes based on parameters we specify. The generated quad will then be configured, ready for receiving any sprites or tiles we choose. By coding the quad generator as an Editor plugin we are creating a useful new engine feature that'll serve us whenever we need a new sprite or tile for our 2D games. The code in this chapter will not actually assign a texture or tile to the quad (that is reserved for later chapters). Here, we'll just focus on creating the quad mesh itself.

Getting Started with the CreateQuad Feature

Starting from an empty Unity Project, let's create a new C# Editor Class for the `CreateQuad` feature we need, as shown in Figure 5-1 (`CreateQuad.cs`). For further information on creating editor classes and their basics, see Chapter 4. The complete source code for this chapter can be found in the companion files at: `Project_Files/Chapter05/source_assets/`. For now, it's important to remember that all Editor Classes must be located inside a folder named `Editor` in the Project Panel. Storing the class outside an Editor Folder means Unity recognizes it as a standard game class (and that's not what we want). In addition, your `CreateQuad.cs` file must include the namespace using `UnityEditor;`. If it doesn't, then you can't use the Editor Classes API in your code. See Listing 5-1 for the initial class code for `CreateQuad.cs`.

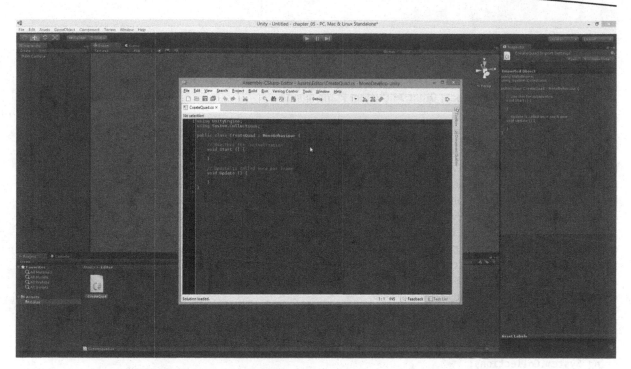

Figure 5-1. *Creating a new C# Editor Class CreateQuad in the Editor folder of the project. This class adds a new feature to the application menu, allowing us to generate parametric quads*

Listing 5-1. CreateQuad.cs

```
//EDITOR CLASS TO CREATE QUAD MESH WITH SPECIFIED ANCHOR
using UnityEngine;
using UnityEditor;
using System.Collections;

public class CreateQuad : ScriptableWizard
{
    [MenuItem("GameObject/Create Other/Custom Plane")]
    static void CreateWizard()
    {
        ScriptableWizard.DisplayWizard("Create Plane",typeof(CreateQuad));
    }
    //Function to create quad mesh
    void OnWizardCreate()
    {
    }
}
```

> **Note**   This class descends from `ScriptableWizard` and not `MonoBehaviour`. The `Update` and `Start`
> functions, auto-generated in the class, have also been removed since they will
> not be required here. Further, the "Create Plane" feature has been added as a menu option
> to the **GameObject ➤ Create Other ➤ Custom Plane** menu.

We also want to give our user (the developer, not the gamer!) some fine control over the quad to
be generated by our tool. We don't just want to generate just *any* sized quad in the scene at *any*
position, and with *any* name. Instead, the user will want to specify its dimensions in width and
height (in *Unity Units*, not pixels), its mesh asset name, and its object name so that each generated
quad can be customized. When generated, the quad mesh will be added as a mesh asset to the
project, and an instance of that asset will be added to the scene. So let's add public variables to
our class to support these properties. GUI text box elements will automatically be added to the
`ScriptableWizard` window on the basis of serialiazble public variable. See Listing 5-2 and Figure 5-2.

Listing 5-2. CreateQuad.cs—Adding Public Variables

```
//EDITOR CLASS TO CREATE QUAD MESH WITH SPECIFIED ANCHOR
using UnityEngine;
using UnityEditor;
using System.Collections;

public class CreateQuad : ScriptableWizard
{
    //Name of Quad Asset
    public string MeshName = "Quad";

    //Game Object Name
    public string GameObjectName = "Plane_Object";

    //Name of asset folder to contain quad asset when created
    public string AssetFolder = "Assets";

    //Width of quad in world units
    public float Width = 1.0f;

    //Height of quad in world units
    public float Height = 1.0f;

    [MenuItem("GameObject/Create Other/Custom Plane")]
    static void CreateWizard()
    {
        ScriptableWizard.DisplayWizard("Create Planc",typeof(CreateQuad));
    }

    //Function to create quad mesh
    void OnWizardCreate()
    {
    }
}
```

Figure 5-2. Adding user properties to the CreateQuad ScriptableWizard window. Using these, the user can control the dimensions and naming of the generated quad mesh

Setting the Quad's Anchor Point

Every game object in a scene has an *anchor point* (or *pivot point*, or *center point*). This point marks the center of rotation and represents the origin of an object's local space. It's also the point where the transformation gizmo is centered when an object is selected in the Viewport. It's an especially important point for any object that moves, rotates, or scales, because it acts as the center from which transformations are applied. Despite its importance you may be surprised to discover that Unity doesn't offer any native feature for changing a mesh's anchor point. Anchor points for premade primitives, such as the cube and sphere, are already locked at the object's center, and imported meshes have their anchor points "baked-in" from 3D modelling software. And you can't change any of these. Thankfully however, when it comes to procedural geometry, the situation is different. There, we *do* have the opportunity of adjusting an object's center point, as we'll see soon. For this reason we also want to let the user choose the location for this center point when generating the quad mesh. It could come in handy. For example, character sprites typically have pivots centered at their feet while gun objects have pivots at their barrels. Take a look in Listing 5-3 at the additional variables we can add to the class to achieve pivot-positioning.

Listing 5-3. Additional Variables to Specify a Center Point

```
//Anchor point for created quad
public enum AnchorPoint
{
        TopLeft,
        TopMiddle,
        TopRight,
        RightMiddle,
        BottomRight,
        BottomMiddle,
        BottomLeft,
        LeftMiddle,
        Center,
        Custom
}

//Position of Anchor
public AnchorPoint Anchor = AnchorPoint.Center;

//Horz Position of Anchor on Plane
public float AnchorX = 0.5f;

//Vert Position of Anchor on Plane
public float AnchorY = 0.5f;
```

Enter this code into the CreateQuad.cs source file for your Quad Generator. When the CreateQuad window is opened from the application menu, you'll see all three public variables Anchor, AnchorX, and AnchorY (as shown in Figure 5-3). The Anchor variable is based on the enumeration AnchorPoint and specifies a range of positional presets for the anchor point: such as the TopLeft of the quad, the BottomRight, and LeftMiddle, and so on. These values are presented in a drop-down list inside the Editor window. The Anchor variable is also related to AnchorX and AnchorY. Each *Anchor* preset corresponds to a specific configuration for the AnchorX and AnchorY values. These two variables are normalized values (ranging from 0 to 1), expressing the center position of the quad mesh in relative terms. This means that a BottomLeft anchor would be at position (0, 0), while a TopRight anchor would be at position (1, 1), and the center of the quad is at (0.5, 0.5). The Custom preset allows you to specify your own AnchorX and AnchorY normalized values to anywhere on the quad mesh. See Figure 5-3 to see how the CreateQuad dialog looks with the Enumeration drop-down list in place, allowing users to select an anchor preset.

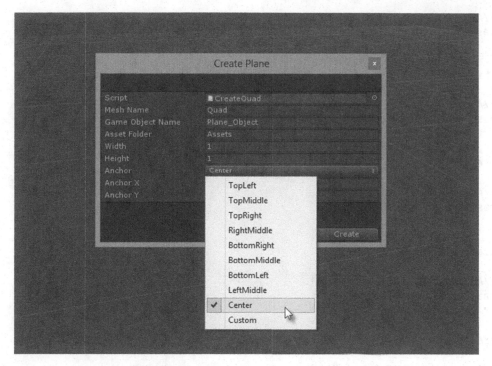

Figure 5-3. Public variables based on enumerations allow users to select values from a drop-down list in Editor windows derived from ScriptableWizard

One GUI issue you may have noticed already with our `ScriptableWizard` window is that, when you select an anchor preset from the drop-down list, the values in the `AnchorX` and `AnchorY` text fields do not change to reflect the preset selection. We want those values to update whenever a preset is selected. To do this, we'll use the `OnInspectorUpdate` event, which is called 10 times per second to give the editor a chance to update its values and fields. More information on this event can be found in the Unity documentation here: `http://docs.unity3d.com/Documentation/ScriptReference/ EditorWindow.OnInspectorUpdate.html`. See Listing 5-4 to see this event in action, updating the `AnchorX` and `AnchorY` fields.

Listing 5-4. Using OnInspectorUpdate

```
//Called 10 times per second
void OnInspectorUpdate()
{
    switch(Anchor)
    {
        //Anchor is set to top-left
        case AnchorPoint.TopLeft:
            AnchorX = 0.0f * Width;
            AnchorY = 1.0f * Height;
        break;
```

```
        //Anchor is set to top-middle
        case AnchorPoint.TopMiddle:
            AnchorX = 0.5f * Width;
            AnchorY = 1.0f * Height;
         break;

        //Anchor is set to top-right
        case AnchorPoint.TopRight:
            AnchorX = 1.0f * Width;
            AnchorY = 1.0f * Height;
        break;

        //Anchor is set to right-middle
        case AnchorPoint.RightMiddle:
            AnchorX = 1.0f * Width;
            AnchorY = 0.5f * Height;
        break;

        //Anchor is set to Bottom-Right
        case AnchorPoint.BottomRight:
            AnchorX = 1.0f * Width;
            AnchorY = 0.0f * Height;
        break;

        //Anchor is set to Bottom-Middle
        case AnchorPoint.BottomMiddle:
            AnchorX = 0.5f * Width;
            AnchorY = 0.0f * Height;
        break;

        //Anchor is set to Bottom-Left
        case AnchorPoint.BottomLeft:
            AnchorX = 0.0f * Width;
            AnchorY = 0.0f * Height;
        break;

        //Anchor is set to Left-Middle
        case AnchorPoint.LeftMiddle:
            AnchorX = 0.0f * Width;
            AnchorY = 0.5f * Height;
        break;

        //Anchor is set to center
        case AnchorPoint.Center:
            AnchorX = 0.5f * Width;
            AnchorY = 0.5f * Height;
        break;

        case AnchorPoint.Custom:
        default:
        break;
    }
```

Specifying the Asset Path

There's an optional extra, or bonus feature, we could add to our Quad Generator to improve its usability even further. Presently, with the AssetFolder variable our user must manually type the complete file path where the quad asset should be generated, such as Assets/MyQuadMeshes/. Now while it's not exactly a terrible inconvenience to do this, we can still make it simpler for the user. Using Editor Classes, such as Selection and AssetDatabase, we can detect which folder in the Project Panel is selected, and from that we can feed the selection into the AssetFolder text field to auto-complete this field for the user. Take a look at the code in Listing 5-5 and Figure 5-4 to see this in action.

Listing 5-5. Getting the User Selection in the Unity Editor with the Selection and AssetDatabase Class

```
//Gets the currently selected asset in the project panel
void GetFolderSelection()
{
    //Check user selection in editor - check for folder selection
    if (Selection.objects != null && Selection.objects.Length == 1)
    {
        //Get path from selected asset
        AssetFolder = AssetDatabase.GetAssetPath(Selection.objects[0]);
    }
}

//Called when window is show
void OnEnable()
{
    GetFolderSelection();
}
```

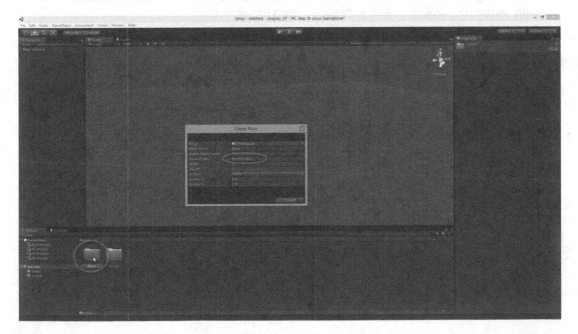

Figure 5-4. Reading the name of the currently selected folder in the Project Panel. Can be used to auto-complete fields

> **Note**   The Selection object enumerates all objects currently selected in the Unity Editor, including scene objects as well as non-scene objects, such as folder selections in the Project Panel. The AssetDatabase class is considered in more detail later in this book in Chapter 6.

Generating the Quad Mesh

The purpose of the CreateQuad editor window we've created is to give the user power and control over the quad generation process. But as soon as the user presses the *Create* button, our class takes over and generates a quad based on their input. The generation process itself goes through three distinct stages, outlined in this section.

- **Generate geometry.** In the first stage, the vertices, edges, and faces of our mesh are generated, along with UV data, and keeping in mind the specified anchor point (or mesh center).

- **Save mesh as an asset.** In the second, the generated mesh is added as an asset of the project at the specified asset path. This mesh will be treated like a regular asset, and it can be dragged and dropped into the scene to create new instantiations.

- **Instantiate mesh in scene.** And in the final stage, the mesh asset is added as a game object in the scene, complete with a Box Collider Component to make collision detection and mouse picking possible.

All three these stages are coded into a single OnWizardCreate function, which is executed automatically when the *Create* button is pressed from the editor.

Step 1—Create Vertices

Let's take a look at the code for Step 1 of this process, which will span several code sections. We'll begin in Listing 5-6.

Listing 5-6.   Creating the Vertices and Faces for the Quad Mesh

```
//Create Vertices
Vector3[] Vertices = new Vector3[4];

//Create UVs
Vector2[] UVs = new Vector2[4];

//Two triangles of quad
int[] Triangles = new int[6];

//Assign vertices based on pivot
```

```
//Bottom-left
Vertices[0].x = -AnchorX;
Vertices[0].y = -AnchorY;

//Bottom-right
Vertices[1].x = Vertices[0].x+Width;
Vertices[1].y = Vertices[0].y;

//Top-left
Vertices[2].x = Vertices[0].x;
Vertices[2].y = Vertices[0].y+Height;
//Top-right
Vertices[3].x = Vertices[0].x+Width;
Vertices[3].y = Vertices[0].y+Height;
```

The code in Listing 5-6 creates three separate arrays, each of a different data type. Vertices for storing all vertices in the mesh, UVs for storing UV data for *each* vertex (elements in this array map to vertices in the Vertices array), and finally the Triangles array, for the faces of the quad. It is set to int array of six elements. This does not mean our quad will have six faces, however. Our quad is formed from two faces—two right-angled triangles aligned together at the hypotenuse. The Triangles array is initialized to six because our mesh has two triangles, and each triangle is made from three vertices (*3×2=6*).

> **Note**   Remember, the first vertex is positioned relative to the anchor point location to ensure the object center will be in the correct place.

Now, after generating the necessary vertices, we must assign the UVs and faces for the mesh. We can do this using the code in Listing 5-7.

Listing 5-7. Assigning UVs and Triangles

```
//Assign UVs
//Bottom-left
UVs[0].x=0.0f;
UVs[0].y=0.0f;

//Bottom-right
UVs[1].x=1.0f;
UVs[1].y=0.0f;

//Top-left
UVs[2].x=0.0f;
UVs[2].y=1.0f;

//Top-right
UVs[3].x=1.0f;
UVs[3].y=1.0f;
```

```
//Assign triangles
Triangles[0]=3;
Triangles[1]=1;
Triangles[2]=2;

Triangles[3]=2;
Triangles[4]=1;
Triangles[5]=0;
```

> **Note**   There are as many UVs as there are vertices in this mesh. Four vertices have been defined.
> Specifically, one for each corner. Each element in the UVs array maps to the Vertices array: 1 to 1, 2
> to 2, etc. The Triangles array refers to indices or index values into the Vertices array. So, Triangle 1
> is composed of three vertices defined through elements 0–2, and is made from three vertices at
> Vertices[3], Vertices[1], and Vertices[2].

Then (in the final part of Step 1) we finally generate the mesh in system memory. This means we convert our Vertex, UVs, and Triangle data into a unified structure Unity recognizes as a mesh. This structure takes the form of a Mesh object, represented by the Mesh class. (More information on this class is found here: http://docs.unity3d.com/Documentation/ScriptReference/Mesh.html). See Listing 5-8.

Listing 5-8. Generating a Mesh Object

```
//Generate mesh
Mesh mesh = new Mesh();
mesh.name = MeshName;
mesh.vertices = Vertices;
mesh.uv = UVs;
mesh.triangles = Triangles;
mesh.RecalculateNormals();
```

Step 2—Create Quad as an Asset

In Step 2 we register the generated quad mesh object as an asset of the project. This adds the mesh as an asset, and it is visible in the Project Panel like any regular asset. Take a look at Listing 5-9.

Listing 5-9. Adding a Quad Mesh Asset to the Project

```
//Create asset in database
AssetDatabase.CreateAsset(mesh, AssetDatabase.GenerateUniqueAssetPath(AssetFolder + "/" + MeshName)
+ ".asset");
AssetDatabase.SaveAssets();
```

> **Note**   The `AssetDatabase` is a class in the Unity API and is the primary interface for managing Project Assets—adding, removing, editing, renaming, and more. The `GenerateUniqueAssetPath` function is a method of the `AssetDatabase`. You can use this to make sure your procedurally generated assets have unique names and do not conflict with existing assets. `GenerateUniqueAssetPath` accepts a proposed name as an argument, and returns either the same name (if it is unique) or a unique but modified name.

Step 3—Instantiate Quad in Scene

In the final step we simply instantiate the newly generated mesh asset in the scene, giving it the user-specified name and a collider component. The code in Listing 5-10 does this.

Listing 5-10. Adding a Quad Mesh Asset to the Project

```
//Create plane game object
GameObject plane = new GameObject(GameObjectName);
MeshFilter meshFilter = (MeshFilter)plane.AddComponent(typeof(MeshFilter));
plane.AddComponent(typeof(MeshRenderer));

//Assign mesh to mesh filter
meshFilter.sharedMesh = mesh;
mesh.RecalculateBounds();

//Add a box collider component
plane.AddComponent(typeof(BoxCollider));
```

Testing the Quad Mesh Generator

So now we've coded the complete quad mesh generator as an editor plugin, and we've come a long way! The complete code for the `CreateQuad.cs` file is shown in Listing 5-11, to clarify how the code should look in its entirety. As mentioned, our code assigns the mesh default UV values, and these don't differ from the UVs assigned by the default Unity Plane object. The crucial difference here is that our quad mesh has fewer vertices and faces, and its UVs can be easily changed, as we'll see in a later chapter.

Listing 5-11. CreateQuad.cs

```
//EDITOR CLASS TO CREATE QUAD MESH WITH SPECIFIED ANCHOR
using UnityEngine;
using UnityEditor;
using System.Collections;

public class CreateQuad : ScriptableWizard
{
    //Name of Quad Asset
    public string MeshName = "Quad";
```

```
//Game Object Name
public string GameObjectName = "Plane_Object";

//Name of asset folder to contain quad asset when created
public string AssetFolder = "Assets";

//Width of quad in world units
public float Width = 1.0f;

//Height of quad in world units
public float Height = 1.0f;

//Anchor point for created quad
public enum AnchorPoint
{
    TopLeft,
    TopMiddle,
    TopRight,
    RightMiddle,
    BottomRight,
    BottomMiddle,
    BottomLeft,
    LeftMiddle,
    Center,
    Custom
}

//Position of Anchor
public AnchorPoint Anchor = AnchorPoint.Center;

//Horz Position of Anchor on Plane
public float AnchorX = 0.5f;

//Vert Position of Anchor on Plane
public float AnchorY = 0.5f;

[MenuItem("GameObject/Create Other/Custom Plane")]
static void CreateWizard()
{
    ScriptableWizard.DisplayWizard("Create Plane",typeof(CreateQuad));
}

//Gets the currently selected asset in the project panel
void GetFolderSelection()
{
    //Check user selection in editor - check for folder selection
    if (Selection.objects != null && Selection.objects.Length == 1)
    {
        //Get path from selected asset
        AssetFolder = AssetDatabase.GetAssetPath(Selection.objects[0]);
    }
}
```

```
//Called when window is show
void OnEnable()
{
    GetFolderSelection();
}

//Called 10 times per second
void OnInspectorUpdate()
{
    switch(Anchor)
    {
        //Anchor is set to top-left
        case AnchorPoint.TopLeft:
            AnchorX = 0.0f * Width;
            AnchorY = 1.0f * Height;
        break;

        //Anchor is set to top-middle
        case AnchorPoint.TopMiddle:
            AnchorX = 0.5f * Width;
            AnchorY = 1.0f * Height;
        break;

        //Anchor is set to top-right
        case AnchorPoint.TopRight:
            AnchorX = 1.0f * Width;
            AnchorY = 1.0f * Height;
        break;

        //Anchor is set to right-middle
        case AnchorPoint.RightMiddle:
            AnchorX = 1.0f * Width;
            AnchorY = 0.5f * Height;
        break;

        //Anchor is set to Bottom-Right
        case AnchorPoint.BottomRight:
            AnchorX = 1.0f * Width;
            AnchorY = 0.0f * Height;
        break;

        //Anchor is set to Bottom-Middle
        case AnchorPoint.BottomMiddle:
            AnchorX = 0.5f * Width;
            AnchorY = 0.0f * Height;
        break;

        //Anchor is set to Bottom-Left
        case AnchorPoint.BottomLeft:
            AnchorX = 0.0f * Width;
            AnchorY = 0.0f * Height;
        break;
```

```
        //Anchor is set to Left-Middle
        case AnchorPoint.LeftMiddle:
            AnchorX = 0.0f * Width;
            AnchorY = 0.5f * Height;
        break;

        //Anchor is set to center
        case AnchorPoint.Center:
            AnchorX = 0.5f * Width;
            AnchorY = 0.5f * Height;
        break;

        case AnchorPoint.Custom:
        default:
        break;
    }
}

//Function to create quad mesh
void OnWizardCreate()
{
    //Create Vertices
    Vector3[] Vertices = new Vector3[4];

    //Create UVs
    Vector2[] UVs = new Vector2[4];

    //Two triangles of quad
    int[] Triangles = new int[6];

    //Assign vertices based on pivot

    //Bottom-left
    Vertices[0].x = -AnchorX;
    Vertices[0].y = -AnchorY;

    //Bottom-right
    Vertices[1].x = Vertices[0].x+Width;
    Vertices[1].y = Vertices[0].y;

    //Top-left
    Vertices[2].x = Vertices[0].x;
    Vertices[2].y = Vertices[0].y+Height;

    //Top-right
    Vertices[3].x = Vertices[0].x+Width;
    Vertices[3].y = Vertices[0].y+Height;

    //Assign UVs
    //Bottom-left
    UVs[0].x=0.0f;
    UVs[0].y=0.0f;
```

```
        //Bottom-right
        UVs[1].x=1.0f;
        UVs[1].y=0.0f;

        //Top-left
        UVs[2].x=0.0f;
        UVs[2].y=1.0f;

        //Top-right
        UVs[3].x=1.0f;
        UVs[3].y=1.0f;

        //Assign triangles
        Triangles[0]=3;
        Triangles[1]=1;
        Triangles[2]=2;

        Triangles[3]=2;
        Triangles[4]=1;
        Triangles[5]=0;

        //Generate mesh
        Mesh mesh = new Mesh();
        mesh.name = MeshName;
        mesh.vertices = Vertices;
        mesh.uv = UVs;
        mesh.triangles = Triangles;
        mesh.RecalculateNormals();

        //Create asset in database
        AssetDatabase.CreateAsset(mesh, AssetDatabase.GenerateUniqueAssetPath(AssetFolder + "/" +
MeshName) + ".asset");
        AssetDatabase.SaveAssets();

        //Create plane game object
        GameObject plane = new GameObject(GameObjectName);
        MeshFilter meshFilter = (MeshFilter)plane.AddComponent(typeof(MeshFilter));
        plane.AddComponent(typeof(MeshRenderer));

        //Assign mesh to mesh filter
        meshFilter.sharedMesh = mesh;
        mesh.RecalculateBounds();

        //Add a box collider component
        plane.AddComponent(typeof(BoxCollider));
    }
}
```

Let's take this code for a quick test run to see it in action and generate some quad meshes. To do this, just run the Quad Generator several times with different values. Select **GameObject ➤ Create Other ➤ Custom Plane** from the application menu, and generate a quad into the scene. When you do this, notice the addition of a new quad mesh asset in the project panel, as well as quad mesh instantiation in the active scene. This mesh appears purple in color because it lacks a material. But any standard material can be assigned. Its UVs are currently configured to show a complete texture, from top-left corner to bottom-right corner. See Figure 5-5.

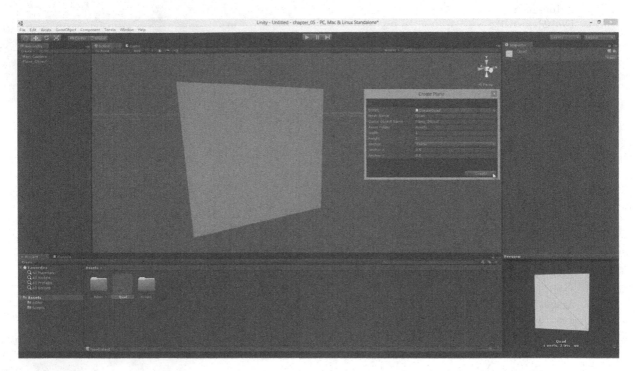

Figure 5-5. Generating quad meshes using the CreateQuad Editor plugin. Newly created quads lack a material and appear purple by default

Tip   The Plane object is one-sided. This means it will not render on its backside. Nor can the object be selected with the mouse in the Viewport from the backside. If you click on the object in the Viewport and find it doesn't select as expected, try rotating the view to see the plane from its front side before selecting.

Don't forget to generate multiple quads, experimenting with different anchor point positions and see the affect this has on transformations in the scene. Then try assigning a material and texture to the quad to see how its default settings look (see Figure 5-6).

Figure 5-6. Debugging the Create Quad plugin: generating multiple quads with different anchors and materials

Summary

This chapter represents an early but significant step in our 2D development workflow. With it, we now have the power to generate optimized quad meshes from the Unity Editor according to a range of parameters we can specify in advance, such as name, size, and anchor point. This kind of flexibility is not open to us if we use either pregenerated primitives or imported meshes. Further, with the simple structure of our quads, the path is now clear to customize our meshes further. For example, we can easily edit our quad's UVs at runtime, and Chapter 7 will show you how. This is useful not just for showing specific regions of textures, but also for showing animations—the UVs can be animated, and this creates an object known as a Flipbook. This now points to the direction for our next work: draw calls, materials, and textures. These features will work hand-in-hand with what we've coded here. In short, after reading this chapter you should be able to:

- Confidentially create Editor plugins based on `ScriptableWizard`
- Understand the benefits of procedural geometry compared to alternatives
- Display drop-down lists in Editor dialogs using `enum` types
- Use `OnInspectorUpdate` to refresh Editor windows
- Understand object anchor points and their relevance for transformations

- Use normalized values to express position and offsets
- Generate meshes from arrays of vertices, UVs, and triangles
- Use the Mesh class to encode a mesh
- Create mesh assets with the AssetDatabase object
- Detect the currently selected object in the Unity Editor
- Instantiate objects and add components from code

Generating Atlas Textures

This chapter ranks as one of the most important in the book. Here, we'll create a new `ScriptableWizard` Editor extension that'll generate *Atlas Textures*. What is an Atlas Texture? And what does creating one achieve? To answer the first question, imagine this: you've created lots of different sprite images for your 2D game (all at different pixel dimensions)—one file for the player, one for each enemy, and one for each prop and power-up. That's probably a lot of files! Then, you copy and paste them all into one, larger image file, consolidating them neatly into rows and columns. In doing this, you've just created an Atlas Texture the manual way. Now why is an Atlas Texture useful? Essentially, they offer us several benefits when we use them in Unity for our objects, as opposed to using many different textures. These benefits are listed here:

- **Atlas Textures reduce scene draw calls**: Unity features a real-time render system. On each frame, this system accepts all scene geometry, materials, shaders, and lighting information as an input, and produces a final rendered image as output. To simplify: the steps the renderer goes through to create an image are known as *draw calls*. Draw calls can be computationally expensive. The number of draw calls required to render any scene depends on the scene content and how its assets are configured. By configuring them smartly, we reduce the number of draw calls, and thereby improve runtime performance. Materials have a significant impact on draw calls. Specifically, two game objects with the same material can be rendered in one draw call. But two objects with different materials must be rendered in different draw calls. By having many textures consolidated into an Atlas, we can assign a single material with an Atlas to many different objects, and have those objects texture themselves correctly through UV Mapping. In this way, we reduce the number of materials needed.

- **Atlas Textures offer us flexibility**: Nearly all textures in Unity, except for GUI textures, must be power-2 compliant; unless we're happy with unpredictable stretching and resampling! This means a texture's pixel dimensions in width and height should be a size, such as: 16, 32, 64, 128, 256, 512, 1024, 2048, or 4096. No other size is practically acceptable. This is limiting because, for 2D games, we typically want our sprites and objects to be different sizes. Atlas Textures help us fix this because, with Atlas Textures, it's only *the Atlas itself* that needs to be power-2 compliant, and not the constituent images from which it's made. Unity doesn't care whether non-power-2 textures are pasted within the Atlas boundaries. All that matters is that the Atlas is a power-2 size.

▪ ***Atlas Textures give us pixel perfection***: Without Atlas Textures, we *could* use our image editor to create sprites at any size and then non-uniformly scale them to the nearest power-2 size, before importing them into Unity as power-2 textures. This method effectively means that Unity will scale and resample your texture back to its correct dimensions when it's applied to an appropriately sized Quad Mesh in the scene. But, the texture quality you'll get from this process at render time will usually not be good. There will often be artifacting, blurring, and a general imprecision, leaving you feeling that the render simply isn't as crisp and as sharp it should be. This is because, in this scenario, we're not achieving pixel perfection. Atlas Textures help us achieve this. Being a power-2 size, Unity doesn't rescale or resample the texture. This means that, provided our textured quads match the proportions of the sprites, and provided the quads are rendered with an orthographic camera, they will always be shown on-screen in a pixel-perfect way.

> **Note**   Chapter 8 covers orthographic cameras and screen space.

▪ ***Atlas Textures are minimalistic***: In short, with an Atlas Texture, you have fewer texture assets to manage and worry about overall in your projects. By loading lots of smaller sprites into a larger texture, you consolidate those textures into one. This might seem only a trivial or secondary benefit, but when dealing with lots of small sprites, it can be a real timesaver.

So here we've seen what an Atlas Texture is and how it helps us. Its benefits are significant enough for almost all 2D games that'll we want to implement them in some form or other. In this chapter we'll add them to our Unity project via an Editor plug-in. This plug-in will allow us to import any number of non-power-2 sized textures into the project (for our sprites), and on the basis of these will automatically generate an optimized power-2 sized Atlas Texture that includes all the imported sprites and is ready to use immediately in our 2D games. After generating this texture, we'll even be able to delete all the previously imported sprites from the project.

Getting Started with Atlas Textures

The Atlas Texture generator is coded as an Editor Class based on `ScriptableWizard`. This means our user (the developer) can import sprite textures and generate atlases from them directly inside the Unity Editor, using only a GUI interface. The previous two chapters explained in-depth how to create a `ScriptableWizard` Editor class (for creating a Batch Rename feature, and a Quad Mesh Generator). In short: create a new C# script file, name your class appropriately, descend from `ScriptableWizard` (and not `MonoBehaviour`), make sure your script includes the directive using `UnityEditor`; and is stored inside a project folder named *Editor*. For this project, I've named the class `TexturePacker`, because it "packs" sprite textures into an Atlas Texture (see Figure 6-1). The initial code for this class should look like Listing 6-1.

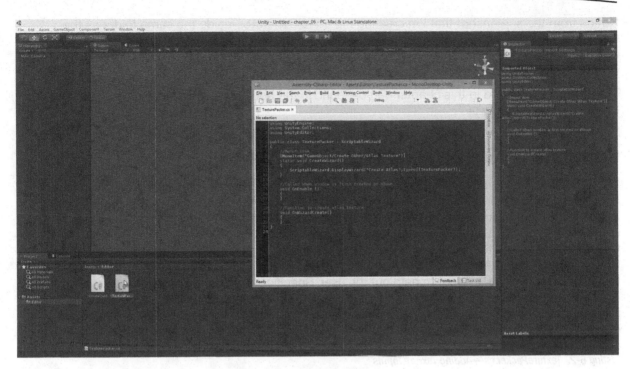

Figure 6-1. Creating a TexturePacker Editor add-on to generate Atlas Textures

Listing 6-1. exturePacker.cs

```
using UnityEngine;
using System.Collections;
using UnityEditor;

public class TexturePacker : ScriptableWizard
{

    //Menu item
    [MenuItem("GameObject/Create Other/Atlas Texture")]
    static void CreateWizard()
    {
        ScriptableWizard.DisplayWizard("Create Atlas",typeof(TexturePacker));
    }

    //Called when window is first created or shown
    void OnEnable ()
    {
    }

    //Function to create atlas texture
    void OnWizardCreate()
    {
    }
}
```

Notice from the screenshot that I'm creating the Atlas Generator inside the same folder as the CreateQuad add-on, coded in the previous chapter. I'm including both files in this project so that later I can generate a quad to work with the Atlas Texture. If you're not using the CreateQuad add-on, you can also use the standard Unity plane asset.

The script files created in this chapter can be found in the book companion files at: Project_Files/Chapter06/.

Configuring Texture Inputs

The Atlas Texture Generator should accept a list of separate sprite textures as input. These inputs are ordinary textures in the project. Then from these, the generator outputs a single and compiled Atlas Texture that includes all inputs. This atlas is generated as a new, power-2 texture asset (4096×4096). Consequently, our editor add-on needs a GUI widget so the user can specify the texture inputs to add to the Atlas. We can add this list widget to the ScriptableWizard window easily by using an array public-variable for the TexturePacker class. But, we can also code additional behavior in the OnEnable event to help out the user. Specifically, when the TexturePacker window is opened, we can search the project panel for any selected textures and then add them automatically to the list to save the user specifying them manually in the Wizard window. This makes Atlas generation ever faster and easier! The code in Listing 6-2 demonstrates how to do this.

Listing 6-2. TexturePacker.cs—Adding Texture Inputs

```
using UnityEngine;
using System.Collections;
using System.Collections.Generic;
using UnityEditor;

public class TexturePacker : ScriptableWizard
{
    //Reference to list of textures
    //Used later for atlas generation
    //Standard unity arrays are very fast
    public Texture2D[] Textures;

    //Menu item
    [MenuItem("GameObject/Create Other/Atlas Texture")]
    static void CreateWizard()
    {
        ScriptableWizard.DisplayWizard("Create Atlas",typeof(TexturePacker));
    }

    //Called when window is first created or shown
    void OnEnable ()
    {
        //Search through selected objects for textures

        //Create new texture list
        List<Texture2D> TextureList = new List<Texture2D>();
```

```
        //Loop through objects selected in editor
        if (Selection.objects != null && Selection.objects.Length > 0)
        {
            Object[] objects = EditorUtility.CollectDependencies(Selection.objects);

            foreach (Object o in objects)
            {
                //Get selected object as texture
                Texture2D tex = o as Texture2D;

                //Is texture asset?
                if(tex != null)
                {
                    //Add to list
                    TextureList.Add(tex);
                }
            }
        }

        //Check count. If >0, then create array
        if(TextureList.Count > 0)
        {
            Textures = new Texture2D[TextureList.Count];

            for(int i=0; i<TextureList.Count; i++)
            {
                Textures[i] = TextureList[i];
            }
        }
    }
    //Function to create atlas texture
    void OnWizardCreate()
    {
    }
}
```

> **Note** Texture sizes of 4096×4096 will often work well for desktop platforms. For many mobile devices, it's likely you'll want to reduce the texture size.

> **Tip** The code in Listing 6-2 will not compile unless you include the namespace System.Collections.Generic. This line has been marked in bold to catch your attention. This line is necessary to use the .NET List class. More information on the List class can be found here: http://msdn.microsoft.com/en-us/library/6sh2ey19.aspx.

Let's discuss the code in Listing 6-2 to see what's happening. First, a new public variable has been added to the TexturePacker class: Texture2D[] Textures. This list contains all textures to be included in the atlas. The user can manually add and remove textures to and from this list using the ScriptableWizard window, which can be opened by selecting **GameObject ➤ Other ➤ Atlas Texture** from the application main menu (see Figure 6-2). However, the OnEnable function (run whenever the ScriptableWizard window is shown) searches through the project panel for selected textures and automatically adds them to the list. It achieves this in code using a multi-step process. First, it uses the static EditorUtility.CollectDependencies function to generate a list of all assets associated with the current selection in the Unity Editor. Then, it cycles through that list and checks each object's data-type, adding all texture assets to a .NET List object. Finally, it adds all validated texture objects in that List to the Textures array member of the class. As a result of this code, textures can be added and removed manually from the ScriptableWizard window, as well as automatically by selecting textures in the project panel before the window is shown. Notice: the textures selected in the Project Panel (in Figure 6-2) were automatically imported as power-2 textures by Unity, even though the textures are not a power-2 size. This doesn't matter, as the Atlas Generator we create handles this event and configures textures optimally.

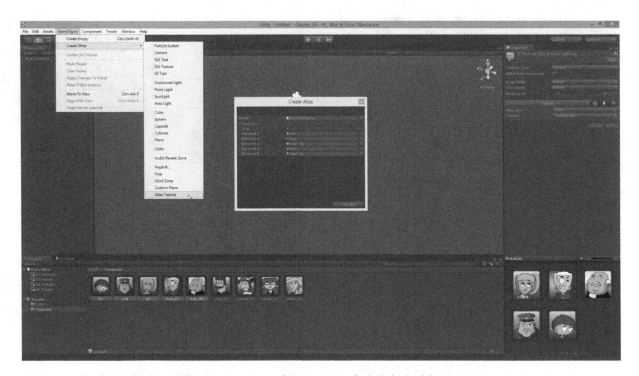

Figure 6-2. *The TexturePacker add-in allows users to select textures to include in the Atlas*

Atlas Textures and UVs

Although an Atlas Texture is really just a single image file featuring many smaller textures, we'll need to keep track of more information than that if the Atlas is to be truly useful for us. The TexturePacker will produce the texture for us, as we'll see. But, if we assign that texture to a plane or a quad object in the scene, the object will show only the whole Atlas Texture from the top-left corner to the bottom-right corner. This is because all quads and planes are by default UV mapped in the 0-1 space. The whole point of having an Atlas is so that we can show only parts of the texture on selected objects, with different objects showing different parts. To achieve this, we'll need not just the Atlas Texture itself, but information about the name of each texture represented in the Atlas and its UV position within the Atlas. To keep track of all this meta-data, we'll create a new C# MonoBehaviour class (not an editor class) called AtlasData. The TexturePacker class will, during its work, instantiate this class and add it as a prefab of the project where it'll encode all the required data for our Atlas. The code for this class is given in Listing 6-3, from the C# file AtlasData.cs. This file represents a standard class and can be stored in any project folder, except the *Editor* folder (see Figure 6-3).

Listing 6-3. AtlasData.cs

```csharp
using UnityEngine;
//-------------------------------------------------
public class AtlasData : MonoBehaviour
{
    //Reference to output texture
    public Texture2D AtlasTexture;

    //List of string for texture file names
    public string[] TextureNames;

    //List of Rects
    public Rect[] UVs;
}
//-------------------------------------------------
```

Figure 6-3. The AtlasData class is created as a standard class derived from MonoBehaviour, and is not an Editor class. Editor classes can make use of standard classes too, as we'll see later

Listing 6-3 is an `AtlasData` class. It encodes information about an Atlas Texture. The variable `AtlasTexture` references the final Atlas Texture asset, the variable `TextureNames` stores the filenames of all sub-images within the atlas, and the variable `UVs` keeps track of UV data for each corresponding texture in the `TextureNames` array. The `UVs` variable encodes texture position in terms of UVs and not pixels. Therefore, an image located at the center of a "4096×4096 atlas texture" would have a position of 0.5, and not 2048.

Note   UV data is measured in a normalized space—that is, between the values 0-1. U refers to the horizontal axis (X dimension) in an image and is called "U" to avoid confusion with the X axis in 3D space. The V direction refers to the vertical axis (Y dimension) in an image. The value (0,0) points to the top-left corner of a texture, and (1,1) points to the bottom-right corner. (0.5, 0.5) refers to the image middle, (1,0) refers to the top-right, and (0,1) to the bottom-left, and so on.

Generating an Atlas – Step 1: Optimizing Texture Inputs

Now it's time to code the Atlas generation functionality from start to finish. This is a multistep process:

In Step one we'll configure all texture inputs with optimized values to ensure the textures are not being stretched or resampled by Unity.

In Step two, we'll copy and paste these optimized textures to the atlas, and record the UV positions of each texture.

In Step three, we'll save out all this data in the form of an `AtlasData` prefab, along with the generated `AtlasTexture` asset, and then finally we'll perform any necessary clean-up operations.

So let's start with coding a texture optimization function, adding it to the `TexturePacker` class (not the `AtlasData` class!). The code for this is in Listing 6-4.

Listing 6-4. TexturePacker.cs—Optimizing a Texture

```
//Function to configure texture for atlasing
public void ConfigureForAtlas(string TexturePath)
{    TextureImporter TexImport = AssetImporter.GetAtPath(TexturePath) as TextureImporter;
    TextureImporterSettings tiSettings = new TextureImporterSettings();
            TexImport.textureType = TextureImporterType.Advanced;
        TexImport.ReadTextureSettings(tiSettings);

    tiSettings.mipmapEnabled = false;
    tiSettings.readable = true;
    tiSettings.maxTextureSize = 4096;
    tiSettings.textureFormat = TextureImporterFormat.ARGB32;
    tiSettings.filterMode = FilterMode.Point;
    tiSettings.wrapMode = TextureWrapMode.Clamp;
    tiSettings.npotScale = TextureImporterNPOTScale.None;
```

```
TexImport.SetTextureSettings(tiSettings);
//Save changes
AssetDatabase.ImportAsset(TexturePath, ImportAssetOptions.ForceUpdate);
AssetDatabase.Refresh();
}
```

The `ConfigureForAtlas` function accepts a fully qualified path to a texture asset in the project, and then configures that texture for being added to the atlas. The texture path should *not* be a local file path on the system (such as `c:\mytextures` on Windows), but a valid Unity Asset Path. This kind of path can be returned from the function `AssetDatabase.GetAssetPath`. We'll see that in action later. Once a valid texture is provided, this function accesses its Texture Import settings through the `TextureImportSettings` class. Effectively, this function is the code equivalent of selecting a texture in the Project Panel and tweaking its settings manually in the Object Inspector. This function, of course, is automating that process for us. Specifically, it converts the texture to an Advanced type, and adjusts a range of properties, including npotScale *(not power-2 scale)*. Once adjusted, the texture is re-imported into the project with updated settings, using the function `AssetDatabase.ImportAsset`.

Now we've got a `ConfigureForAtlas` function, we'll code a `GenerateAtlas` function. This function generates the final Atlas Texture and makes use of `ConfigureForAtlas`. The first few lines of this function appear in Listing 6-5 and represent Step 1 of the Atlas generation process (optimizing texture inputs).

Listing 6-5 does not feature the complete `GenerateAtlas` function. We complete this function over the course of subsequent sections.

Listing 6-5. TexturePacker.cs—Optimizing a Texture Before Atlas Generation

```
//Function to generate Atlas Texture
public void GenerateAtlas()
{
    //Generate Atlas Object
    GameObject AtlasObject = new GameObject("obj_"+AtlasName);
    AtlasData AtlasComp = AtlasObject.AddComponent<AtlasData>();
    //Initialize string array
    AtlasComp.TextureNames = new string[Textures.Length];
    //Cycle through textures and configure for atlasing
    for(int i=0; i<Textures.Length; i++)
    {
        //Get asset path
        string TexturePath = AssetDatabase.GetAssetPath(Textures[i]);
        //Configure texture
        ConfigureForAtlas(TexturePath);
        //Add file name to atlas texture name list
        AtlasComp.TextureNames[i] = TexturePath;
    }
```

Note   The public string variable `AtlasName` has been added to the `TexturePacker` class. This is allows the user to assign the generated Atlas a human-readable name.

This code begins the Atlas generation process. It temporarily creates a new AtlasData object in the scene to store the Atlas metadata. Then it cycles through all texture inputs and plugs them in to the ConfigureForAtlas function. Notice also that the AtlasData object is being populated with a list of texture names, representing the textures to be added to the atlas.

Generating an Atlas – Step 2: Atlas Generation

This part continues with the GenerateAtlas function. Here we'll move onto to Step 2 and generate the Atlas Texture itself. This process is detailed in Listing 6-6, and makes use of the Unity API function PackTextures (part of the Texture2D class) to generate Atlas Textures.

Listing 6-6. TexturePacker.cs – Continuing with the Atlas Generation Function

```
//Generate Atlas
Texture2D tex = new Texture2D(1, 1, TextureFormat.ARGB32, false);
AtlasComp.UVs = tex.PackTextures(Textures, Padding, 4096);

//Generate Unique Asset Path
string AssetPath = AssetDatabase.GenerateUniqueAssetPath("Assets/" + AtlasName + ".png");//Write
texture to file
byte[] bytes = tex.EncodeToPNG();
System.IO.File.WriteAllBytes(AssetPath, bytes);
bytes = null;

//Delete generated texture
UnityEngine.Object.DestroyImmediate(tex);

//Import Asset
AssetDatabase.ImportAsset(AssetPath);

//Get Imported Texture
AtlasComp.AtlasTexture = AssetDatabase.LoadAssetAtPath(AssetPath, typeof(Texture2D)) as Texture2D;

//Configure texture as atlas
ConfigureForAtlas(AssetDatabase.GetAssetPath(AtlasComp.AtlasTexture));
```

Listing 6-6 is the heart of the Atlas generation process. The function Texture2D.PackTextures accepts an array of texture objects and pastes them into a single texture, separating them from one another by pixel padding, as specified in the Padding variable. This variable has been added to the class as a public member, allowing the user to control padding from the ScriptableWizard window. The PackTextures function returns an array of Rect UV values, which are stored in the AtlasData.UVs member. After the texture is generated, it is saved to a PNG file using the functions EncodeToPng and System.IO.File.WriteAllBytes. This file is then imported into the project as the Atlas Texture.

> **Note**   Code sample 6-6 uses of many important and useful functions in the Unity API. The following URLs feature more information on these functions:
>
> PackTextures
>
> `http://docs.unity3d.com/Documentation/ScriptReference/Texture2D.PackTextures.html`
>
> GenerateUniqueAssetPath
>
> `http://docs.unity3d.com/Documentation/ScriptReference/AssetDatabase.GenerateUniqueAssetPath.html`
>
> EncodeToPNG
>
> `http://docs.unity3d.com/Documentation/ScriptReference/Texture2D.EncodeToPNG.html`
>
> LoadAssetAtPath
>
> `http://docs.unity3d.com/Documentation/ScriptReference/Resources.LoadAssetAtPath.html`

> **Note**   There's an alternative way to create Atlas Textures, although it's not discussed in further detail beyond this note. You can use the Texture Creation software *Texture Packer found at:* `http://www.codeandweb.com/texturepacker`. Using this application you can package individual textures into a single atlas using a GUI interface. The metadata for the atlas (the texture names and UVs) is exported to a file in the JSON (JavaScript Object Notation) language. Therefore, to use atlases from this software, you need to code or buy a JSON parser. There's also a free, community-developed JSON parser here at: `http://wiki.unity3d.com/index.php/SimpleJSON`

Generating an Atlas – Step 3: Saving the Atlas Prefab

The final part of Atlas generation involves saving out the atlas data to a Prefab asset in the project and performing clean-up operations on the objects created during the generation process. This really involves only a few lines of extra code, so in Listing 6-7 I'll provide the complete TexturePacker class for clarity, so you can see how the whole thing works together, including the final lines of code. I've made highlights in bold to lines not explicitly included in previous code samples.

Listing 6-7. Full Listing of TexturePacker.cs

```
using UnityEngine;
using UnityEditor;
using System.Collections.Generic;
//-----------------------------------------------
public class TexturePacker : ScriptableWizard
{
    //Name of Atlas Texture
    public string AtlasName = "Atlas_Texture";
```

```
//Amount of padding in atlas
public int Padding = 4;
//Reference to list of textures
public Texture2D[] Textures;
//------------------------------------------------
//Called when dev selects window from main menu
[MenuItem("GameObject/Create Other/Atlas Texture")]
static void CreateWizard()
{
    ScriptableWizard.DisplayWizard("Create Atlas",typeof(TexturePacker));
}


//------------------------------------------------
//Called when window is first created or shown
void OnEnable ()
{
    //Search through selected objects for textures

    //Create new texture list
    List<Texture2D> TextureList = new List<Texture2D>();

    //Loop through objects selected in editor
    if (Selection.objects != null && Selection.objects.Length > 0)
    {
        Object[] objects = EditorUtility.CollectDependencies(Selection.objects);
        foreach (Object o in objects)
        {
            //Get selected object as texture
            Texture2D tex = o as Texture2D;
            //Is texture asset?
            if(tex != null)
            {
                //Add to list
                TextureList.Add(tex);
            }
        }
    }
    //Check count. If >0, then create array
    if(TextureList.Count > 0)
    {
        Textures = new Texture2D[TextureList.Count];
        for(int i=0; i<TextureList.Count; i++)
        {
            Textures[i] = TextureList[i];
        }
    }
}
//------------------------------------------------
//Function to create atlas texture
```

```
void OnWizardCreate()
{
    GenerateAtlas();
}
//------------------------------------------------
//Function to generate Atlas Texture
public void GenerateAtlas()
{
    //Generate Atlas Object
    GameObject AtlasObject = new GameObject("obj_"+AtlasName);
    AtlasData AtlasComp = AtlasObject.AddComponent<AtlasData>();
    //Initialize string array
    AtlasComp.TextureNames = new string[Textures.Length];
    //Cycle through textures and configure for atlasing
    for(int i=0; i<Textures.Length; i++)
    {
        //Get asset path
        string TexturePath = AssetDatabase.GetAssetPath(Textures[i]);
        //Configure texture
        ConfigureForAtlas(TexturePath);
        //Add file name to atlas texture name list
        AtlasComp.TextureNames[i] = TexturePath;
    }
    //Generate Atlas
    Texture2D tex = new Texture2D(1, 1, TextureFormat.ARGB32, false);
    AtlasComp.UVs = tex.PackTextures(Textures, Padding, 4096);
    //Generate Unique Asset Path
    string AssetPath = AssetDatabase.GenerateUniqueAssetPath("Assets/" + AtlasName + ".png");
    //Write texture to file
    byte[] bytes = tex.EncodeToPNG();
    System.IO.File.WriteAllBytes(AssetPath, bytes);
    bytes = null;
    //Delete generated texture
    UnityEngine.Object.DestroyImmediate(tex);
    //Import Asset
    AssetDatabase.ImportAsset(AssetPath);
    //Get Imported Texture
    AtlasComp.AtlasTexture = AssetDatabase.LoadAssetAtPath(AssetPath, typeof(Texture2D)) as
    Texture2D;
    //Configure texture as atlas
    ConfigureForAtlas(AssetDatabase.GetAssetPath(AtlasComp.AtlasTexture));
    //Now create prefab from atlas object
    AssetPath = AssetDatabase.GenerateUniqueAssetPath("Assets/atlasdata_" + AtlasName + ".prefab");
    //Create prefab object
    Object prefab = PrefabUtility.CreateEmptyPrefab(AssetPath);
    //Update prefab and save
    PrefabUtility.ReplacePrefab(AtlasObject, prefab, ReplacePrefabOptions.ConnectToPrefab);
    AssetDatabase.SaveAssets();
    AssetDatabase.Refresh();
    //Destroy original object
    DestroyImmediate(AtlasObject);
}
```

```
//-------------------------------------------------
//Function to configure texture for atlasing
public void ConfigureForAtlas(string TexturePath)
{
    TextureImporter TexImport = AssetImporter.GetAtPath(TexturePath) as TextureImporter;
    TextureImporterSettings tiSettings = new TextureImporterSettings();
    TexImport.textureType = TextureImporterType.Advanced;
    TexImport.ReadTextureSettings(tiSettings);
    tiSettings.mipmapEnabled = false;
    tiSettings.readable = true;
    tiSettings.maxTextureSize = 4096;
    tiSettings.textureFormat = TextureImporterFormat.ARGB32;
    tiSettings.filterMode = FilterMode.Point;
    tiSettings.wrapMode = TextureWrapMode.Clamp;
    tiSettings.npotScale = TextureImporterNPOTScale.None;

    TexImport.SetTextureSettings(tiSettings);
    //Save changes
    AssetDatabase.ImportAsset(TexturePath, ImportAssetOptions.ForceUpdate);
    AssetDatabase.Refresh();
}
//-------------------------------------------------
}
```

Listing 6-7 represents the complete Atlas generation code. The new additions, for creating a Prefab asset, make use of two main features: GenerateUniqueAssetPath, and the PrefabUtility class. The function GenerateUniqueAssetPath simply produces a unique path as a string for saving the asset, ensuring the asset always has a unique name. The PrefabUtility is a helper class for creating and defining Prefab assets.

Testing the Atlas Texture

We've now coded two complementary classes: AtlasData and TexturePacker. Together these generate an Atlas Texture from texture inputs. Let's give this code a test run. To begin, import a group of image files into your Unity project. If you don't have any easily available, then I've provided some images in the book companion files at Project_Files/Chapter06/. These are character images from my Unity-based game *Bounders and Cads*, in case you're interested. Once imported, leave all the default settings intact (see Figure 6-4).

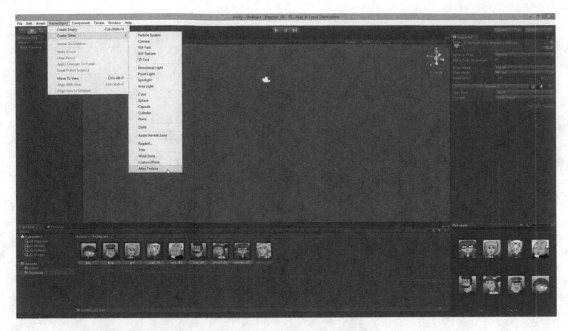

Figure 6-4. Importing texture assets into the project, ready for creating atlas textures

Note   More information on Bounders and Cads can be found at
`http://www.waxlyricalgames.com/boundersandcads/`. This game was created using Unity 3.5.

Select some or all the imported textures and open the TexturePacker window by selecting
GameObject ➤ Create Other ➤ Atlas Texture from the application menu. This shows the
TexturePacker window, and the *Textures* list should be auto-populated with the textures selected
in the Project Panel, as a result of the OnEnable event (see Figure 6-2). From the TexturePacker
window, assign the Atlas a name (MyAtlas) and specify a padding value (*4 pixels*), and then click
the *Create* button to generate the Atlas Texture. This process may take time on some systems,
depending on the number of input textures (see Figure 6-5).

Figure 6-5. An Atlas Texture generated from inputs. The atlas includes both the texture and the associated Prefab metadata. The Prefab includes information about the textures within the Atlas and their UV positions

The generation process produces two files from the inputs: First, a 4096×4096 Atlas Texture, which is assigned custom import values. Second, a Prefab object with an `AtlasData` Component defining metadata for the images included in the Atlas. These values are the name of each texture in the Atlas and its UV coordinates. Both the Atlas Texture and the `AtlasData` Prefab are added as assets of the project and are featured in the Project Panel. Go ahead and explore the AtlasData object further. Select it in the Project Panel and expand its `TextureNames` and `UV` members in the Object Inspector to see the recorded atlas data (see Figure 6-6).

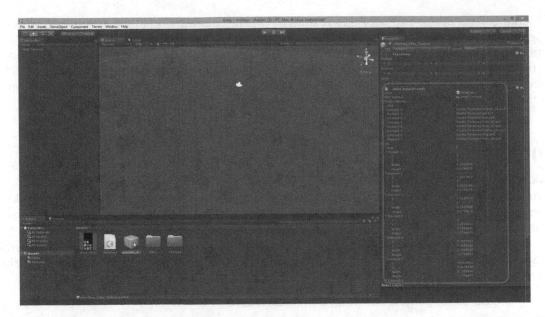

Figure 6-6. *The AtlasData object records UV and Texture name data. This information will be used later to customize the UV mapping of Texture Quads to show the correct regions of the Atlas*

Now let's generate a new quad or plane object in the scene to receive our Atlas Texture. To do this, you can use either the Textured Quad Generator add-in from the previous chapter, or simply create a Unity Plane Primitive. Here, I'll use our Textured Quad add-in. Then just drag and drop the Atlas Texture from the Project Panel onto the mesh in the scene Viewport. This assigns the Atlas Texture to the mesh by auto-generating a material (see Figure 6-7).

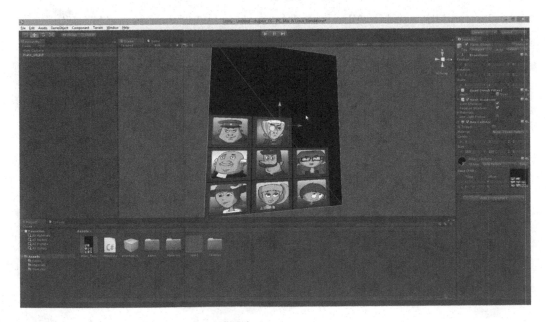

Figure 6-7. *The Atlas Texture is assigned to a Quad Mesh in the scene*

From Figure 6-7 you'll see that our Atlas Texture functionality is working in the sense that, when the Atlas Texture is assigned to a Plane Mesh in the scene, the whole atlas is shown and includes all our input textures. Of course, while the atlas is working *in this sense*, we don't usually want to show the whole texture on an object; only part of it. To achieve this, we need control over of an object's UV mapping data. Specifically, we need to edit an object's UV mapping to reference specific regions within the Atlas. This subject is considered in more depth in the next chapter.

Summary

The importance of generating Atlas Textures should not be understated for most 2D games. Most 2D games feature lots of sprites, backgrounds, props, characters, objects, and animations. Atlas Textures offer a convenient and efficient method for storing this data in memory, especially when compared to storing all images in separate files. The work of this chapter is therefore a pivotal stage in our 2D development workflow. Using Atlas Textures we can improve runtime performance, import non-power-2 textures into our games, achieve pixel perfection, and make asset management simpler during development. Specifically, by this stage you should be able to:

- Create editor plugins based on ScriptableWizard

- Know what an Atlas Texture is

- Understand the rationale for Atlas Textures and the benefits they offer

- Use the Texture2D class for creating Atlas Textures

- Instantiate objects from code and create assets from prefabs

- Export textures to PNG files

- Adjust texture import settings from code

- Understand the need for Atlas metadata, such as texture names and UV data

- Understand how UVs control an object mapping to the texture

- Use the Atlas Generator add-in to create your own Atlas Textures

7

UVs and Animation

The previous chapter explained how to develop a GUI editor add-in that allows users to add selected textures in the project panel to a larger atlas texture. Atlas Textures help us improve the performance of our 2D games. In generating the atlas, we also saved meta-data. This included all filenames of textures inside the atlas, and their UV positions within the atlas. In closing that chapter, we tested the add-on functionality by assigning an Atlas Texture to a procedural Quad Mesh in the scene, to see how it looked in the Viewport. The problem we faced was that the quad mesh rendered the complete atlas texture, rather than just a region of it (see Figure 7-1). The problem was not with the Atlas Texture, but with the mesh itself; with its UV mapping. By default, the UV mapping for Quad Meshes is configured to show a complete texture. To show only a region, the UV mapping must be adjusted at the vertex level. That is, we must dig deeper into the mesh construction and edit its vertices. We'll do that in this chapter, as we create a new editor add-in to control mesh UV mapping. This add-on lets us select a textured quad in the scene and entirely customize its UV mapping to show any region within the Atlas Texture (or within any texture!). In addition, we'll also create another class to change UV mapping over time, creating a flipbook animation effect or an animated sprite effect.

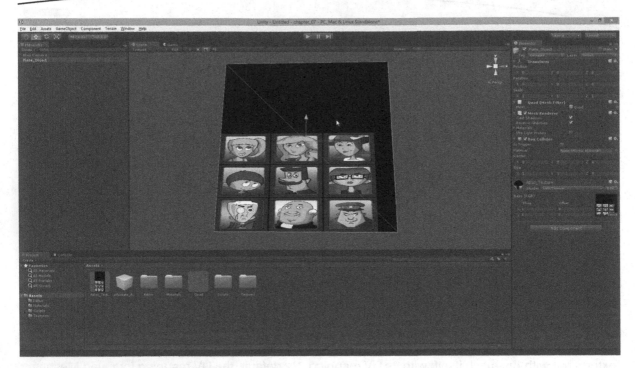

Figure 7-1. By default, textured quads are generated with UV mapping to show a complete texture, from the top-left corner to the bottom-right corner. This does not meet the needs of Atlas Textures. To fix this, we'll need to edit the mesh UV mapping

Creating a Dockable Editor

So far in this book we've built three editor add-ons (if you've been following every chapter): a *Batch Rename* tool, a *Create Quad* tool, and a *Create Atlas Texture* tool. Despite the enormous differences in behavior between these tools, they still have an important characteristic in common relating to their usability and design. Specifically, a developer uses them all to run one-hit operations; that is, a "one click and you're done" paradigm. For example, to rename multiple objects, just select the objects in the scene and then run the rename tool. To generate a Quad Mesh, open up the *Create Quad* window and press the *Create* button, and so on. This workflow has served us well so far. But, the task that faces us now (*editing* mesh UVs) is different in this regard. Our scene may have potentially many different Quad Mesh objects that must be edited (not just one or two), and we'll want to perform those edits quickly and intuitively from the editor, without having to visit the application menu, launching different ScriptableWizard windows one after the other. Instead, it would be great if we could have a non-modal and dockable window, such as the Object Inspector, showing all relevant UV properties we can edit and have applied to the selected object (see Figure 7-2). Fortunately for us, we can achieve this behavior using the EditorWindow class.

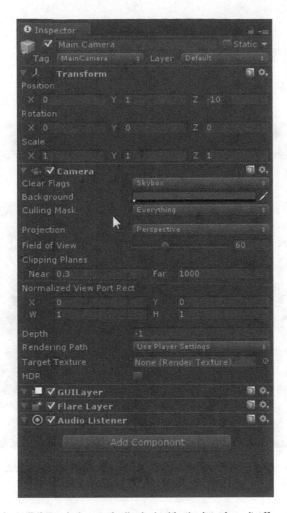

Figure 7-2. The Object Inspector is an Editor window typically docked in the interface. It offers intuitive property editing features

So let's create an EditorWindow class for the UV editing feature. To do this, follow the standard procedure for creating any new editor class, *except* this time the class should descend from EditorWindow and not ScriptableWizard. ScriptableWizard works fine for pop-up dialogs launched from the menu, but for more integrated behavior we need EditorWindow. Take a look at Listing 7-1 for our class skeleton. Figure 7-3 shows the project at this stage, configured and ready for coding.

Listing 7-1. UVEdit.cs

```csharp
using UnityEngine;
using UnityEditor;
using System.Collections;

public class UVEdit : EditorWindow
{
    [MenuItem ("Window/Atlas UV Editor")]
    static void Init ()
```

```
    {
        //Show window
        GetWindow (typeof(UVEdit),false,"Texture Atlas", true);
    }
}
```

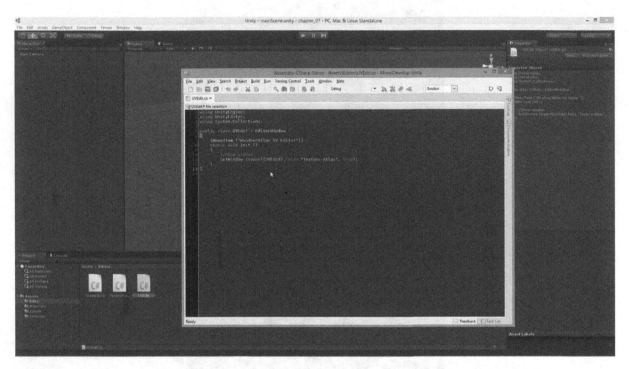

Figure 7-3. *Ready to code the UV editing Editor class. This class is stored inside the Editor folder and descends from EditorWindow, not ScriptableWizard*

The script files created in this chapter can be found in the book companion files at: Project_Files/Chapter07/.

Note   If you save and compile the code in Listing 7-1, a new entry will be added the Unity Application menu: **Window ➤ Atlas UV Editor**. Clicking this shows an empty but dockable window. All controls and widgets for this window must be drawn manually inside an OnGUI event, which is shown soon.

Starting an Editor GUI — Selecting an Atlas

The ScriptableWizard class really makes it easy for us to incorporate GUI elements into an Editor window. Using ScriptableWizard, we don't need to create any GUI code—it automatically creates GUI fields for every public and serializable variable in the class, allowing us to quickly generate a GUI. The EditorWindow class, in contrast, doesn't play by those rules. If you add public variables to an EditorWindow class, they will not automatically show up in the Editor window, even if they're serializable variables. The EditorWindow class expects you to create the GUI manually using OnGUI event, and using the GUI and EditorGUI classes in the Unity API. This makes creating an EditorWindow a more cumbersome task, but it offers us more control and flexibility over how the add-on will look.

More information on the GUI, EditorGUI, GUILayout,and EditorGUILayout classes can be found in the Unity documentation here:

> **Note**   http://docs.unity3d.com/Documentation/ScriptReference/GUI.html
>
> http://docs.unity3d.com/Documentation/ScriptReference/GUILayout.html
>
> http://docs.unity3d.com/Documentation/ScriptReference/EditorGUI.html
>
> http://docs.unity3d.com/Documentation/ScriptReference/EditorGUILayout.html

Unity offers us the classes GUI, EditorGUI, GUILayout, and EditorGUILayout for creating and rendering GUIs. The classes GUI and GUILayout are typically used to make GUIs *for your games,* and EditorGUI and EditorGUILayout are used for creating Editor add-on GUIs. However, GUI and GUILayout can also be used for making Editor GUIs—these are dual purpose classes.

UV Editor—Adding an Input for the Atlas Prefab

So let's get started. The UV Editor add-on, when in use, is supposed to be permanently open and docked beside the Object Inspector. It should allow users to select Quad Meshes and then edit their UV mapping to render the intended regions of the Atlas Texture. To achieve this, our editor interface will need lots of widgets. This includes: labels for giving instructions and for labelling elements, and text fields to accept user input, such as UV coordinates. One of the most important fields, however, lets the user choose which Atlas Texture we're using for the selected object (a project can have more than one Atlas Texture). This value is important because it gives us a context for editing mesh UVs. When we know the atlas we're using we can show the user a list of textures within the atlas. One of these can be selected to configure the mesh UVs. So because this value is so important, let's add it as the first field in the Editor interface. The atlas data (such as texture names and mesh UVs) is stored inside the AtlasData Prefab object, which is generated alongside the Atlas Texture (see Chapter 6 for more information). Therefore, we'll need to create a GUI field that lets the user pick this AtlasData object. We can achieve this by adding the following OnGUI event to our UVEdit class, as shown in Listing 7-2.

Listing 7-2. UVEdit.cs–Updating the UI in OnGUI

```
using UnityEngine;
using UnityEditor;
using System.Collections;

public class UVEdit : EditorWindow
{
    //Reference to atlas data game object
    public GameObject AtlasDataObject = null;
    [MenuItem ("Window/Atlas UV Editor")]
    static void Init ()
    {
        //Show window
        GetWindow (typeof(UVEdit),false,"Texture Atlas", true);
    }
    void OnGUI ()
    {
        //Draw Atlas Object Selector
        GUILayout.Label ("Atlas Generation", EditorStyles.boldLabel);
        AtlasDataObject = (GameObject) EditorGUILayout.ObjectField("Atlas Object", AtlasDataObject,
typeof (GameObject), true);
    }
}
```

> **Note**   The Unity GUI and `EditorGUI` framework is not object-oriented in the traditional sense; rather, it's a *declarative* framework. This means that to create widgets in the interface, such as text boxes and labels, you *do not* instantiate any text box or label or widget objects. You simply call a function in the OnGUI event, such as `GUILayout.Label` and `GUILayout.Button` *(see Listing 7-2)* to render the appropriate widget, and Unity handles the rest automatically. More information on this framework can be found here: `http://docs.unity3d.com/Documentation/Components/GUIScriptingGuide.html`.
>
> It must be noted here that OnGUI is typically called several times *per frame* (not per second). This therefore makes OnGUI a very expensive function in computational terms. This might not be so much of an issue when creating Editor GUIs on power development systems, but it could easily become a crippling burden for games, especially games on mobile devices. Indeed, many developers avoid the Unity GUI framework altogether and just "roll their own", or they use Asset store add-ins, such as EZGUI or NGUI (although these add-ons are for making in-game GUIs and not Editor GUIs).

Listing 7-2 uses the `EditorGUILayout.ObjectField` method to draw an Object Field input inside the Editor window. Using this, the user can click and select an Atlas Texture in the Project Panel to load into the field. This function always returns a reference to the object currently loaded into the field. Consequently, the member variable `AtlasDataObject` will either be null, if no Atlas Texture is selected, or reference a valid Atlas Texture. See Figure 7-4 to see the Object Field at work in the `EditorWindow`.

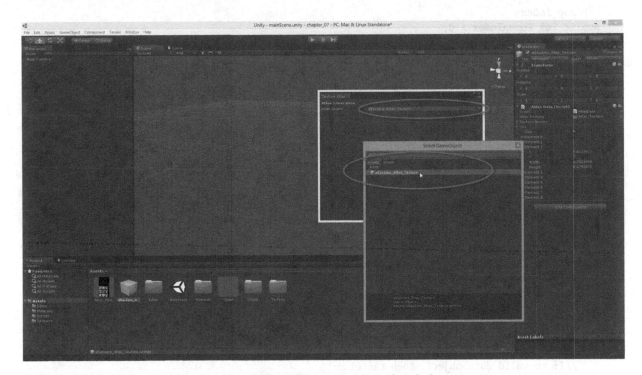

Figure 7-4. Object Fields allow users to select assets in the project panel or objects in the scene

Continuing with the GUI—Selecting a Texture

Let's keep moving with the UV Editor GUI. We've created an input field in the `EditorWindow` for selecting a valid atlas object in the Project Panel. This object should be of type `AtlasData`. Now, on the basis of this object, we'll present the user with a list of textures inside the atlas, allowing them to choose one and have the UVs automatically adjusted for the selected quad. This makes the UV Editor act like a specialized texture picker. To achieve this we can use a drop-down (or pop-up list). Take a look at the code in Listing 7-3.

Listing 7-3. UVEdit.cs – Using a Drop-Down List to Select Textures

```
using UnityEngine;
using UnityEditor;
using System.Collections;
```

```csharp
public class UVEdit : EditorWindow
{
    //Reference to atlas data game object
    public GameObject AtlasDataObject = null;
    //Reference to atlas data
    public AtlasData AtlasDataComponent = null;

    //Popup Index
    public int PopupIndex = 0;

    [MenuItem ("Window/Atlas UV Editor")]
    static void Init ()
    {
        //Show window
        GetWindow (typeof(UVEdit),false,"Texture Atlas", true);
    }

    void OnGUI ()
    {
        //Draw Atlas Object Selector
        GUILayout.Label ("Atlas Generation", EditorStyles.boldLabel);
        AtlasDataObject = (GameObject) EditorGUILayout.ObjectField("Atlas Object", AtlasDataObject,
        typeof (GameObject), true);

        //If no valid atlas object selected, then cancel
        if(AtlasDataObject == null)
            return;

        //Get atlas data component attached to selected prefab
        AtlasDataComponent = AtlasDataObject.GetComponent<AtlasData>();

        //If no valid data object, then cancel
        if(!AtlasDataComponent)
            return;

        //Show popup selector for valid textures
        PopupIndex = EditorGUILayout.Popup(PopupIndex, AtlasDataComponent.TextureNames);

        //When clicked, set UVs on selected objects
        if(GUILayout.Button("Select Sprite From Atlas"))
        {
        }
    }
}
```

> **Note** For Listing 7-3 to work fully you'll need to have generated and selected an Atlas Texture in your project. The image list will only show if a valid Atlas Texture object is provided in the Atlas Object Field at the top of the EditorWindow. This code will not *yet* change any mesh UVs, but it will display a drop-down box, listing all textures in the atlas.

The code in Listing 7-3 adds two new class variables: AtlasDataComponent and PopupIndex. The former retrieves a reference to the AtlasData object attached as a component to the AtlasData Prefab. The latter is an integer, which is returned during each OnGUI event by the EditorGUILayout.Popup method. This method displays a drop-down list in the Editor window, listing all texture names in the atlas (these are read from the AtlasData member TextureNames). This method returns an integer index to the currently selected item, where 0 means the first or topmost item. Using this control, users can select a texture inside the atlas (see Figure 7-5).

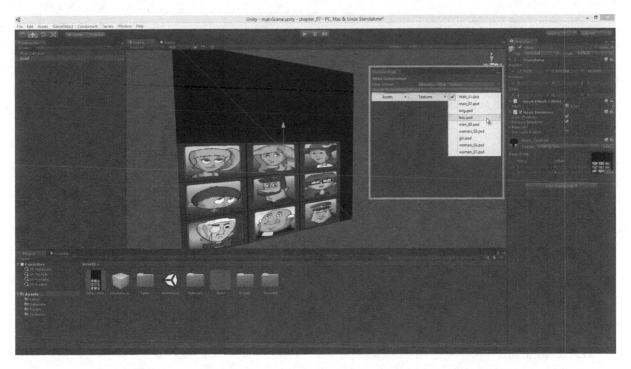

Figure 7-5. EditorGUILayout shows a pop-up list from which the user can choose an option. This is used here to select a texture in the atlas to assign to the selected object

UVs and Manual Mode

Using the UV Editor window to select an atlas and a texture within it is excellent. It means we get *enough* information to autoconfigure the UV mapping for any Quad Mesh (we'll see how to actually do that soon.). But still, I can't escape the desire for even more control here (Maybe I'm just a control freak). Let's give the user additional input fields where they can type-in the UV values for each vertex of the quad, if they want to. For most atlases created by our custom-made atlas generator, we'll not need these fields, because the UVs for each texture are saved in AtlasData. For our own atlases, the standard atlas and texture drop-down fields should be enough. But for imported atlases or non-atlas textures with no associated AtlasData object, it could prove a handy feature to have. It allows us complete control over a quad's UVs. The code in Listing 7-4 amends the EditorWindow class for this feature.

Listing 7-4. UVEdit.cs—Defining UV Inputs

```
using UnityEngine;
using UnityEditor;
//------------------------------------------------
public class UVEdit : EditorWindow
{
    //Reference to atlas data game object
    public GameObject AtlasDataObject = null;
    //Reference to atlas data
    public AtlasData AtlasDataComponent = null;

    //Popup Index
    public int PopupIndex = 0;

    //Popup strings for sprite selection mode: sprites or custom (sprites = select sprites from atlas,
    custom = manually set UVs)
    public string[] Modes = {"Select By Sprites", "Select By UVs"};

    //Sprite Select Index - selection in the drop down box
    public int ModeIndex = 0;

    //Rect for manually setting UVs in Custom mode
    public Rect CustomRect = new Rect(0,0,0,0);

    //------------------------------------------------
    [MenuItem ("Window/Atlas Texture Editor")]
    static void Init ()
    {
        //Show window
        GetWindow (typeof(UVEdit),false,"Texture Atlas", true);
    }
```

```
//-------------------------------------------------
void OnGUI ()
{
    //Draw Atlas Object Selector
    GUILayout.Label ("Atlas Generation", EditorStyles.boldLabel);
    AtlasDataObject = (GameObject) EditorGUILayout.ObjectField("Atlas Object", AtlasDataObject,
    typeof (GameObject), true);
    //If no valid atlas object selected, then cancel
    if(AtlasDataObject == null)
        return;

    //Get atlas data component attached to selected prefab
    AtlasDataComponent = AtlasDataObject.GetComponent<AtlasData>();

    //If no valid data object, then cancel
    if(!AtlasDataComponent)
        return;

    //Choose sprite selection mode: sprites or UVs
    ModeIndex = EditorGUILayout.Popup(ModeIndex, Modes);

    //If selecting by sprites
    if(ModeIndex != 1)
    {
        //Show popup selector for valid textures
        PopupIndex = EditorGUILayout.Popup(PopupIndex, AtlasDataComponent.TextureNames);
        //When clicked, set UVs on selected objects
        if(GUILayout.Button("Select Sprite From Atlas"))
        {
        }
    }
    else
    {
        //Selecting manually
        GUILayout.Label ("X");
        CustomRect.x = EditorGUILayout.FloatField(CustomRect.x);
        GUILayout.Label ("Y");
        CustomRect.y = EditorGUILayout.FloatField(CustomRect.y);

        GUILayout.Label ("Width");
        CustomRect.width = EditorGUILayout.FloatField(CustomRect.width);
        GUILayout.Label ("Height");
        CustomRect.height = EditorGUILayout.FloatField(CustomRect.height);
        //When clicked, set UVs on selected objects
        if(GUILayout.Button("Select Sprite From Atlas"))
        {
        }
    }
}
}
```

Code branches and other flow control structures, such as if statements and return statements, affect the appearance of the Editor window and determine which widgets are drawn. If a GUILayout draw function is not called (such as GUILayout.Button), then the associated widget will not be shown for that OnGUI call. Listing 7-4 takes advantage of this to create two different modes for the UV Editor window: Select By Sprites and Select By UVs. The Select By Sprites method controls UV mapping for a selected quad based on the specified atlas and texture. The Select By UVs method controls UV mapping manually, leaving the user to specify UV values for each vertex.

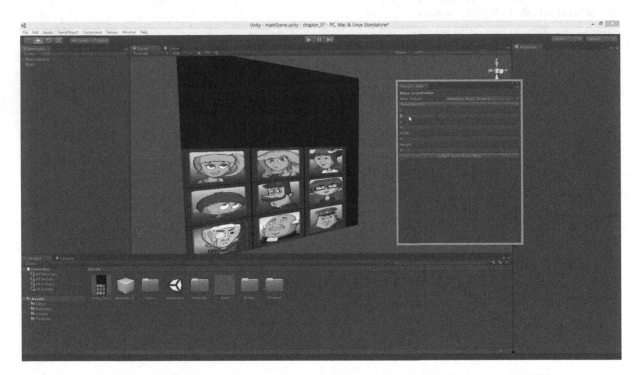

Figure 7-6. The UV Editor manual mode offers full control over the UV values for each vertex in a selected Quad Mesh

Editing Mesh UVs

Here's the part where our Editor window adjusts the UVs of the selected Quad Mesh to match either the selected texture in the atlas (if the editor is in standard mode) or the manually specified UV values (if in UV mode). Regardless of the mode however, all we essentially need to do to is get a Rect structure of *new* UVs and use that to overwrite the existing UVs of the quad. To achieve this procedure, we can add the following member function to the UV Editor class, as shown in Listing 7-5.

Listing 7-5. Function UpdateUVs in UVEdit.cs

```
//Function to update UVs of selected mesh object
void UpdateUVs(GameObject MeshObject, Rect AtlasUVs, bool Reset = false)
{
    //Get Mesh Filter Component
    MeshFilter MFilter = MeshOject.GetComponent<MeshFilter>();
    Mesh MeshObject = MFilter.sharedMesh;
```

```
//Vertices
Vector3[] Vertices = MeshObject.vertices;
Vector2[] UVs = new Vector2[Vertices.Length];

//Bottom-left
UVs[0].x=(Reset) ? 0.0f : AtlasUVs.x;
UVs[0].y=(Reset) ? 0.0f : AtlasUVs.y;

//Bottom-right
UVs[1].x=(Reset) ? 1.0f : AtlasUVs.x+AtlasUVs.width;
UVs[1].y=(Reset) ? 0.0f : AtlasUVs.y;

//Top-left
UVs[2].x=(Reset) ? 0.0f : AtlasUVs.x;
UVs[2].y=(Reset) ? 1.0f : AtlasUVs.y+AtlasUVs.height;

//Top-right
UVs[3].x=(Reset) ? 1.0f : AtlasUVs.x+AtlasUVs.width;
UVs[3].y=(Reset) ? 1.0f : AtlasUVs.y+AtlasUVs.height;

MeshObject.uv = UVs;
MeshObject.vertices = Vertices;

AssetDatabase.Refresh();
AssetDatabase.SaveAssets();
}
```

> **Note**   Listing 7-5 does not list the entire UVEdit class; only the newly added UpdateUVs function inside the class.

Listing 7-5 bears some resemblance to the mesh generation code for creating procedural quads in Chapter 5. It makes use of the MeshFilter component to access and edit a vertex buffer- a list of vertices and UVs based on the AtlasUVs Rect argument, featuring the new UV values. The Reset argument (when true) will reset the quad UVs to their defaults.

> **Note**   Listing 7-5 uses the MeshFilter.SharedMesh member to access the Quad Mesh object, as opposed to MeshFilter.Mesh. The code could have used either. Making changes to SharedMesh will update the Mesh Asset, and thus all changes will be propagated to every instance. Making changes to Mesh will affect only *specific instances* of the mesh. You'll need to make decisions for your own projects about which setup most suits your needs.

Putting It All Together—Finishing the UV Editor

So let's put together our final UV Editor source file and compile it before going for a test run in the Unity Editor. The final UVEdit class appears in full, in Listing 7-6. Most of this code has been featured already in previous samples, but this listing does include additional lines too. These appear in OnGUI, to link the GUI front end (and its input fields) with the UV editing functionality (as defined in the UpdateUVs function).

Listing 7-6. UVEdit.cs–Linking Inputs to UV Editing

```
using UnityEngine;
using UnityEditor;
//------------------------------------------------
public class UVEdit : EditorWindow
{
    //Reference to atlas data game object
    public GameObject AtlasDataObject = null;

    //Reference to atlas data
    public AtlasData AtlasDataComponent = null;

    //Popup Index
    public int PopupIndex = 0;

    //Popup strings for sprite selection mode: sprites or custom (sprites = select sprites from atlas,
    custom = manually set UVs)
    public string[] Modes = {"Select By Sprites", "Select By UVs"};

    //Sprite Select Index - selection in the drop down box
    public int ModeIndex = 0;

    //Rect for manually setting UVs in Custom mode
    public Rect CustomRect = new Rect(0,0,0,0);

    //------------------------------------------------
    [MenuItem ("Window/Atlas Texture Editor")]
    static void Init ()
    {
        //Show window
        GetWindow (typeof(UVEdit),false,"Texture Atlas", true);
    }
    //------------------------------------------------
    void OnGUI ()
    {
        //Draw Atlas Object Selector
        GUILayout.Label ("Atlas Generation", EditorStyles.boldLabel);
        AtlasDataObject = (GameObject) EditorGUILayout.ObjectField("Atlas Object", AtlasDataObject,
        typeof (GameObject), true);
        //If no valid atlas object selected, then cancel
        if(AtlasDataObject == null)
            return;
```

```
//Get atlas data component attached to selected prefab
AtlasDataComponent = AtlasDataObject.GetComponent<AtlasData>();

//If no valid data object, then cancel
if(!AtlasDataComponent)
    return;

//Choose sprite selection mode: sprites or UVs
ModeIndex = EditorGUILayout.Popup(ModeIndex, Modes);

//If selecting by sprites
if(ModeIndex != 1)
{
    //Show popup selector for valid textures
    PopupIndex = EditorGUILayout.Popup(PopupIndex, AtlasDataComponent.TextureNames);

    //When clicked, set UVs on selected objects
    if(GUILayout.Button("Select Sprite From Atlas"))
    {
        //Update UVs for selected meshes
        if(Selection.gameObjects.Length > 0)
        {
            foreach(GameObject Obj in Selection.gameObjects)
            {
                //Is this is a mesh object?
                if(Obj.GetComponent<MeshFilter>())
                    UpdateUVs(Obj, AtlasDataComponent.UVs[PopupIndex]);
            }
        }
    }
}
else
{
    //Selecting manually
    GUILayout.Label ("X");
    CustomRect.x = EditorGUILayout.FloatField(CustomRect.x);
    GUILayout.Label ("Y");
    CustomRect.y = EditorGUILayout.FloatField(CustomRect.y);
    GUILayout.Label ("Width");
    CustomRect.width = EditorGUILayout.FloatField(CustomRect.width);
    GUILayout.Label ("Height");
    CustomRect.height = EditorGUILayout.FloatField(CustomRect.height);
    //When clicked, set UVs on selected objects
    if(GUILayout.Button("Select Sprite From Atlas"))
    {
        //Update UVs for selected meshes
        if(Selection.gameObjects.Length > 0)
        {
            foreach(GameObject Obj in Selection.gameObjects)
            {
```

```
                    //Is this is a mesh object?
                    if(Obj.GetComponent<MeshFilter>())
                        UpdateUVs(Obj, CustomRect);
                }
            }
        }
    }
}
//---------------------------------------------------
//Function to update UVs of selected mesh object
void UpdateUVs(GameObject MeshOject, Rect AtlasUVs, bool Reset = false)
{
    //Get Mesh Filter Component
    MeshFilter MFilter = MeshObject.GetComponent<MeshFilter>();
    Mesh MeshObject = MFilter.sharedMesh;

    //Vertices
    Vector3[] Vertices = MeshObject.vertices;
    Vector2[] UVs = new Vector2[Vertices.Length];
    //Bottom-left
    UVs[0].x=(Reset) ? 0.0f : AtlasUVs.x;
    UVs[0].y=(Reset) ? 0.0f : AtlasUVs.y;
    //Bottom-right
    UVs[1].x=(Reset) ? 1.0f : AtlasUVs.x+AtlasUVs.width;
    UVs[1].y=(Reset) ? 0.0f : AtlasUVs.y;
    //Top-left
    UVs[2].x=(Reset) ? 0.0f : AtlasUVs.x;
    UVs[2].y=(Reset) ? 1.0f : AtlasUVs.y+AtlasUVs.height;
    //Top-right
    UVs[3].x=(Reset) ? 1.0f : AtlasUVs.x+AtlasUVs.width;
    UVs[3].y=(Reset) ? 1.0f : AtlasUVs.y+AtlasUVs.height;
    MeshObject.uv = UVs;
    MeshObject.vertices = Vertices;
    AssetDatabase.Refresh();
    AssetDatabase.SaveAssets();
}
//---------------------------------------------------
}
```

> **Note**   Listing 7-6 shows the full source for UVEdit. The OnGUI function handles button clicks to confirm the editor settings and update the UVs for the selected quad. Notice: OnGUI updates the UVs for *all* selected Quad Meshes, meaning multiple quads can be selected and edited simultaneously.

Listing 7-6 should compile successfully in the Unity Editor. Once compiled, test your plugin. To do that, ensure you've generated an Atlas Texture (with the Atlas Generator) and a Quad Mesh (using the Quad Mesh generator, and not the default Unity Plane Mesh). The generated quad is always added to the scene with purple shading, meaning it features no material—so be sure to assign it a material with the Atlas Texture. Then you're ready to go: First, click **Window ➤ Atlas Texture Editor** from the application menu to show the Atlas Texture Editor. As shown in Figure 7-7.

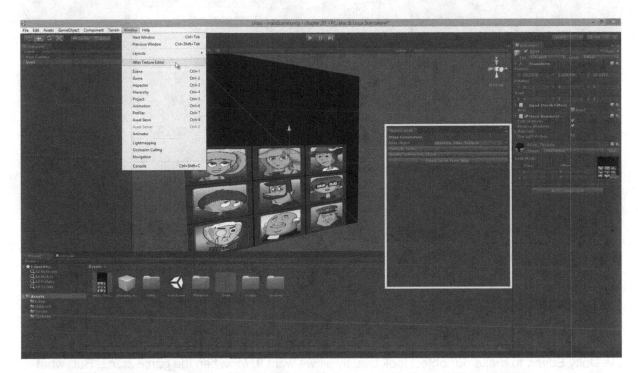

Figure 7-7. *Select Window ➤ Atlas Texture Editor from the application menu to display the UV Editor. This Editor can also be docked into the Unity interface, just like an Object Inspector window*

When the UV Editor window appears, drag and drop the `AtlasData` prefab from the Project Panel into the `Atlas Object` input field. When you do this, additional options appear below to control how the UV is to be defined. Click the *Mode* drop-down box and choose *Select By Sprites,* to enable Sprite Selection mode. This mode allows you to select a texture in the atlas. Then use the texture drop-down to pick a texture by name. *Before* clicking the *Select Sprite From Atlas button*, be sure all Quad Meshes are selected in the scene. Clicking this button updates the selected object's UV data (see Figure 7-8).

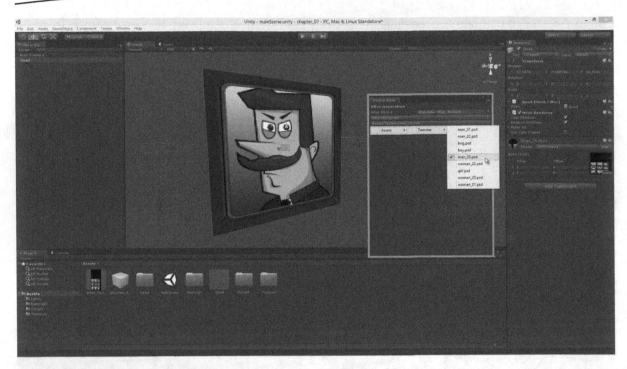

Figure 7-8.   Congratulations! Your UV Editor plugin now controls the UV data for selected quads

Flipbook Animation

The UV Editor add-on that we've created is a really powerful tool for editing object mapping *at design time*. It means that *while we're developing,* we may tweak any quad's mapping right from the Unity Editor, to make our object look exactly as we want it, *for when the game starts*. But, what about *after* the game is up and running? How do we change an object's mapping at runtime? Or better yet, how do we change a quad's mapping in quick succession over time, frame by frame, to creation animation—just like the cartoons made by flipping through the pages of a sketch book? In short, we can run all our UV mapping code in standard Unity classes too—not just Editor classes. This makes it easy to change an object's UV mapping at runtime. In this section we'll see how that's done by creating a Flipbook Animation class to animate a quad over time. This class works by reading frames from an Atlas Texture and then playing them back in sequence on a quad, one frame after another.

Note   Flipbook animations are especially useful for creating animated sprites, such as enemies and player characters. Typically, these elements display walk animations, along with attacks, jumps, crouches, falls, deaths and more.

Let's make our Flipbook Animation class featured filled! It'll have several controllable playback options. Specifically, we'll have control over the following properties:

- **Frame Rate**. We'll be able to choose how many frames per second are played back from the Atlas Texture. This setting is used to control playback speed. Higher values result in faster animations.

- **Play Method**. Lets us have control over playback direction. Specifically, the flipbook will be able to play animations forward, backward, (back and forth in a loop—ping pong), in a random order, and in a custom order that we specify. This should be enough to cover most scenarios.

- **Auto Play**. We'll also have a Boolean flag to control auto-playback. When set to true, the flipbook animation will play automatically as the scene begins. If set to false, then the animation must be manually initiated in code.

Now let's see the complete `Flipbook` class, as shown in Listing 7-7, and then further explanation will follow.

Listing 7-7. FlipBookAnimation.cs

```
//FLIP BOOK ANIMATION COMPONENT
//-----------------------------------------------
using UnityEngine;
using System.Collections;
//-----------------------------------------------
public class FlipBookAnimation : MonoBehaviour
{
    //Public variables
    //---------------------------------------------
    //Enum for Play Types
    public enum PlayType {Forward=0, Reverse=1, PingPong=2, Custom=3, Randomized=4};

    //Enum for Loop Type
    public enum LoopType {PlayOnce=0, Loop=1};

    //Public reference to list of UVs for frames of flipbook animation
    public Rect[] UVs;

    //Reference to AutoPlay on Start
    public bool AutoPlay = false;

    //Public reference to number of frames per second for animation
    public float FramesPerSecond = 10.0f;

    //Public reference to play type of animation
    public PlayType PlayMethod = PlayType.Forward;

    //Public reference to loop type
    public LoopType LoopMethod = LoopType.PlayOnce;
```

```csharp
//Public reference to first frame. Custom setting used ONLY if PlayMethod==Custom. Otherwise,
auto-calculated
public int CustomStartFrame = 0;

//Public reference to end frame. Custom setting used ONLY if PlayMethod==Custom. Otherwise,
auto-calculated
public int CustomEndFrame = 0;

//Public reference to play status of flipbook animation
public bool IsPlaying = false;

//Methods
//------------------------------------------------
// Use this for initialization
void Start ()
{
    //Play animation if auto-play is true
    if(AutoPlay)
        StartCoroutine("Play");
}
//------------------------------------------------
//Function to play animation
public IEnumerator Play()
{
    //Set play status to true
    IsPlaying = true;

    //Get Anim Length in frames
    int AnimLength = UVs.Length;

    //Loop Direction
    int Direction = (PlayMethod == PlayType.Reverse) ? -1 : 1;

    //Start Frame for Forwards
    int StartFrame = (PlayMethod == PlayType.Reverse) ? AnimLength-1 : 0;

    //Frame Count
    int FrameCount = AnimLength-1;

    //if Animation length == 0 then exit
    if(FrameCount <= 0) yield break;

    //Check for custom frame overrides
    if(PlayMethod == PlayType.Custom)
    {
        StartFrame = CustomStartFrame;
        FrameCount = (CustomEndFrame > CustomStartFrame) ? CustomEndFrame - CustomStartFrame :
        CustomStartFrame - CustomEndFrame;
        Direction = (CustomEndFrame > CustomStartFrame) ? 1 : -1;
    }
```

```
        //Play back animation at least once
        do
        {
            //New playback cycle
            //Number of frames played
            int FramesPlayed = 0;
            //Play animation while all frames not played
            while(FramesPlayed <= FrameCount)
            {

                //Set frame - Get random frame if random, else get standard frame
                Rect Rct = (PlayMethod == PlayType.Randomized) ?
UVs[Mathf.FloorToInt(Random.value * FrameCount)] : UVs[StartFrame + (FramesPlayed * Direction)];
                SetFrame(Rct);

                //Increment frame count
                FramesPlayed++;
                //Wait until next frame
                yield return new WaitForSeconds(1.0f/FramesPerSecond);
            }
            //If ping-pong, then reverse direction
            if(PlayMethod == PlayType.PingPong)
            {
                Direction = -Direction;
                StartFrame = (StartFrame == 0) ? AnimLength-1 : 0;
            }
        }while(LoopMethod == LoopType.Loop); //Check for looping
        //Animation has ended. Set play status to false
        IsPlaying = false;
    }
    //-------------------------------------------------
    //Function to stop playback
    public void Stop()
    {
        //If already stopped, then ignore
        if(!IsPlaying)
            return;
        StopCoroutine("Play");
        IsPlaying = false;
    }
    //-------------------------------------------------
    //Function to set specified frame of mesh based on Rect UVs
    void SetFrame(Rect R)
    {
        //Get mesh filter
        Mesh MeshObject = GetComponent<MeshFilter>().mesh;

        //Vertices
        Vector3[] Vertices = MeshObject.vertices;
        Vector2[] UVs = new Vector2[Vertices.Length];
```

```
        //Bottom-left
        UVs[0].x=R.x;
        UVs[0].y=R.y;
        //Bottom-right
        UVs[1].x=R.x+R.width;
        UVs[1].y=R.y;
        //Top-left
        UVs[2].x=R.x;
        UVs[2].y=R.y+R.height;
        //Top-right
        UVs[3].x=R.x+R.width;
        UVs[3].y=R.y+R.height;
        MeshObject.uv = UVs;
        MeshObject.vertices = Vertices;
    }
    //-------------------------------------------------
    //Function called on component disable
    void OnDisable()
    {
        //Stop coroutine if playing
        if(IsPlaying)
            StopCoroutine("Play");
    }
    //-------------------------------------------------
    //Function called on component enable
    void OnEnable()
    {
        //If was playing before disabled, then start playing again
        if(IsPlaying)
            StartCoroutine("Play");
    }
    //-------------------------------------------------
}
```

This class is included in the book companion files. Its purpose is to display a timed sequence of frames from an Atlas Texture on the surface of a quad object in the scene. The two core class methods for achieving this are Play and SetFrame. The member variable Rect UVs[] features an array of UVs for all frames in the animation, and these refer to positions within the Atlas Texture. You could create an editor plugin to set these UV values automatically for the FlipBookAnimation, but here I have entered them manually using the properties stored in the Atlas Data object, created with the Atlas Texture. The SetFrame function is responsible for accepting an index into the UVs array (Frame Number) and updating the UV mapping of the quad automatically. The Play function is implemented as a Unity Coroutine, which runs every frame to update the animation, depending on the playback type. Figure 7-9 shows the FlipBookAnimation in action.

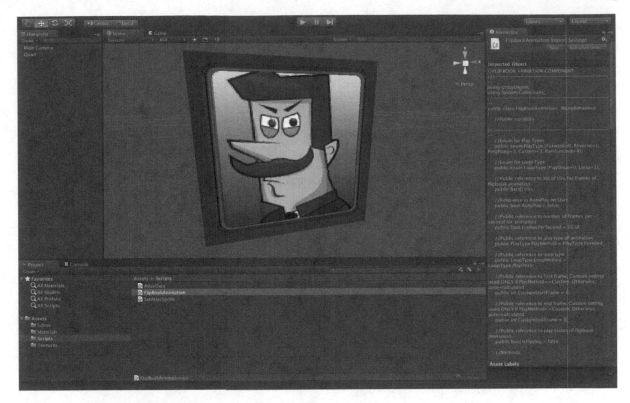

Figure 7-9. *FlipBookAnimation at work*

Summary

This chapter pulls together much of the work we've created so far in this book; so much so that it's now possible to assess just how far we've come. We can build procedural quads from an editor extension, create Atlas Textures, and now control the mapping of quads to align with the texture. In addition, with the FlipBookAnimation component we can now animate textures too, and this opens up new possibilities for creating sprites and other dynamic objects. Things are looking great so far, but there's still an outstanding and nagging problem that bothers me. In our work so far, all objects are seen in perspective. This means our textures are never shown in a pixel-perfect way. We never see them as they are intended to be seen—flat and directly on-screen. The result is that we always see a resampled and rescaled image on a 3D object. This might look fine in some cases, but it doesn't give us the graphical crispness and precision that we may typically want to achieve. That subject is the focus of Chapter 8. After reading this chapter you should be able to:

- Create *a dockable editor extension using Editor window*
- Use the OnGUI method to custom draw window widgets
- Understand the OnGUI workflow for interface rendering

- Feel confident using standard widget controls, such as Label, Box, TextField, and so on

- Read input from GUI controls

- Understand how to control an object's UV mapping programmatically

- Change UV mapping at run time

- Animate UV mapping with a FlipBookAnimation class

- Understand frame rate and animation speed

- Control animation direction: forward, backward, and so on

Chapter 8

Cameras and Pixel Perfection

Now you've seen how to create the infrastructure for a truly 2D game in Unity, at least in terms of textures and geometry. In the past few chapters we've created editor plug-ins to generate quads and atlas textures. The quads are formed from four corner vertices and two polygons. By combining the quads with atlas textures, and UV mapping, we can display specific regions of an atlas on the quad surface. Further, we can animate the UV mapping to show flip-book animations, like traditional sketchbook animations where its pages are flipped through one after the other. But there's a crucial ingredient missing in our 2D formula. Sure, we *can* create quads and atlas textures, *but* all the quads we create are shown using a standard Unity camera in a perspective view. This means all our 2D elements are subject to the standard "laws of perspective." See Figure 8-1. The implications of this are considered more fully in the list that follows.

Figure 8-1. Textured Quad in perspective view. Texture is not pixel-perfect and there is no obvious relationship between world space (in Unity Units) and screen space (in Pixels)

- **Objects are rendered in perspective** Perspective drawing is the name given to any 2D image that aims to replicate a sense of three dimensions and depth, as perceived by the human eye. Because the eye is curved and is always situated in 3D space at a specific vantage point, all other objects that we see must necessarily appear distorted. This distortion is called *foreshortening*, and it's a characteristic feature of perspective imagery. In essence, it means five things:

  - Objects nearer to the viewer appear larger than distant objects.

  - Objects further away appear closer to the horizon line than nearer objects.

  - Objects in the distance appear less detailed than nearer objects.

  - Objects nearer to us appear in front (on top) of distant objects.

  - Objects that are rotated from us appear distorted or skewed.

- These five features are essential to creating 3D images, but they can damage the impact of 2D graphics and 2D games, inadvertently revealing that everything is really flat. 2D games need finer control over perspective—they need either to play some extra tricks or else they need to play no tricks at all. The standard unity camera, in its default configuration doesn't give us the control we need. Therefore, we'll have to fix that.

- **Textures are not pixel-perfect** If an object is rendered in perspective, and if perspective entails distortion, then it follows that the object's texture is not being seen at its true aspect. This means that textures drawn in perspective can never be pixel-perfect, except by accident when the camera happens to align exactly with our texture. But for 2D games we typically want pixel-perfection. We want our textures to appear on-screen as crisply and sharply as they look in Photoshop or GIMP. So we'll have to fix that here too.

- **Perspective renders do not map to 2D space** World Space units in Unity are termed *Unity Units* (UU). These units measure and mark positions in 3D space. They are generic units insofar as they mean whatever you want them to mean: 1 millimeter, 1 inch, 1 mile, and so on. But for the Unity physics system, they correspond to real world meters: meaning 1 UU = 1m. For this reason, most developers treat Unity Units as Meters. Now, while this system of units works for 3D objects and scenes, it poses a logistical problem for 2D games, which rely on pixels. This is because we have no guarantee about how Unity Units (in 3D) correspond to on-screen pixels (in 2D) in our final renders. After all, we're dealing with two different coordinate spaces: world space and screen space. If we generate a quad in the scene using our quad generator plug-in, for example, we find that it exists in 3D space and not 2D space—it's ultimately a 3D object. So, given this, how we can we possibly position the quad (or the camera!) in the scene to get control over where the object finally appears on-screen in terms of pixels? For example, how can we size a quad to be 50 pixels wide by 50 pixels high? How can we show a quad on screen at, say, 15×15 pixels from the top-left corner? This chapter will show you how.

Perspective versus Orthographic Cameras

By default every new scene in Unity is created with a camera object, named MainCamera. Unless you delete this camera manually or explicitly add a new one, Unity will always use the MainCamera as the viewpoint from which the scene is rendered at run-time. This camera is configured as a *perspective* camera, meaning that it renders the scene how you might typically expect any real-world camera would. But 2D games often require a different type of camera, known as an *orthographic* camera. Let's see how this works. Figure 8-2 shows a new scene with the default camera selected and at its normal settings.

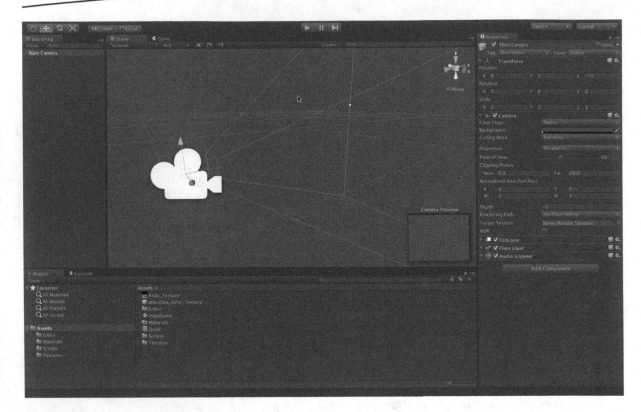

Figure 8-2. Empty new scene created with a perspective camera

Click on the *Projection Mode* drop-down list from the Object Inspector, and change the Camera's mode from *Perspective* to *Orthographic*. The change takes effect instantly. If your scene has other objects and meshes within the camera view (*Frustum*), then you'll probably notice an immediate difference in how the scene looks in the *Game* tab. In Orthographic mode, objects may look noticeably smaller, or larger, or flatter. In almost all cases, however, a traditional 3D scene will probably not look as you intend. See Figure 8-3 for an orthographic scene. As a result of orthographic projection several cubes take on an *isometric* appearance in the *Game* tab—although they continue to be shown in perspective in the *Scene* tab.

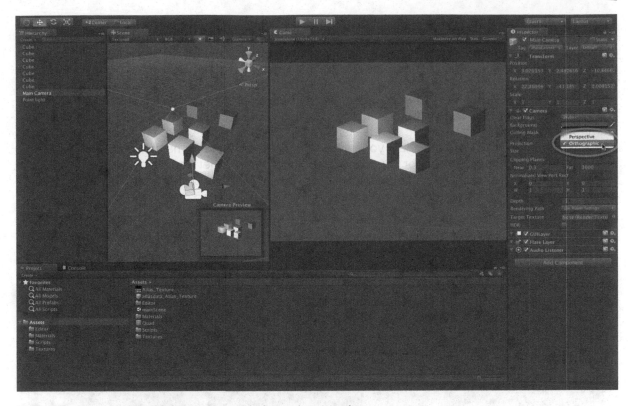

Figure 8-3. Orthographic projection can be used for isometric perspectives

> **Note**   Notice how all near edges of the cubes (see Figure 8-3) run parallel to each other and remain
> parallel. In perspective, all parallel lines should meet at a common vanishing point. In orthographic mode,
> this perspective rule (along with most rules) are abandoned.

In Orthographic mode several key laws of perspective are abandoned, which can give it a somewhat awkward and weird appearance initially. First, parallel lines don't converge at vanishing points. They remain parallel because there are no vanishing points anymore. Second, objects don't change size with distance from the camera: you can move objects nearer and further from the camera (or you can move the camera) and objects retain their size (the only way to change size is with *scaling*). And third, the camera's viewing angle on an object is retained no matter where it's translated, so long as the camera is not rotated. This last point requires clarification by way of example. Essentially, if a camera is centred on a cube, facing it head-on and looking at its front face, then the camera will retain its viewing angle on the cube, even if the camera or cube is panned sideways or up and down. Only rotation affects a camera's viewing angle on an object.

So far so good: we've now converted a perspective camera to an orthographic one. It's easy to do, but things are still not looking quite right. Objects probably don't appear at their correct sizes automatically in the Game tab, and we still don't have a 1:1 world unit to pixel ratio on-screen. We'll take care of that in the next section.

World Units and Pixels

Orthographic cameras flatten out the scene renders in a way that's especially suited for 2D games, as well as to 3D games seeking to capture a retro feel. However, this effect is only noticeable when other objects exist in the scene and are in view of the camera. In this section we'll configure our scene and camera so that world units correspond to pixels, and this will (finally) let us piece together a truly 2D scene in Unity. To get started, let's create a blank new scene in Unity—this will be our starting point. It's not really going to be the starting point for any game or project specifically. It'll just be a small, test project. I want to show you how to configure the camera manually for 2D, so you'll have all the knowledge you need for your own 2D projects. First off, let's add a new quad mesh to the empty scene to act as a sprite object, using our quad mesh generator plugin. If you haven't already coded this, I recommend doing so before continuing. Chapter 5 details this process.

However, because we want our textures to be pixel-perfect, and also to establish a 1:1 relationship between world units and pixels, be sure to generate your quad to a size that matches the texture you want to show. In this case, I'll size my quad to 150×184 world units, because the character texture I'll be using is 150×184 pixels. Consider Figure 8-4. One issue to note here is that you could also generate your quad at 1x1 and then upsize it afterwards to 150×184 using the Scale tool. Doing this however sometimes causes an issue or quirk, specific to the Windows platform (it seems), where your object is always 1 pixel less than it should be in both width and height. You can technically fix this by compensating the scale uniformly with an additional 1 pixel, but you can avoid this issue altogether by simply sizing your quads appropriately at generation time. Therefore, I recommend avoiding the Scale tool where possible.

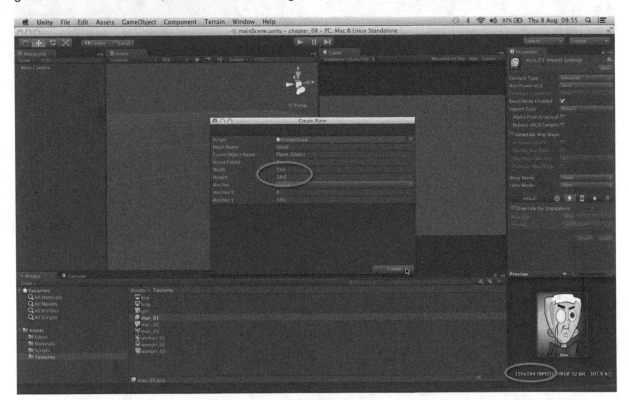

Figure 8-4. *Generate a Quad Mesh whose sizes (in Unity Units) match the size of the texture you want to show (in Pixels). Doing this ensures pixel perfection. Notice, I've also set the pivot (center) to the top-left position*

> **Note**   The project files created in this chapter can be found in the book companion files at:
> Project_Files/Chapter08/.

Position Objects

Position the Quad at the world space origin of (0,0,0) if it's not there already—we want this world space position to map onto the screen space origin at the top-left screen position. Do the same for the camera (set its position to 0,0,0) but set it back slightly on the Z-axis (depth axis), away from the Quad Mesh to avoid any intersection and overlap between the two objects. Be sure to remove any rotation from the Quad and the camera, if any are applied. Change the camera *Projection* type from *Perspective* to *Orthographic*, and align the camera view in the scene to be parallel and centered to the Quad Mesh: the camera should face the Quad Mesh head-on. The default settings for the Orthographic camera might make the Quad look either too small or too large in the Game tab—but we'll fix this shortly. Take a look at Figure 8-5.

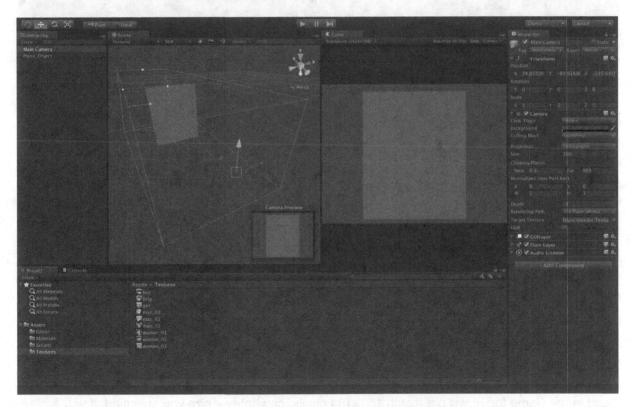

Figure 8-5. Setting up the camera and Quad Mesh for a 1:1 relationship between pixels and world space

Field of View

The orthographic camera, when selected in the scene, will show a wireframe bounding box representing its field of view. Unlike perspective cameras, which have a trapezoidal-shaped field of view, the orthographic camera has a truly rectangular shaped one, which ultimately accounts for its lack of perspective distortion. Anything inside this field of view will be visible to the camera. You can control the size of this volume using the *Near* and *Far Clipping Planes* setting for the camera. So, if your Quad Mesh is not visible in the *Game* tab (as shown in Figure 8-5), then make sure it's within the camera field of view. See Figure 8-6 for a clearer view of the camera clipping planes.

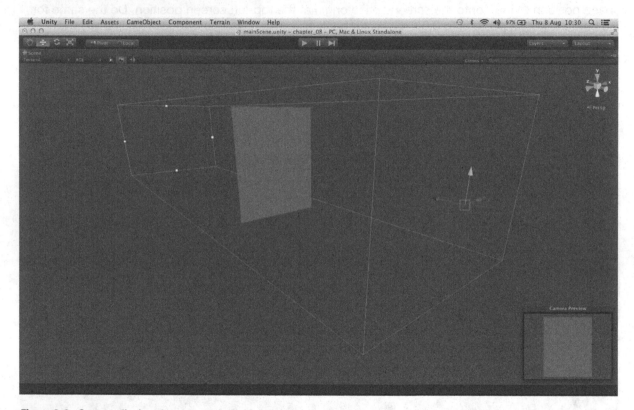

Figure 8-6. Camera clipping planes control what is within the camera field of view. Anything before the near clipping plane or beyond the far clipping plane will not be rendered

Camera Size

Typically the default orthographic settings don't produce 1:1 ratio between world space and screen space. More must be done to achieve this. Right now, if you measure the pixel dimensions of your Quad in the *Game* tab, it will not match 150×184 pixels, or whatever size you specified. If you tweak the *Size* setting for the camera in the Object Inspector, you'll see the field of view dimensions change, and this affects the size of meshes in the Game tab. This setting is crucial to establishing a 1:1 pixel ratio. But what should it be? What is the correct value? The answer to this question is: it depends. Consider Figure 8-7 to see the *Size* field in action.

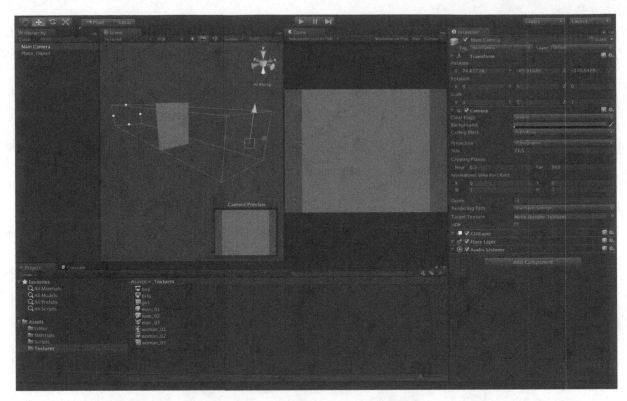

Figure 8-7. *Camera Size controls the dimensions of its field of view. This is directly related to mesh sizes in pixels for the final render*

In short, to establish a 1:1 pixel relationship between world and screen space, the camera *Size* must be half the vertical resolution of your game. If your game window is 800×600 pixels, then *Size* should be 300, because 600 / 2 = 300. If your game is 1024×768, then *Size* should be 384, because 768 / 2 = 384. If your game is designed to run at different resolutions, and if those resolutions can be changed by the user at runtime, then you'll need to script your camera to adjust its *Size* value on each resolution change. For this project I'll set the resolution to 800×600. To do this, select **Edit ➤ Project Settings ➤ Player** from the application menu. Then enter the values 800×600 for the *Default Width* and *Height* in the Object Inspector (see Figure 8-8).

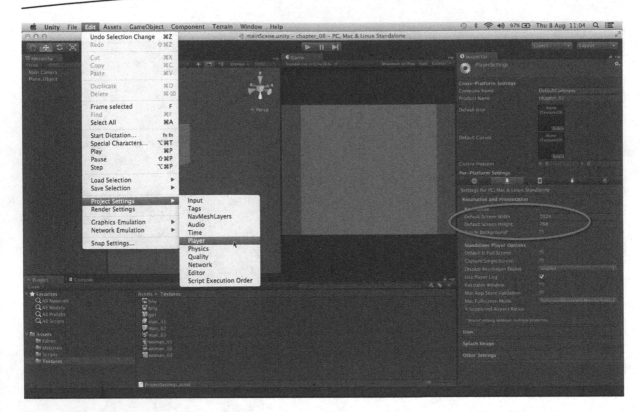

Figure 8-8. Setting game resolution in the Unity Player Settings dialog

Once you've specified the game resolution in the *Player Settings* dialog, be sure to set the *Default Aspect* for the *Game* tab. This makes your game actually run at your target resolution in the *Game* tab, as opposed to simply any resolution that best fits the *Game* tab based on your Unity editor configuration (*Free Aspect*). If you're running Unity on a low resolution layout, you may need to run your game with the *Game* tab maximized, to display your game correctly. To set the *Game* tab resolution, click the *Aspect* drop-down box from the *Game* tab toolbar and select your target resolution of 800×600, as shown in Figure 8-9.

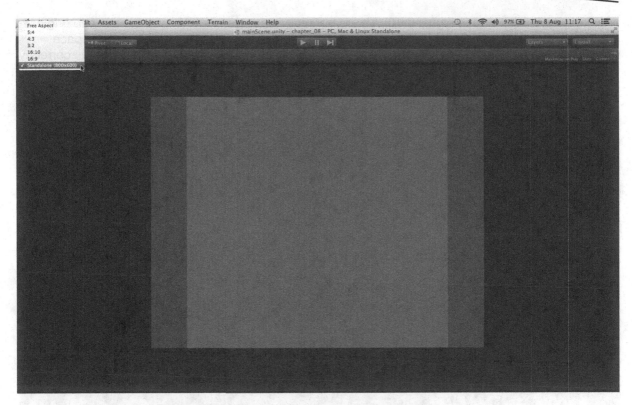

Figure 8-9. Fixing the game resolution using the Aspect drop-down list on the Game tab

Note   Setting the game resolution on the Game tab does not affect the actual resolution when the game
runs as a standalone build. It simply sets game resolution for testing and running in the Game tab. In short,
it gives you a more accurate view and representing of your game during testing.

Finally, set the camera *Size* to 300, since 600 / 2 = 300. And voila! Now your camera displays world
units as pixels. This means, for example, that a Quad Mesh whose scale is (1,1,1) and whose size is
100×100 world units will display in the camera view as 100×100 pixels in size. In my case, my Quad
Mesh displays at 150×184 pixels—the correct size for my textures.

Pixel Positioning

Okay, so now we have much more control over exactly how large or small game objects appear
on-screen, in terms of pixels, but what about pixel-positioning on-screen? Right now, the camera is
centered at the world origin (except for its Z-axis) and the Quad Mesh is also centered at the world
origin, but the Quad appears at the center of the screen, and not at the top-left corner, which is the

origin of screen space (see Figure 8-10). This is not really what we want. We want these two origins to align so that when an object is at the world space origin, it'll also appear at the screen space origin. This will help us map screen space to world space, so we can easily position objects correctly on-screen using only XY pixel positions.

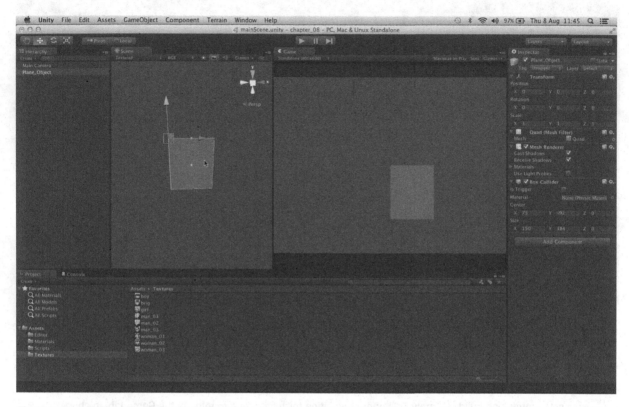

Figure 8-10. Misalignment between world space and screen space origins. Quad Mesh positioned at world origin appears at the screen center. Remember, the object pivot is at the top-left vertex in this case; meaning that its top-left corner is aligned to the screen center; not the object center

There are many different ways we can get the two coordinate spaces to align exactly, both world and screen. One "crude" way is to use code to offset all world space positions to align with the screen origin. This method involves iteratively adding or subtracting an offset from the transform of all game objects. This method will certainly work, but it'll wreak havoc with development. This is because all objects will only appear in the right places at runtime and not design-time; making it difficult to preview and build our levels in the editor. A simpler and better way is to offset the camera position, and this is the method I'll use here. Currently, the camera is positioned at the origin in terms of X and Y, and our Quad Mesh appears at the screen center. This means we can align screen and world space by negatively offsetting the camera to half the screen height and width. For me, the camera should be positioned at (X: 400, Y: –300). See Figure 8-11. Congratulations! You've now aligned screen space to world space and can position elements based on XY pixel values.

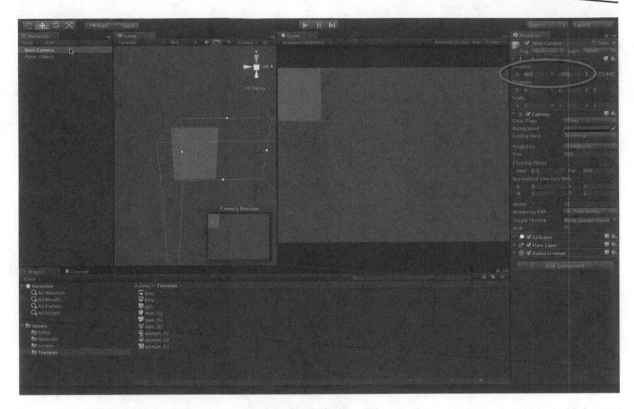

Figure 8-11. Offsetting the camera to align screen space to world space

> **Note**   In this example, the screen-space origin refers to the top-left corner of the screen. Downwards movement on the Y-axis is measured in negative terms, meaning the screen-bottom position is –600 and not 600. You may want to re-align the camera or change the screen space origin to the bottom-left corner of the screen to work only with positive values.

Pixel Perfection

Let's now take our camera work so far for a test run and see pixel perfection in action for the textures. To do this, I'll use the UV Mapping Editor plugin, created in the previous chapter, to assign texture data to the Quad Mesh. To do this, just drag and drop an Atlas Texture onto the Quad to assign it, and then use *Window — Atlas Texture Editor* from the application menu to assign UV mapping to the selected object (see Figure 8-12).

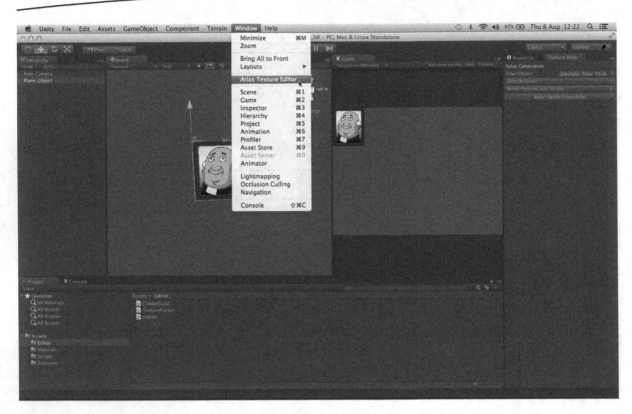

Figure 8-12. Assigning texture data to the Quad to show with pixel perfection

Note   *You can only access the UV Editor plugin if your project includes the* UVEdit.cs *class, created in Chapter 7.*

Be sure to maximize the *Game* tab (spacebar press) to view your scene at its complete target resolution, and your texture should now appear as crisply and sharply as it would in any photo editor software—as well as at the same pixel dimensions. No artifacting, no distortion, and no strange graphical glitches—just one sharp and clean looking texture, thanks to Atlas Textures and Orthographic Cameras (see Figure 8-13).

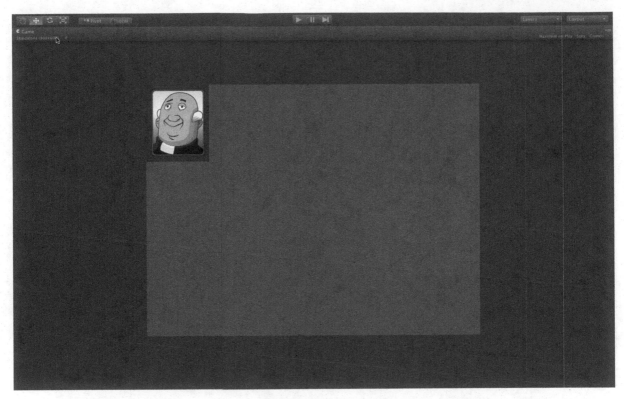

Figure 8-13. Maximizing the Game tab to view the game at full target resolution complete with pixel perfect textures

One issue that may arise later in development is that a gamer or tester runs your game at a different resolution from the one you intended. You can configure Unity to fix or freeze your target resolution so the user has no option but to use the resolution you specify. But, often you'll want to give the gamer some control over resolution, to help them get the best experience for their system. For 2D games this possibility is especially problematic because they rely so heavily on pixel positions and screen space, which is intimately connected to resolution. Sometimes developers go so far as to create different versions of the game for different resolutions! But at other times, developers opt for some-kind of scaling solution where renders are scaled to fit the target resolution—either up-scaled or down-scaled. But scaling means your textures no longer appear at their original sizes on-screen, and thus you essentially lose pixel-perfection. In such scenarios you'll need to develop a damage limitation strategy. The full details involved in this process are beyond the scope of this book, but one really helpful technique that I'll detail here is to use *anti-aliasing*. Typically this setting is disabled in Unity, for all *Build* versions except the highest quality ones. To enable *anti-aliasing,* click **Edit ➤ Project Settings ➤ Quality** from the application menu. This displays the Quality Settings dialog in the Object Inspector (see Figure 8-14).

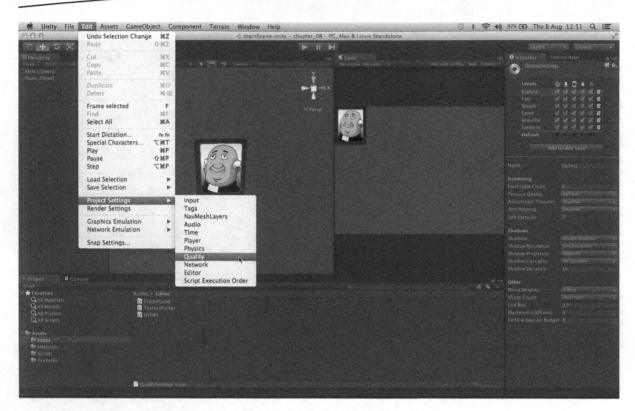

Figure 8-14. The Quality Settings offers high-level quality control over graphical assets at runtime

> **Note**   The Quality Settings dialog offers pre-sets for different build versions: the user can choose which preset to apply for their game. By default, users can select quality pre-sets from the standard Unity configuration dialog that shows when an application is run. Otherwise, pre-set selection can be offered in-game through GUI controls.

From the *Quality Settings* dialog click the *Anti-Alias* drop-down and select *2x Multi-Sampling*. You can select higher quality presets (at higher performance penalties), but typically 2x is sufficient for most games. Be sure this setting is specified either for all your quality presets, or for any presets intended for multiresolution support (see Figure 8-15). If your game supports only one resolution, then anti-aliasing need not apply.

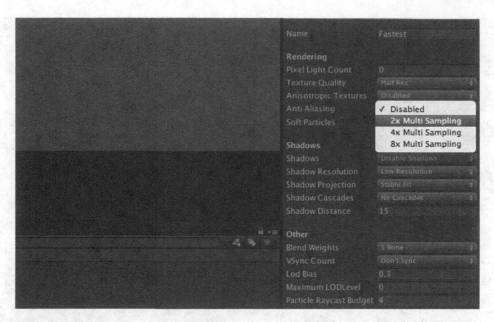

Figure 8-15. Setting anti-aliasing from the Quality dialog to improve 2D texture quality across multiple resolutions

Other Useful Camera Tricks

You've now seen how to create and configure orthographic cameras that align 1:1 with world space, allowing measurements in the two coordinate systems (screen and world) to be practically interchangeable. The importance of this for 2D games cannot be understated. But still, there are likely other tricks and techniques you'll want to achieve with cameras, and not only in 2D games, but in games more generally. This section takes a look at some of these.

Depth

Depth order (Z-Ordering) is important for 2D games because it controls which objects should appear in front of others. Given two game objects, the one with the lowest depth will appear in front of the other. This is because lower-depth objects are closer to the camera. In traditional 2D games this problem was usually solved with the painter's algorithm: objects were sorted in a list based on their distance from the camera, and then rendered in that order from furthest to nearest. The nearest objects were always rendered last to ensure they were drawn over distant objects. Unity, however, uses its own custom and internal process for rendering, which prioritizes objects and rendering in quite a different way. Thankfully, however, this doesn't prove a problem for us. Why? Because we can simply use an object's Z-Position (depth position) to control draw order. Objects nearer to the camera will automatically draw on-top of more distant objects. If you want an object to appear in front of all others in the scene, then ensure its Z (Depth) value is nearer to the camera than any other object (see Figure 8-16).

Figure 8-16. Control game object Z-Order (Depth) using the Z (Depth) value of an object's Transform component. The woman sprite is offset further back on the Z-axis and appears behind the male character sprite in the game Viewport

> **Note**   Z-Position (Depth) doesn't affect object size or vertical position on-screen for Orthographic cameras. An object will always be rendered at the same size, regardless of its real distance from the camera. Further, an object will not appear to recede toward the horizon line as it moves deeper in the scene. To achieve depth effects like this in 2D, you'll need to simulate them by manually decreasing an object's scale as it moves away, as well as change its Y (up-down) position.

Advanced Depth

Sometimes, the standard way of depth sorting objects in Unity is just not enough for 2D games. Typically, it will be enough. But occasionally it won't. Sometimes you'll need to temporarily show one object in front of another without changing its true position in the scene, even when that object is positioned at the back, or is completely off-screen. You may want to show a pop-up-dialog or a mini-map, for example, or you may want to show a different region of the level in a pop-up window—such as when a button press activates a door-open sequence. In these cases it's useful to keep objects at their existing positions in the scene, but simply show them at the front of a render. You can achieve this by using multiple cameras and adjusting their *Depth* setting, as well as *Viewport Rect* setting. Let's see how that works.

> **Caution**   Multiple cameras that are layered and rendered onto each other entail multiple renders and draw calls. This can in principle lead to extreme performance penalties. So, use multiple cameras sparingly.

I've created a new scene with two Quad Mesh objects positioned at completely different places in the scene, and there are two cameras as well—each camera facing a different Quad Mesh (see Figure 8-17). One camera has a Depth value of –1, and another has a value of 0. You'll see from the *Game* tab in Figure 8-17 that only one of the cameras is showing up. By default the camera with the highest *Depth* is rendered on-top of all other cameras.

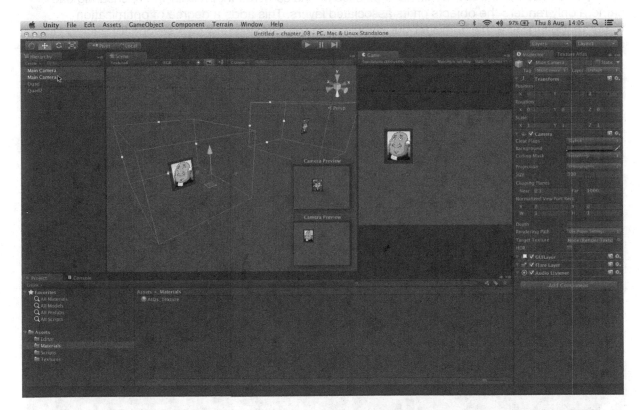

Figure 8-17.   Here is scene with two objects and two cameras at different places in the scene. Cameras with a higher Depth setting are rendered in front

> **Note**   The scene featured in Figure 8-17 is saved as MultipleCameras, and is a part of the Unity Project associated with this chapter.

So how can I composite the views of both cameras into one render that will show both quad objects, without my having to change the positions of anything? Achieving this is a two-step process, discussed next.

Assign Objects to Layers

First, if we're rendering from multiple cameras we typically don't want them to render the same things or objects—that would be a doubling-up of work and a waste of resources. Typically, the cameras are supposed to render different objects. To optimize this rendering workflow, we assign the objects in our scene to different layers based on the cameras that render them, ensuring each camera only renders the objects on its associated layers. This adds a degree of optimization to our rendering. To achieve this for our sample scene, create two new layers—one for each quad. Click **Layers ➤ Edit Layers** from the Unity interface (as shown in Figure 8-18).

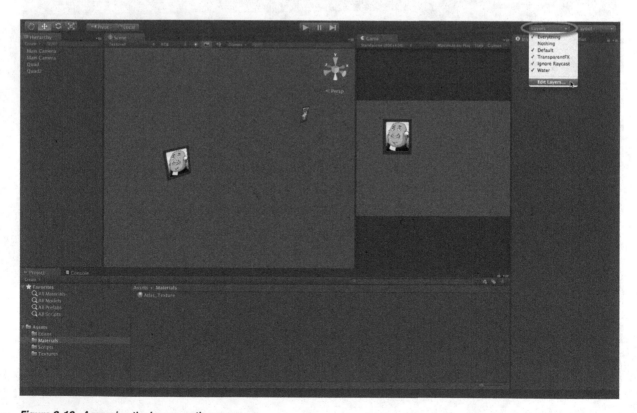

Figure 8-18. Accessing the layer creation menu

From the Layer Creation menu, add two new layers. I've named these LayerObject1 and LayerObject2. These are not especially helpful or descriptive names generally speaking. They're fine for our sample project, but in your own projects it's good practice to choose meaningful names, to avoid confusion and to save time. See Figure 8-19.

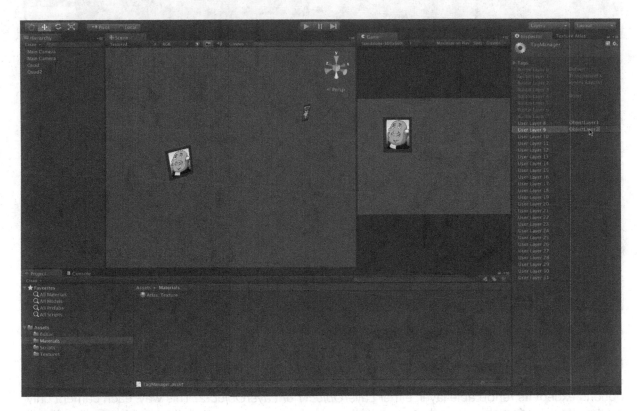

Figure 8-19. *Creating new layers*

Select each object in the scene and assign it to its appropriate layer. Use the layers to group together all objects to be rendered by the same camera. If two objects are to be rendered by different cameras, they should exist on separate layers. To assign an object to a layer, select the object and click the layer drop-down to select the layer (see Figure 8-20).

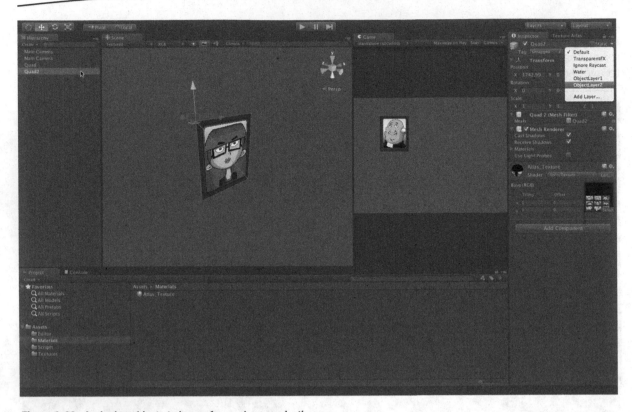

Figure 8-20. Assigning objects to layers for render organization

Next select each camera, and use the *Culling Mask* setting from the Object Inspector to limit the cameras renderable objects only to its associated layer. This means removing a check mark from all options except its renderable layer, either *LayerObject1 or LayerObject2*. This way, each camera only renders its assigned objects and no more. (Alternatively, you can select Nothing for the Culling Mask to deselect everything, and then choose the item to be rendered.) See Figure 8-21.

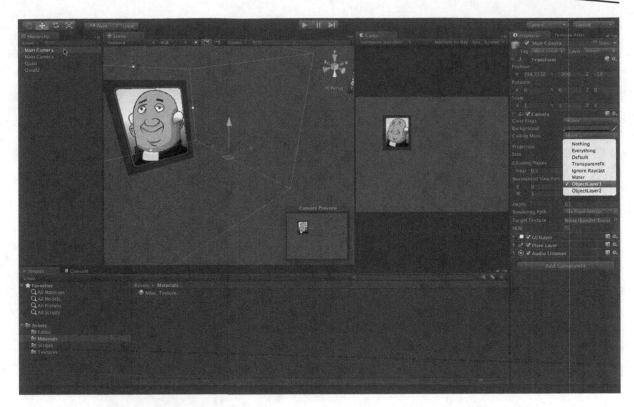

Figure 8-21. Assigning cameras to layers

Clearing the Depth Buffer

Now that we've configured the render layers, it's time to set up the cameras to composite their renders together, showing the output from both in a single image. To do this, select the topmost camera (the camera with the highest depth) and change its *Clear Flags setting* in the Object Inspector from *Skybox* to *Depth Only (see Figure* 8-22).

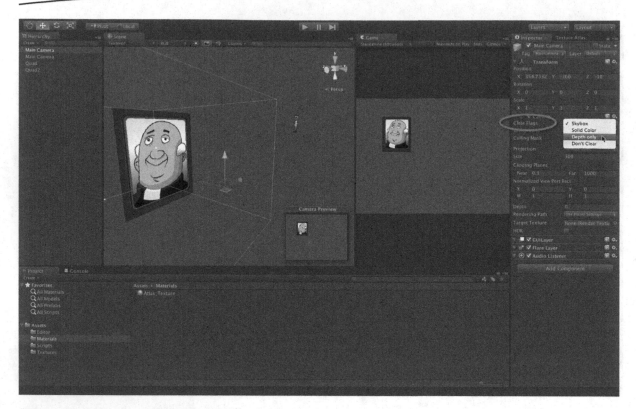

Figure 8-22.   Configuring the topmost camera to show-through to cameras beneath

By setting the Clear Flags to Depth Only we instruct the topmost camera to turn its background transparent to reveal the camera layers beneath. We can even apply these settings to additional cameras further down the depth chain to create a complete stack of layered cameras that render together into a single image, even though they exist in completely different parts of the scene. Using this technique we gain high-level control of the rendering depth of scenes (see Figure 8-23).

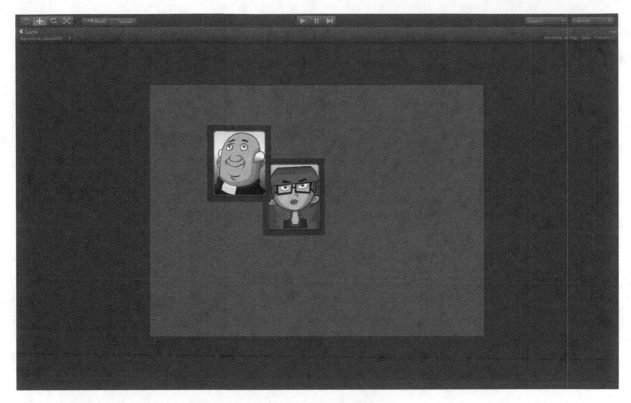

Figure 8-23. Rendering together multiple cameras using the Clear Flags setting

Summary

This chapter builds on the former ones. On reaching this stage you can now probably piece together something resembling a 2D game. You've seen how to create Quads, generate Atlas Textures, customize UV mapping, and now how to configure a 1:1 relationship between world and screen space. This relationship is important because it means we can position and size objects in Unity scenes with pixel-perfection, to match-up exactly with our original visualizations and plans in Photoshop or GIMP. After reading this chapter you should be able to:

- Understand the difference between Perspective and Orthographic cameras
- Create Orthographic cameras
- Configure cameras to establish a 1:1 world to screen space map
- Position and size objects in 2D space
- Understand how to control the depth and render order of scene objects
- Understand how to offset cameras to align screen and world space origins
- Set the game resolution
- Understand how to use the Quality Settings dialog
- Use camera depth, flags, and culling masks to control render depth

Chapter 9

Input for 2D Games

In this chapter we'll talk about user input for 2D games, specifically input from the keyboard, mouse, and mobile devices. Input is critical for any game, whether 2D or not. Without input, a game cannot be interactive. For most 2D games, we need to read input that maps directly to 2D space, in terms of pixel positions. However, because Unity is a 3D engine and our objects exist in three-dimensional space, we'll also need to convert screen space positions to world space positions. For this chapter, I'll be working from a premade, basic 2D project, which is included in the book companion files (in `Project_Files/Chapter09/`); however, you can work along with your own projects instead, if you want to. Some points covered in this chapter include:

- Read live input from the keyboard and mouse

- Show a cursor graphic that tracks mouse movement across the screen

- Detect mouse clicks and touches on specific game objects in the scene.

- Read touch and location input from mobile devices like iPads and Android tablets, and

- Write input handling code that compiles conditionally, depending on the target platform.

The last point means writing one code set for handling desktop input, another for mobile input, and having Unity compile the right versions for the appropriate platform automatically. Figure 9-1 demonstrates our starting point: a basic 2D scene, featuring one plane with an Atlas Texture.

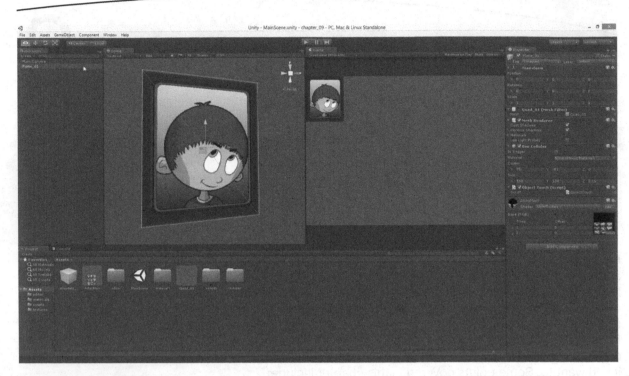

Figure 9-1. *Starting Unity scene. This scene can be found in the book companion files in Project_Files/Chapter09*

Detecting Mouse Clicks on Objects Automatically

The most straightforward user input to detect in Unity is mouse clicks. Unity features a fast and efficient work flow for detecting mouse clicks on any objects in the scene, provided those objects have a Collider Component attached (this includes Box Colliders, Capsule Colliders, and any other type of Collider). This section explores further how to detect and respond to this input. To get started, load up the sample project associated with this chapter (Project_Files/Chapter09/), or create your own 2D scene from scratch, ensuring your camera is orthographic and your scene has a textured quad in view of the camera. The camera has been aligned in the world so that the screen space origin is at the bottom-left corner; meaning positive X spans across the screen width, and positive Y across the screen height from bottom to top (see Figure 9-1).

Note   This chapter extends on material covered in previous chapters; specifically, Chapters 4, 5, 6, 7, and 8.

Select the textured quad in the scene and make sure there's a Collider Component attached. For this example, I've used a Box Collider. You can attach colliders to your objects, if they don't have one already, by choosing **Component ➤ Physics ➤ Box Collider** from the application menu (your object should be selected before choosing this option). The purpose of the Collider is to act as a bounding box for the object, approximating its volume and bulk using a simple primitive, such as a box or capsule. Consequently, take care to size your Colliders appropriately, keeping them as tight fitting as possible while encompassing the extents of your object. You can change the size of an attached Collider using the *Center* and *Size* properties in the Object Inspector (see Figure 9-2).

Figure 9-2. *Assigning a collider to a textured quad in preparation for detecting mouse clicks*

> **Tip**   Although textured quads are essentially flat planes in 3D space, it's a good idea to give their colliders some depth and volume in the Z axis (depth axis). This helps Unity detect collisions with those objects more reliably. So, if you're having trouble detecting mouse clicks and other collisions for your objects, check out their colliders.

Once you've got an object with a Collider, you may detect and respond to mouse clicks on the object easily, by using a script file that implements an OnMouseDown event. To create this, generate a new C# script file in the project, selecting **Assets ➤ Create ➤ C# Script** from the application menu. Attach this as a component to the Textured Quad object, and then open the script file in MonoDevelop to add an OnMouseDown function. Take a look at Listing 9-1 to see my implementation that prints a message to the console when the object is clicked with the mouse. Figure 9-3 illustrates the results.

Listing 9-1. ObjectTouch.cs

```
using UnityEngine;
using System.Collections;
```

```
public class ObjectTouch : MonoBehaviour
{
    //Called on mouse down
    void OnMouseDown()
    {
        Debug.Log ("You clicked me");
    }
}
```

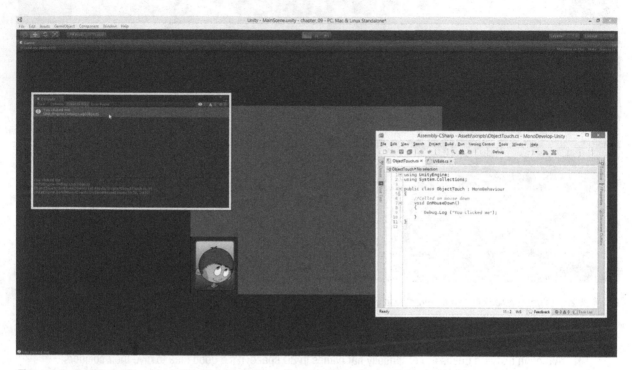

Figure 9-3. Testing OnMouseDown functionality. This requires an object with a collider attached

The OnMouseDown function is not the only event supported by MonoDevelop to work with mouse events and colliders. There's also OnMouseUp, called whenever the user releases the mouse button (this function is called even when the cursor is not hovering over the object). There's also OnMouseEnter and OnMouseExit, which are called when the cursor hovers over and hovers off the object, respectively. This can be useful for creating GUI button hover states, such as *Over* and *Neutral* states. For more information, see the Unity Documentation for MonoBehaviour at: http://docs.unity3d.com/Documentation/ScriptReference/MonoBehaviour.html.

Detecting Mouse Clicks on Objects Manually

The OnMouse events for MonoBehaviour work efficiently and are often useful when you need to detect and respond to mouse clicks. But they have some important limitations, as we'll see here. That's why it's necessary to have alternative methods and work-flows in your coding toolbox. One limitation is that OnMouseDown takes Z-Order (depth) into consideration. This means: if you have two overlapping objects in the scene, one in front of the other, then OnMouseDown will only fire for clicks on the front object, and not on the back object. In many situations (such as for GUIs) this may be what you want, but (for example) if your click is supposed to represent gun fire at a target object, then you may want your weapon to shoot two enemies at once. Another limitation of these events is that they won't fire for mobile devices. In Unity, touch and tapping events don't implicitly map to mouse events. Therefore, a mobile touch event will not trigger a mouse down event, and vice versa. The second issue we'll examine later in this chapter. For now, let's address the first issue. Specifically, let's see how to detect the cursor position manually and then convert its screen space position into world space to see which objects have been clicked.

> **Tip** If you're continuing your work in Unity directly from the previous section, be sure to remove or disable the OnTouch component to avoid any mouse click detection and confusion while working with mouse clicks in this section.

To work with mouse input manually (as well as keyboard and mobile input), Unity offers the appropriately named Input class. This class is not event driven but is a *polling class*. This means it doesn't explicitly tell you when input happens through events and function calls. Rather, you ask it questions (such as in the Update function) about the current state of input devices (such as "Is the mouse button being pressed?"), and it will tell you the answer. You can read the mouse button state with a call to Input.GetMouseButton, and the mouse cursor position with the property Input.mousePosition. Take a look at Listing 9-2 to see these two functions at work. Notice, I've created a new script file to handle mouse input manually. I've called this file MouseInputManual.cs.

Listing 9-2. MouseInputManual.cs

```
using UnityEngine;
using System.Collections;

public class MouseInputManual : MonoBehaviour
{
    // Update is called once per frame
    void Update ()
    {
        //Is left button being pressed?
        if(Input.GetMouseButton(0))
            Debug.Log("Left Button Pressed");

        //Is middle button being pressed?
        if(Input.GetMouseButton(2))
            Debug.Log("Middle Button Pressed");

        //Is right button being pressed?
        if(Input.GetMouseButton(1))
            Debug.Log("Right Button Pressed");
```

```
        //Get mouse x position on screen
        float X = Input.mousePosition.x;
        float Y = Input.mousePosition.y;
    }
}
```

> **Note**   The property mousePosition records the absolute mouse cursor position in screen coordinates, from the origin of screen space (bottom-left). It's not a deltaPosition value, which expresses the difference in mouse movement since the previous frame.

> **Note**   The mouse middle button has an ID of 2 and not 1, which corresponds to the right button. This is because earlier mice were released with left and right buttons only—no middle buttons.

So now let's see how we can convert a cursor position into 3D space so we can detect which object has been clicked. This is achieved by using the Physics system and Rays. A *Ray* is a mathematical construct that can be imagined as an invisible laser projecting outward from the camera lens along a straight line into the scene. Using this concept, we can project a ray from the mouse click position on the screen, outwards into the scene, and see what objects the ray intersects. This helps us detect which objects we clicked on. Let's start by seeing how we can detect the first and nearest object we click on (that is, *nearest to the camera*). Take a look at Listing 9-3, and then we'll explore it step by step.

Listing 9-3. MouseInputManual.cs—Using Rays

```
using UnityEngine;
using System.Collections;

public class MouseInputManual : MonoBehaviour
{
    // Update is called once per frame
    void Update ()
    {
        //Clicked mouse button
        if (Input.GetMouseButton(0))
        {
            //Generate ray from main camera and mouse position
            Ray R = Camera.main.ScreenPointToRay(Input.mousePosition);

            //Will store info about nearest object hit
            RaycastHit HitInfo;

            //Test to see if ray intersects with any colliders
            if (Physics.Raycast (R, out HitInfo))
```

```
        {
            //Object was hit, get game object that was hit
            GameObject HitObject = HitInfo.collider.gameObject;

            //Print GameObject name to console
            Debug.Log (HitObject.name);
        }
    }
  }
}
```

This code starts by detecting for a mouse click with `Input.GetMouseButton`. Once a click is detected, it calls the `ScreenPointToRay` function of the `Camera` object to generate a ray structure, based on the camera view and the mouse position. It should be mentioned here that for this functionality to work correctly you should call `ScreenPointToRay` on the active camera (the camera you're using for the player view). Next, the function casts the ray into the scene with `Physics.Raycast`, and the nearest intersection is returned in the `HitInfo` structure. Figure 9-4 shows this function at work.

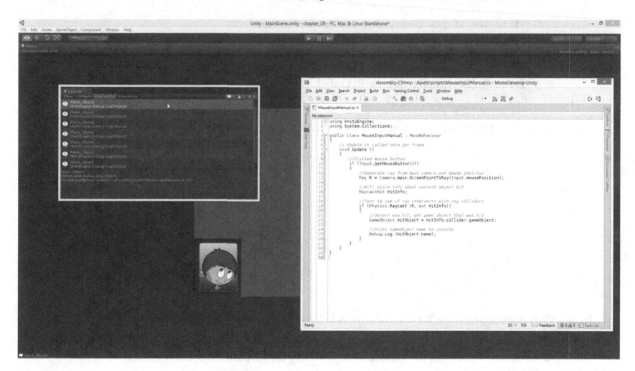

Figure 9-4. Using a Physics.Raycast to detect mouse clicks on the nearest object in the scene

Everything should be working great with the mouse detection code. But this code doesn't really do anything different from the simpler `OnMouseDown` event we used earlier. It detects a mouse click on only the nearest object. But there still could be multiple objects in the scene behind the nearest one that would have received the click if the nearer one hadn't existed. So how we can detect for an intersection with all objects? The answer is to use `Physics.RaycastAll` instead of `Physics.Raycast`. Listing 9-4 shows an amended function that uses `RaycastAll` to get all objects under the mouse click during a click. Take a look at Figure 9-5 to see multiple intersections at work.

Listing 9-4. MouseInputManual.cs — Using RayCastAll

```
using UnityEngine;
using System.Collections;

public class MouseInputManual : MonoBehaviour
{
    // Update is called once per frame
    void Update ()
    {
        //Clicked mouse button
        if (Input.GetMouseButtonDown(0))
        {
            //Generate ray from main camera and mouse position
            Ray R = Camera.main.ScreenPointToRay(Input.mousePosition);

            //Will store info about all intersections
            RaycastHit[] HitInfo = Physics.RaycastAll(R);

            //Test to see if ray intersects with any colliders
            if (HitInfo != null)
            {
                //Loop through all intersections
                foreach (RaycastHit Hit in HitInfo)
                {
                    //Object was hit, get game object that was hit
                    GameObject HitObject = Hit.collider.gameObject;

                    //Print GameObject name to console
                    Debug.Log (HitObject.name);
                }
            }
        }
    }
}
```

Note   Unity doesn't guarantee the order of objects in the HitInfo array. Physics.RaycastAll could return all intersections in any order, not necessarily from nearest to furthest. If distance or nearness is important to you, you should check the distance of the intersected object using the RaycastHit.distance member.

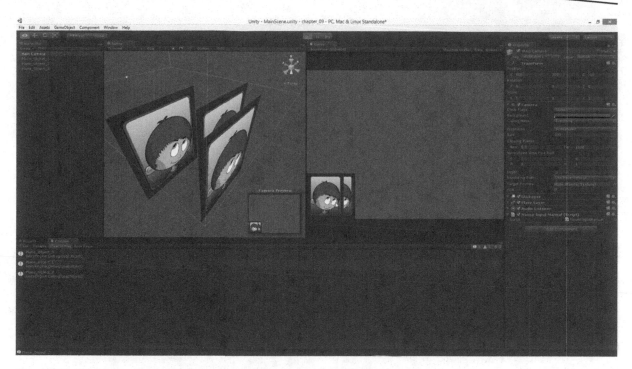

Figure 9-5. Using a Physics RaycastAll to detect mouse clicks on all objects in the scene

Listing 9-4 works much like Listing 9-3. The critical difference is the use of Physics.RaycastAll to generate an array of all intersections with the mouse, as opposed to simply the nearest intersection. Notice also that I've used Input.GetMouseButtonDown instead of Input.GetMouseButton. What is the difference between these two? The latter function (GetMouseButton) returns true on *every* frame for *as long as* the mouse button is being held down. The former (GetMouseButtonDown) returns true only once for each button press. GetMouseButton is useful for executed repeated behavior while the button is depressed, and GetMouseButtonDown is useful for executing on-off behavior on each independent mouse click.

Coding a Mouse Cursor

For most desktop 2D games (PC, Mac, and Linux) you'll want a cursor graphic that overrides the standard system cursor and tracks mouse movement. In this section I'll show how you to create this feature using the project files associated with this chapter (Project_Files/Chapter09/). These files include a cursor graphic file cursor.psd, *which has all the necessary transparency data baked in*. Open the texture settings for this cursor (which should be added as a texture for the project) and set its size to 64×64 pixels (its native resolution). See Figure 9-6.

Figure 9-6. *Preparing a cursor graphic in Unity*

Create a new a quad asset at 64×64 units, with its origin set to the bottom-left. This Quad object will be used for the mouse cursor. When the Quad is generated in the scene, make sure its Z (depth) position is nearer to the camera than all other scene objects—otherwise your cursor will appear behind them! See Figure 9-7 to see my scene setup.

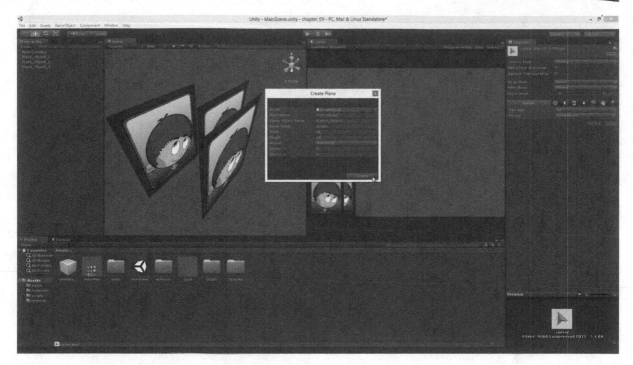

Figure 9-7. Creating a Quad Mesh for the cursor graphic

Select the cursor object in the scene and assign it the cursor texture. Set the material to the **Unlit ➤ Transparent CutOut shader** to apply the alpha transparency, removing the texture background. Then, remove the cursor's Collider component (created by default). If you don't do this, your cursor will become an object for mouse clicking, just like any regular object with a collider. Typically, we don't want to detect mouse clicks on the cursor (see Figure 9-8).

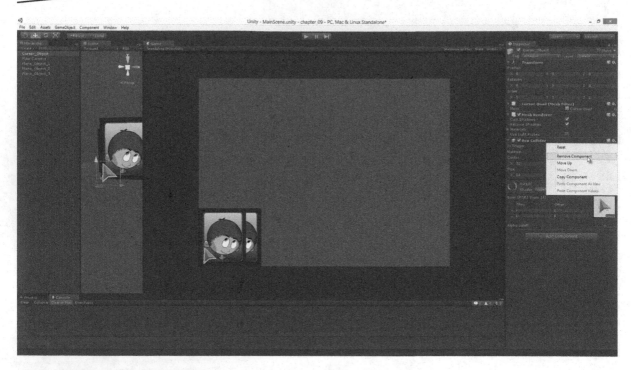

Figure 9-8. Removing the cursor's collider component to exclude it from mouse click detection

Create a new C# Script file in the project named Cursor.cs, which will contain all the code required for the mouse cursor. Attach this script file as a component on the cursor object in the scene, and then open the script file in MonoDevelop. The code in Listing 9-5 demonstrates the complete source file for the cursor.

Listing 9-5. Cursor.cs

```
using UnityEngine;
using System.Collections;

public class Cursor : MonoBehaviour
{
    //Hotspot Offset
    public Vector2 CursorOffset = Vector2.zero;

    //Override system cursor?
    public bool ShowSystemCursor = false;

    //Transform component
    private Transform ThisTransform = null;

    // Use this for initialization
    void Start ()
    {
        //Cache transform
        ThisTransform = transform;
```

```
    //Hide or show system cursor
    Screen.showCursor = ShowSystemCursor;
}

// Update is called once per frame
void Update ()
{
    ThisTransform.position = new Vector3(Input.mousePosition.x + CursorOffset.x,
Input.mousePosition.y + CursorOffset.y, ThisTransform.position.z);
}
}
```

By attaching this script to the mouse cursor object you'll get a full-featured cursor that tracks mouse movement. There are two critical stages to this script. The first is the Screen.showCursor statement in the Start event. This property is part of the Unity Screen class and used to control the visibility of the *system cursor* right from application start-up. The system cursor refers to the default mouse cursor provided by the operating system. This continues to be visible unless explicitly hidden by an application. The second stage is in the Update function, where the position of the cursor graphic mirrors the mouse position, as read from the Input class. This mouse position is also modified by the CursorOffset Vector member. This member offsets the cursor graphic to a custom-pivot or center, representing the point at which cursor clicks are made. This value differs depending on the cursor graphic you use: for my cursor graphic a value of −14, and −61 work well, offsetting the graphic to the correct position. Take a look at Figure 9-9 to see the cursor in action. Congratulations! You should now have a functional cursor in your game.

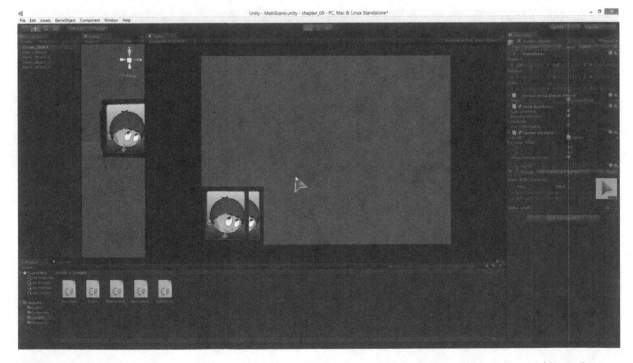

Figure 9-9. *The cursor graphic at work in the scene using the Cursor.cs script. Notice the system cursor is overlaid onto the cursor graphic because ShowSystemCursor is enabled*

> **Note**   An alternative to coding a manual cursor in the way outlined in this section is to use the native Cursor
> class, which is new to Unity 4.1. I've used a manual cursor here to keep compatibility with all versions of
> Unity 4. More information on this class can be found at:
> http://docs.unity3d.com/Documentation/ScriptReference/Cursor.html.

Working with Keyboard Input

Keyboard input is another method you probably want to work with for desktop games—especially
for action or intense games, such as platformers and RPGs. These games typically have run, jump,
and attack actions, and these usually map directly to specific keys on the keyboard. Reading
keyboard input in Unity is achieved through the Input class. In this section, we'll code a keyboard
override for the mouse cursor object so that directional arrow presses (and WASD) will move the
cursor around the screen. This code will be added to the Cursor.cs script coded in the previous
section. Take a look at Listing 9-6 to see the changes made to implement keyboard handling.

Listing 9-6. Cursor.cs—Controlling the Cursor with the Keyboard

```
using UnityEngine;
using System.Collections;

public class Cursor : MonoBehaviour
{
    //Hotspot Offset
    public Vector2 CursorOffset = Vector2.zero;

    //Override system cursor?
    public bool ShowSystemCursor = false;

    //Speed of cursor movment for keyboard override (pixels per second)
    public float CursorSpeed = 100.0f;

    //Should enable keyboard override?
    public bool EnableKeyboardOverride = false;

    //Transform component
    private Transform ThisTransform = null;

    // Use this for initialization
    void Start ()
    {
        //Cache transform
        ThisTransform = transform;

        //Hide or show system cursor
        Screen.showCursor = ShowSystemCursor;
    }
```

```
    // Update is called once per frame
    void Update ()
    {
        //Should we control cursor movement with keyboard?
        if(EnableKeyboardOverride)
        {
            //Amount of Movement
            float Move = CursorSpeed * Time.deltaTime;

            //Update keyboard movement
            if(Input.GetKey(KeyCode.W) || Input.GetKey(KeyCode.UpArrow))
                ThisTransform.Translate(0, Move, 0);

            if(Input.GetKey(KeyCode.S) || Input.GetKey(KeyCode.DownArrow))
                ThisTransform.Translate(0, -Move, 0);

            if(Input.GetKey(KeyCode.A) || Input.GetKey(KeyCode.LeftArrow))
                ThisTransform.Translate(-Move, 0, 0);

            if(Input.GetKey(KeyCode.D) || Input.GetKey(KeyCode.RightArrow))
                ThisTransform.Translate(Move, 0, 0);

            return;
        }

        //No keyboard override. Update with mouse movement

        //Update position from mouse movement
        ThisTransform.position = new Vector3(Input.mousePosition.x + CursorOffset.x,
Input.mousePosition.y + CursorOffset.y, ThisTransform.position.z);
    }
}
```

> **Note**   In Unity, each key on the keyboard is identified by a unique code (key code), which is expressed as a number. These codes are used by the Input class to read and identify keys. The codes for all keys can be found in the Unity documentation at:
> http://docs.unity3d.com/Documentation/ScriptReference/KeyCode.html.

Listing 9-6 is the modified cursor class to handle input from the keyboard to control the cursor position. It reads keyboard input using the Input.GetKey function. Again, like the mouse functions, this is a polling-function. We query to see whether a specified key is pressed, and the Input class tells us. Additionally, the Input class also supports the method GetKeyDown and GetKeyUp. GetKey returns true for every frame as long as the specified key is depressed, while the GetKeyDown and GetKeyUp variations only return true once for each independent press and release respectively.

Virtual Axes and Buttons—Input Abstraction

The functions used so far have read input from both the keyboard and mouse in a very direct way. Effectively, these functions "hard coded" the controls into the source code because we checked for specified keys, and for mouse clicks and mouse movements. Though there's nothing wrong per se in doing this (it works!), it does nonetheless restrict the user because they cannot customize the controls. We could of course refine our code further and implement a more abstracted system that did allow for user customization, but Unity already ships with this feature in the form of virtual axes and virtual buttons. In general, it's good practice to work with these features, rather than reading input directly as we have done so far. By using the virtual axes and buttons, we can still respond to input (just as before) but the user has the flexibility of customizing and changing the controls through the *Input Manager*. We can access the Input Manager from the Unity Editor by choosing **Edit ➤ Project Settings ➤ Input** from the application menu. This allows us to add, remove, and edit existing axes from which we can read input. Figure 9-10 shows the Input Manager in the Unity Editor.

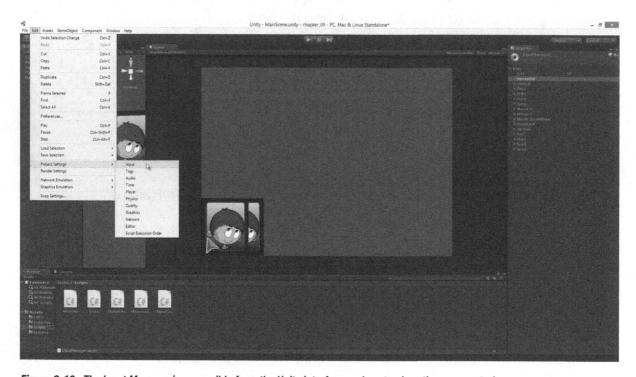

Figure 9-10. *The Input Manager is accessible from the Unity interface and customizes the user controls*

If you click on the "Fire1" axis in the Object Inspector, you'll see by default it has been assigned to the left-control key on the keyboard and the left-click button on the mouse. This means that when the user clicks the left-mouse button or presses left-control on the keyboard, the virtual button "Fire1" is classified as being depressed. This intermediary system (or abstraction) means that if our games listen for input on the virtual axes, as opposed to raw input, then the user can transparently change the controls without breaking our code (see Figure 9-11).

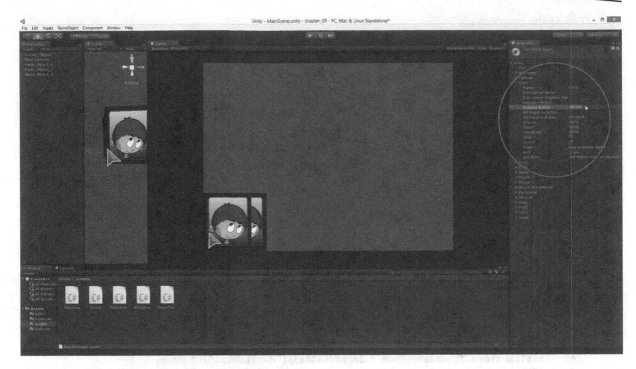

Figure 9-11. Configuring input through the Input Manager

So how do we work with virtual axes in code? In short, to read position information that corresponds to left and right (on the keyboard) we call Input.GetAxis("Horizontal"). To read vertical position data, we call Input.GetAxis("Vertical"). These functions return a value between –1 and 1 to indicate the direction being pressed: –1 for left, 1 for right, and 0 for no input for the horizontal axis and 1 for up, –1 for down, and 0 for no input on the vertical axis. Listing 9-7 shows how we can completely rewrite the keyboard functionality for our Cursor.cs file to handle cursor movement. Notice how much shorter the code is too—keyboard handling is reduced to only one compound expression!

Listing 9-7. Cursor.cs—Controlling the Cursor with Virtual Axes

```
using UnityEngine;
using System.Collections;

public class Cursor : MonoBehaviour
{
    //Hotspot Offset
    public Vector2 CursorOffset = Vector2.zero;

    //Override system cursor?
    public bool ShowSystemCursor = false;

    //Speed of cursor movment for keyboard override (pixels per second)
    public float CursorSpeed = 100.0f;

    //Should enable keyboard override?
    public bool EnableKeyboardOverride = false;
```

```
    //Transform component
    private Transform ThisTransform = null;

    // Use this for initialization
    void Start ()
    {
        //Cache transform
        ThisTransform = transform;

        //Hide or show system cursor
        Screen.showCursor = ShowSystemCursor;
    }

    // Update is called once per frame
    void Update ()
    {
        //Should we control cursor movement with keyboard?
        if(EnableKeyboardOverride)
        {
            //Amount of Movement
            float Move = CursorSpeed * Time.deltaTime;

            //Update keyboard movement
            ThisTransform.Translate(Move * Input.GetAxis("Horizontal") * Move,
Input.GetAxis("Vertical") * Move, 0);

            return;
        }

        //No keyboard override. Update with mouse movement

        //Update position from mouse movement
        ThisTransform.position = new Vector3(Input.mousePosition.x + CursorOffset.x,
Input.mousePosition.y + CursorOffset.y, ThisTransform.position.z);
    }
}
```

How about virtual button presses, such as mouse clicks and fire buttons? For these we use the method Input.GetButton. Remember "Fire1" is associated with mouse clicks and left-control button presses on the keyboard. We can listen for these input events using the code in Listing 9-8.

Listing 9-8. Listening for Virtual Buttons

```
// Update is called once per frame
void Update ()
{
    if(Input.GetButton("Fire1"))
    {
        //Fire 1 pressed
    }
}
```

Mobile Input—Android, iOS, and Windows Phone

The mobile platforms have thrown spanners into the works of many a Unity developer, because they work a little differently from regular input devices like keyboards and mice. One common assumption made about Unity is that mobile device input will map directly onto mouse input so that, if an application supports mouse controls, it will also support tap input on mobile devices. This is not correct by default, although (with some scripting) a Unity application can be engineered to work like this. The other problem that arises is that developers often require code branching for mobile input. Desktop platforms should respond to keyboard and mouse, and mobile devices to touch, and we don't want to waste time processing the input systems of one platform for another. So, it becomes useful to implement code branching. This can be achieved by if or switch statements, but there is another and more optimal method, as we'll see. So let's take a closer look at mobile input.

Detecting Touch Events on Mobiles

The touch event finds its closest counterpart in the mouse click event, although it differs to a degree because multiple fingers can touch the screen simultaneously. This makes the touch event more like a multi-location mouse click. Whenever the user touches the screen of a mobile device, a touch event is generated by the Unity Input class for each touching finger, and each event has a Phase (TouchPhase class), which describes the state of the touch. The phase can be: Began, Moved, Stationary, Ended, *or* Cancelled. The phase of a touch is set to Began as the finger contacts the screen. It is set to Moved (if and when) the finger slides while still in contact with the screen. It is set to Stationary if the finger is in contact with the screen but doesn't move. It is set to Ended when the finger is removed from the screen, and it is set to Cancelled if input is cancelled completely. If all you need to do is simply get the screen location of the first touch event (akin to a mouse click), then you can use the code in Listing 9-9.

Listing 9-9. Getting the First Touch Input

```
// Update is called once per frame
void Update ()
{
    if(Input.touchCount>0)
    {
        //Screen position of touch
        Vector2 TouchLocation = Input.GetTouch(0).position;

        //Get phase of touch
        TouchPhase TPhase = Input.GetTouch(0).phase;
    }
}
```

The Input.TouchCount keeps a real-time list of all active touches on the screen, and the Input.GetTouch method provides individual access to the touches in the array. This means you can get all information on all active touches with the code in Listing 9-10.

Listing 9-10. Getting All Touches

```
// Update is called once per frame
void Update ()
{
    if(Input.touchCount>0)
    {
        for(int i =0; i<Input.touchCount; i++)
        {
            //Screen position of touch
            Vector2 TouchLocation = Input.GetTouch(0).position;

            //Get phase of touch
            TouchPhase TPhase = Input.GetTouch(0).phase;

            //Touch begins
            if(TPhase.Equals(TouchPhase.Began))
            {
                //Click equivalent
            }
        }
    }
}
```

Mapping Touches to Mouse Input

Many developers are only interested in a single touch event, and they simply want their mobile games to map directly onto mouse input so both their desktop and mobile games share the same input handling code. Unity does not offer this functionality out-of-the-box, but you can add it manually using much of the code we've seen already. In Listing 9-11 a new C# class has been created (MobileMouseMap.cs) that establishes a mobile touch to mouse click input map for any objects that have a collider attached. It constructs a physics raycast based on touch location, and then initiates an OnMouseDown event for all object intersections.

Listing 9-11. MobileMouseMap.cs

```
using UnityEngine;
using System.Collections;

public class MobileMouseMap : MonoBehaviour
{
    // Update is called once per frame
    void Update ()
    {
        if(Input.touchCount>0)
        {
            //Screen position of touch
            Vector2 TouchLocation = Input.GetTouch(0).position;

            //Get phase of touch
            TouchPhase TPhase = Input.GetTouch(0).phase;
```

```
        //Touch begins
        if(TPhase.Equals(TouchPhase.Began))
        {
            //Generate ray from main camera and mouse position
            Ray R = Camera.main.ScreenPointToRay(TouchLocation);
            RaycastHit HitInfo;

            //If intersection
            if(Physics.Raycast(R, out HitInfo))
            {
                //Click equivalent - call mouse event
                HitInfo.collider.gameObject.SendMessage("OnMouseDown");
            }
        }
    }
  }
}
```

Conditional Code Compilation

There's no getting around it: desktop input is different from mobile input. The devices work a little differently, and this often requires us to respond differently in code to user input. Sometimes we can get around it and use input maps, as shown in the previous section, to minimize the impact this has on our code. But often we cannot get around it so easily. At these times we simply need to use different blocks of code: one to handle desktop input, and one to handle mobile input. Now while it's possible to use conditional statements to switch between the blocks of code at run-time, it can often be easier and more efficient to use *Conditional Code Compilation*. In essence this allows us to select regions of our code in the source files and then assign them to a specific target platform (Windows, or Mac, or mobile). Doing this allows Unity to understand which regions it should compile and which regions it should just turn into code-comments for the current build. The syntax for using Conditional Code Compilation would work as follows (in Listing 9-12) for isolating desktop input code.

Listing 9-12. Isolating Desktop Input with Conditonal Code Compilation

```
// Update is called once per frame
void Update ()
{
    #if UNITY_STANDALONE || UNITY_EDITOR || UNITY_WEBPLAYER || UNITY_DASHBOARD_WIDGET
    //Clicked mouse button
    if (Input.GetMouseButtonDown(0))
    {
        //Generate ray from main camera and mouse position
        Ray R = Camera.main.ScreenPointToRay(Input.mousePosition);

        //Will store info about all intersections
        RaycastHit[] HitInfo = Physics.RaycastAll(R);

        //Test to see if ray intersects with any colliders
        if (HitInfo != null)
        {
```

```
            //Loop through all intersections
            foreach (RaycastHit Hit in HitInfo)
            {
                //Object was hit, get game object that was hit
                GameObject HitObject = Hit.collider.gameObject;

                //Print GameObject name to console
                Debug.Log (HitObject.name);
            }
        }
    }
    #endif
}
```

> **Note**   Using Conditional Compilation, in combination with platform-specific functionality, can not only increase the readability of your functions, but make them more versatile and reusable. In short, it can save you from having to write and rewrite different functions, maintaining separate code bases.

> **Note**   You can switch target platform in the Unity Editor by opening the *Build dialog* with **File ➤ Build**. From there, select your target platform and click the button Switch Platform. See Figure 9-12.

Figure 9-12. Using the Build dialog to change your target platform

In Listing 9-12 all desktop input code is inserted between the pre-processor directives #if and #endif, *as highlighted in bold for clarity*. This setup forces Unity to recognize this code as valid only if the current build platform is a desktop platform (Windows, Mac, or Linux), the Unity Editor, a Web Page Build, or is a Dashboard Widget. If the target build platform is anything different (such as a mobile platform), Unity will convert this code into comments before the compilation process, meaning this code will not be included in the build. Using this technique, we can isolate mobile input using the code in Listing 9-13.

Listing 9-13. Isolating Mobile Input with Conditional Code Compilation

```
// Update is called once per frame
void Update ()
{
    #if UNITY_IPHONE || UNITY_ANDROID || UNITY_BLACKBERRY || UNITY_WP8
    if(Input.touchCount>0)
    {
        //Screen position of touch
        Vector2 TouchLocation = Input.GetTouch(0).position;

        //Get phase of touch
        TouchPhase TPhase = Input.GetTouch(0).phase;

        //Touch begins
        if(TPhase.Equals(TouchPhase.Began))
        {
            //Generate ray from main camera and mouse position
            Ray R = Camera.main.ScreenPointToRay(TouchLocation);
            RaycastHit HitInfo;

            //If intersection
            if(Physics.Raycast(R, out HitInfo))
            {
                //Click equivalent - call mouse event
                    HitInfo.collider.gameObject.SendMessage("OnMouseDown");
            }
        }
    }
    #endif
}
```

Note   More information on conditional code compilation can be found at: http://docs.unity3d.com/Documentation/Manual/PlatformDependentCompilation.html.

Summary

This chapter marks the end of the input section and also the end of an important section of the book. This chapter concludes our foundations and groundwork section for creating 2D games. What remains is for us to put these skills to the test in creating a small 2D project. This occupies us for the next two chapters (Chapters 10 and 11). Before proceeding further it's worth recapping what we've learned here. By now you should be able to:

- Use the `Input` class with confidence

- Understand how to read raw input from the mouse (clicks and position)

- Read raw input from the keyboard (key presses)

- Create a cursor graphic that tracks mouse movement

- Understand the benefits of abstracting input with virtual axes and buttons

- Read user configurable input with `GetAxis` and `GetButton`

- Understand how to use the Input Manager

- Read input from mobile devices as touch events

- Understand how to map mobile input to mouse input

- Understand how to attach lines of code to specific platforms for conditional compilation

Chapter 10

Getting Started with a 2D Game

By this stage you should have a firm grasp on the most fundamental issues underpinning 2D games in Unity, including procedural geometry, Atlas Textures, UV mapping, orthographic cameras, and 2D input. The preceding chapters focused on each of these issues in isolation, one at a time, and examined their implementation details and specifics. This chapter, and the one that follows, puts these ideas into practice in the form of a 2D game project. Specifically, we'll make a simple 2D card matching game—the kind that tests your memory on position and placement, as we'll see. Take a look at Figure 10-1 to see the project in action. In creating this, we'll put to use all the skills and ideas we've seen so far. Additionally, at the end of this chapter, our project will take an interesting and arguably more complicated twist—one which you may or may not expect. I'll leave that to be a surprise! So let's get started now with our card matching game.

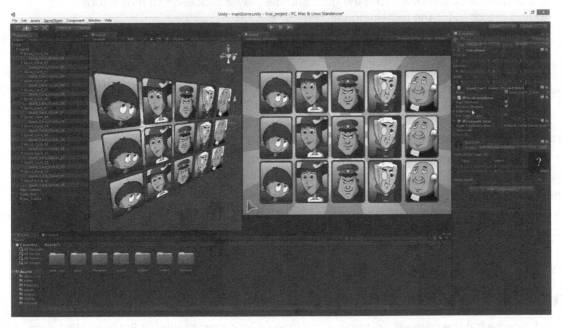

Figure 10-1. The 2D Game Project created in this chapter and the next: a card matching game

Game Design—Card Matching

All games begin from a design, no matter how simple or complex. Sometimes that design may be only in your head, and at other times it'll be encoded in a formal game design document (GDD). For our game we'll make a design document, but a really short one. This document defines the game and its rules. We could approach this document in different ways, including digressing into lengthy descriptions (and that is certainly one method of approaching design). But let's instead take a minimalist design approach instead. Thus, the complete game design is expressed over the following points:

- *Game title*: Match 3 Cards

- *Game description*: This game features a *grid* of custom playing cards arranged in 5×3 rows(5 cards wide and 3 cards tall). There are a total of 5 card types, and the grid features 3 identical copies of each card type. Thus, the grid features 15 cards. The game consists of *rounds* and *turns*. At the beginning of a round the cards are shuffled and arranged randomly in the grid, after which each card is covered by a token so the player cannot know which card is where. The player then takes a turn by picking any one token on the grid to reveal the card beneath. With the card visible the player must then pick subsequent tokens to reveal other cards. The aim of each turn is to consecutively find all three copies of the same card type. If a mistake is made such that the player picks two cards of a different type, the tokens picked for that turn are then returned to the grid to re-cover the cards as before, and the player must try again on a new turn. If the player finds all three copies of the same card type, the cards and their tokens are permanently removed from the grid, and the player proceeds to a new turn to find matches for the remaining card types.

- *Game win condition*: The game is completed when the round is over and all card types have been matched and removed from the grid.

> **Tip**   It's a very easy thing, especially in the world of 2D games, to call a game "simple" or "small" or "little", such as: "oh, that's a *simple little* game!" I recommend avoiding this kind of language and consciousness when creating games. It typically leads to underestimation; to an inability to appraise the true depth and extent of the work involved. This underestimation frequently expresses itself in a lack of prior planning, which so often causes abortive projects: projects that are started but are never finished. So the tip here is: when you make a game, appraise the workload with appropriate focus, outside of aesthetic judgements and platitudes about the supposed simplicity or complexity of the game.

Getting Started with the Game

We've now defined what the game is and how it's played so let's start making it in Unity! We begin (as always) a new Unity project by selecting File ➤ New Project from the application menu and assigning the project a name. For this game, I'll name the project CardMatch (but you can use any name you like), as shown in Figure 10-2. I do not import any packages for this project. The complete files for this chapter can be found in the book companion files at `Project_Files/Chapter10/`.

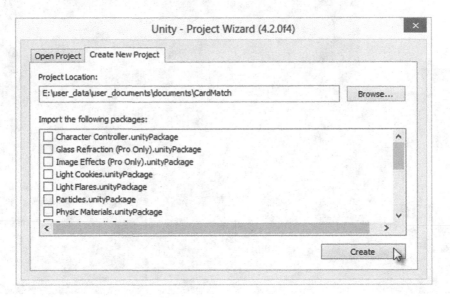

Figure 10-2. Creating a new project for the card matching game

Importing Assets

This game project relies on many different assets; not only on the card and cursor graphics that we'll be using (as shown in Figure 10-1), but also on all the script files for our 2D Editor extensions that we've made throughout this book. Our project uses procedural geometry, atlas textures, UV mapping and more. The total collection of assets we'll use can be found in the course companion files for this chapter at `Project_Files/Chapter10/assets_to_import`. Alternatively, if you've followed along with every chapter, you can import your own script files. So let's import all the assets now. To start with that, I'll create folders in the Project Panel for all the asset types: scripts, scenes, textures, materials, quads, editor, and atlas_data. See Figure 10-3 for the folders I created.

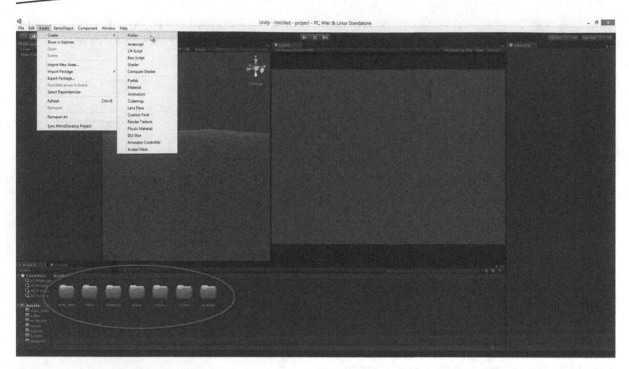

Figure 10-3. *Organizing assets into folders*

Tip   Notice from Figure 10-3 that I'm using the 2D-game interface layout I discussed in Chapters 1 and 2 of this book. By arranging your interface Game and Scenes tabs side by side you often get a more fluid development experience when creating 2D games.

Keeping your assets in different folders is recommended housekeeping. It keeps your project tidy and organized, making it easier for you to work with.

Once the asset folders are created, go ahead and import all the assets into the project using the drag-and-drop method, discussed in Chapter 1. Be sure to import all assets into their respective folders: editor script files inside the editor folder, all PSD texture files inside the textures folder, and so on. As mentioned, all assets for this project are found in the project files at: `Project_Files/Chapter10/assets_to_import`. See Figure 10-4.

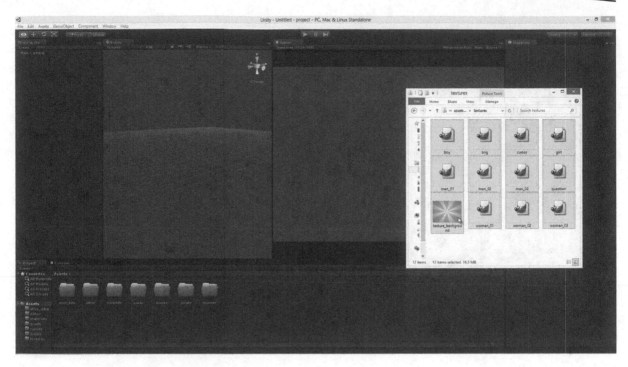

Figure 10-4. Importing assets into the project

> **Note**   The script files contain a Cursor class (cursor.cs) for creating a mouse cursor (this class was
> created in Chapter 9). From Unity 4.1 forward, support has been added for custom cursors with the Cursor
> class. However, I shall use the custom class made for this book to increase compatibility backward to Unity 4.0.

Generating an Atlas Texture

For this project I've actually provided you with more card textures than are really needed—we won't
be using them all. They're included in case you do want to use them, or if you want to expand this
project into something grander. However, because we have all these texture assets (including the
cursor and background graphic), and because we could potentially use them here if we wanted, let's
include them inside one large texture atlas. As explained in Chapter 6, the main reason for using
an atlas is to reduce draw calls and improve render performance (see Chapter 6 for more details).
To generate an atlas we must first have the Atlas Texture editor class (TexturePacker.cs) imported
into the project (inside the editor folder). Then select all the textures inside the Textures folder in the
Project Panel. With the textures selected, choose GameObject ➤ Create Other ➤ Atlas Texture from
the application menu (see Figure 10-5). Accept the default settings and click Create to generate the
atlas. (If the option GameObject ➤ Create Other ➤ Atlas Texture is not visible from the menu, be
sure your TexturePacker class is imported properly).

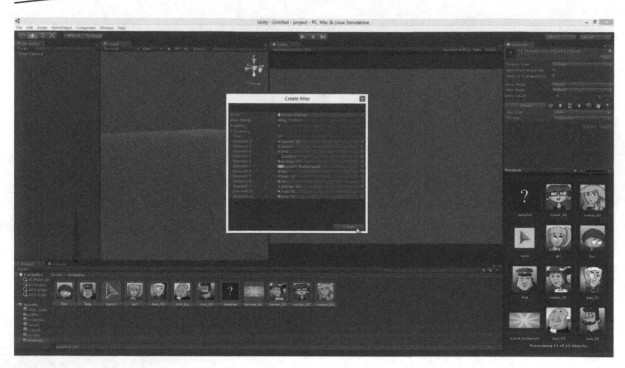

Figure 10-5. Generating an Atlas Texture for the project

Generating an Atlas Texture creates two files: the 4096×4096 Atlas Texture itself, and the atlas meta-data, which includes the UV information for all images within the atlas. Be sure to drag and drop these newly created assets into the atlas_data folder of the project, and if you plan to deploy this game to mobile devices, then check the Atlas Texture size (changing it to 2048 or 1024) for better performance, if applicable. Chapter 13 features more information on mobile development and optimization. For this project, I'll leave the atlas size at 4096×4096.

Generating Card and Cursor Quads

Our game really consists of only eight main elements or objects: five unique card types, one token or cover to conceal each card in the grid, one background element, and one cursor element. Each of these types requires its own Quad mesh—so we need eight Quad meshes. Let's generate these now using our Quad Generator Editor plugin. For each generated Quad, make sure its origin is set to the bottom-left corner (screen-space origin) and its size matches the texture that will be applied to it. Each card graphic and the cover are 150×184 pixels, and the cursor graphic is 64×64 pixels. To start the Quad Generator, select GameObject ➤ Create Other ➤ Custom Plane from the application menu. (Remember, the Quad Generator Editor plugin—CreateQuad.cs—must be imported into the project first). See Figure 10-6.

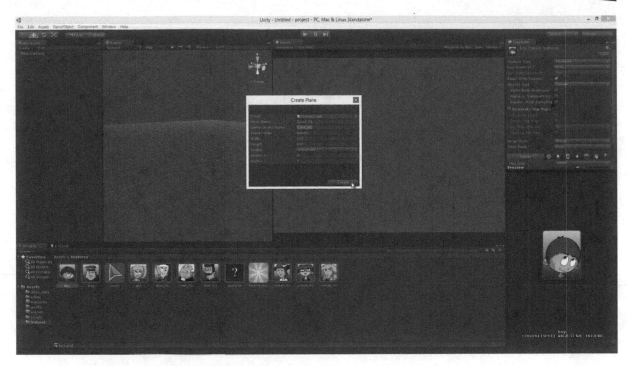

Figure 10-6. Generating textured Quads for game sprites

Assigning Materials and UVs

The Quad generator produces Quad meshes in the project and also instantiates an instance in the scene. The scene now should feature eight new instances, one for each Quad. These should be left as they are and will form the basis of all other objects we'll create for the game. If you've already deleted these objects from the scene, don't worry—you can simply instantiate new instances by dragging and dropping the Quad mesh assets from the Project Panel and into the scene via the Viewport. By default, these objects are created with a default purple color applied to them. This signifies the objects have no valid material applied. We'll fix that issue now as well as assign each object the appropriate texture from the atlas. Start by creating a new material, choosing Assets ➤ Create ➤ Material from the application menu (name it mat_atlas). Move this material to the material folder in the Project Panel if necessary. Once the material is created, assign it an Unlit ➤ Transparent Cutout Shader in the Object Inspector, and select the Atlas Texture for the Base RGB slot. See Figure 10-7.

Figure 10-7. Creating a transparent Cutout material for the Atlas Texture. Notice from the Hierarchy Panel how I've given all objects in the scene meaningful names

After the material is created it should be assigned to all Quad objects in the scene, including the Cursor object (unless you're using the native Unity cursor class). Doing this assigns the atlas to each object, but no object appears correctly because its UV mapping is not yet configured. To fix this, we'll use the UV Mapping Editor extension created back in Chapter 7. Ensure this editor extension (UVEdit.cs) is added to the project. See Figure 10-8 to see the UV mess we get by default when assigning our material to the Quads in the scene, without UV mapping.

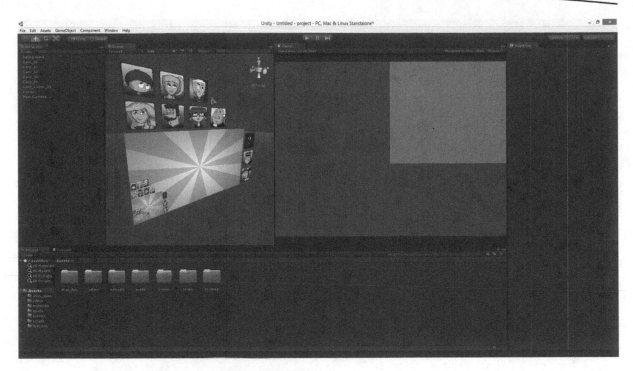

Figure 10-8. Assigning the Cutout material to the scene objects

Access the UV Editor by selecting Window ➤ Atlas Texture Editor from the application menu. Load-in the atlas data by dragging and dropping the `atlas_data` object (created by `TexturePacker.cs`) from the Project Panel into the Atlas Object field of the Atlas Texture Editor. The Editor reads the atlas meta-data and allows us to pick textures inside the Atlas from a drop-down list. Go ahead and select each object in the scene, assigning it the appropriate texture from the atlas. The scene, of course, contains fewer card types than we have images in the atlas, meaning that you'll need to make decisions about which graphics you want to use for the cards. You can see my choices in Figure 10-9.

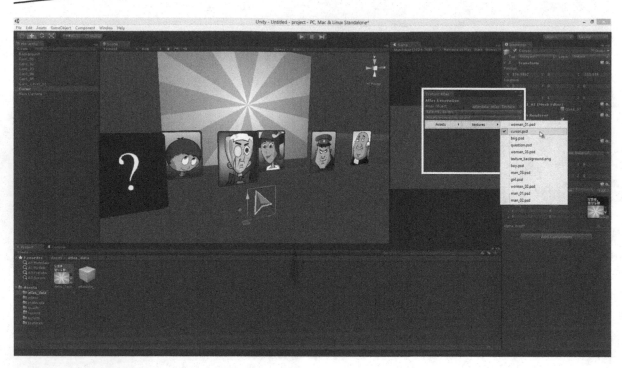

Figure 10-9. Assign objects in the scene textures from the atlas

Note   The Card Cover object is associated with the Question.psd material. This is because it shows a question mark icon as it covers the card behind.

Feel free to transform your objects away from each other to assign them textures more easily. The positions of objects in the scene are not important at this stage: we'll transform them into position later.

Camera and Resolution

Things are looking good with the project so far! The scene camera is still not correctly configured. We saw how to do this in Chapter 9, but we'll cover how to do it here in summary. The resolution for this game is the "famous" 800×600, which was often the default resolution for games in the late '90s. So set the resolution to 800×600 either from the Player Settings dialog, accessible via the application menu at Edit ➤ Project Settings ➤ Player, or via the Game tab through the Aspect drop-down list on the toolbar. See Figure 10-10.

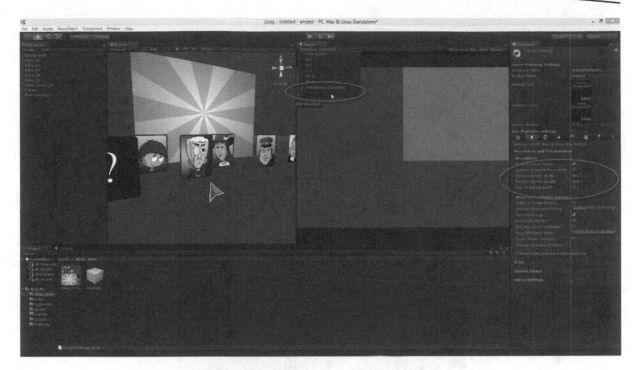

Figure 10-10. Setting the game resolution to 800×600

The resolution is set and the Game tab resizes its boundaries to match, giving us a clearer picture of how the final game will look. But there's still no 1:1 correspondence between world space and screen space: that is, Unity Units do not currently correspond to Pixels. We'll fix this through a two-step process using the scene camera. First, select the camera in the scene and choose Orthographic from the Projection field in the Object Inspector. Then second, set the camera size to 300 (which is half the vertical resolution). See Figure 10-11. Doing this displays the scene at its native pixel resolution.

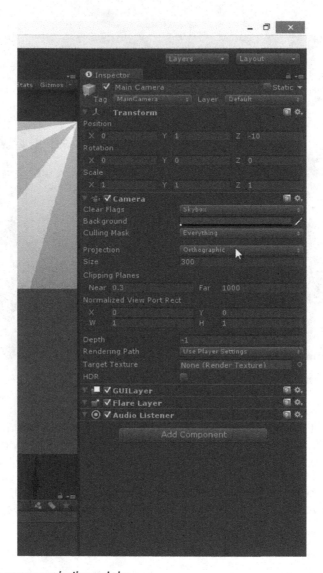

Figure 10-11. Configuring the camera projection and size

Let's not forget to offset the camera position to align the world and screen space origins. This means that objects positioned at (0,0,0) in world space will appear at position (0,0) in screen space. In this case, the screen space origin is at the bottom-left corner of the screen. To offset the camera, set its X position to 400, and its Y position to 300. In addition, adjust its Z position to pull the camera backward in the scene so its viewing frustum contains all the 2D objects we expect to see (after all, even orthographic cameras cannot see what's behind them!). See Figure 10-12. Once you've done this, you've just configured your game project ready for development. You'll see that it took us quite a few steps to get there: and part of this comes because we're configuring a 3D engine to act apart from its default behaviour as a 2D engine. Even so, you could shorten this process a little for your future projects, simply by configuring all the generalizable aspects (such as camera configuration) in a template project, which you copy and paste as the starting point for all your subsequent 2D projects.

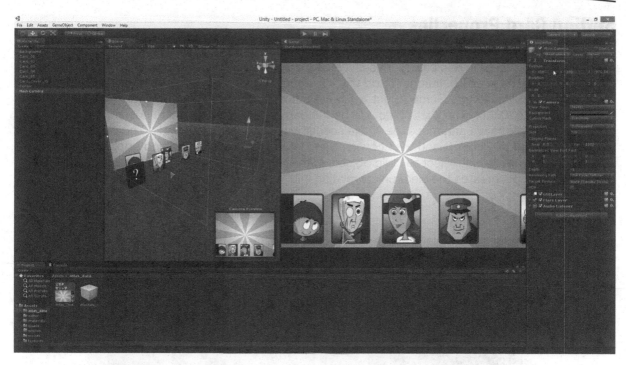

Figure 10-12. Positioning the camera for a 2D project. Our project is now configured for development

> **Note**   You can also transfer assets between projects using Asset Packages. You can export your scenes and
> assets and transfer them to a separate project. To export a package, select your assets in the Project Panel,
> and then choose Assets ➤ Export Package from the application menu.

Configuring the Scene—Setting Up the Cards

The development of a 2D Unity project can be broken into two distinct phases: the first is about
configuring the environment and tools for a 2D work-flow, and the second is about implementing
the project itself. We've now completed the first phase (in configuring our Quads, Atlas Textures,
and Cameras), and it's the second phase that'll occupy us for the remainder of the chapter. The
first issue we'll address is configuring the main objects in the scene: namely, the cards and the card
covers. The scene features five unique card objects, and one card cover. Each of the five cards
will be duplicated so the scene features three copies of each card, and the cover object will be
duplicated so that each card has its own cover. We could do this duplication right now, but there are
some properties that we need to set for each card first. By setting these properties first, we'll ensure
the properties are copied over to any duplicates we make after.

Setting Card Properties

The scene right now features five unique card objects, soon to be duplicated to give us three copies of each type (a total of fifteen cards). This is a reasonable number of objects, and so we should start organizing the scene hierarchy. To do this, I'll create two new objects in the scene: root and cards. I do this by selecting GameObject ➤ Create Empty from the application menu. I'll also set their positions to (0,0,0). The Root object will be the parent of all objects in the scene (including the camera). This means we can move the whole scene by moving the root object. The Cards object will be the parent of all cards and their covers. See Figure 10-13. Go ahead and apply this structure to your objects now—just select all child objects in the Hierarchy Panel and drag them onto their parents. Doing this creates the hierarchical relationship.

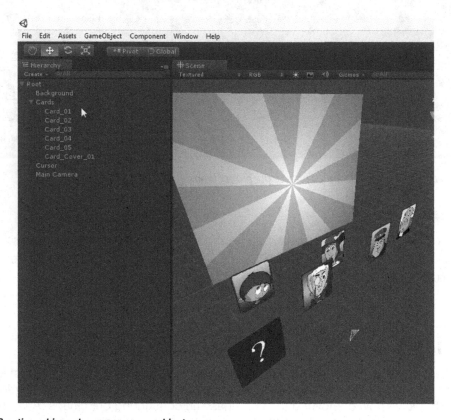

Figure 10-13. *Creating a hierarchy among scene objects*

Let's also tag all card objects (not the card cover) with the same tag "Card." Why? Because this will help us later in script whenever we need access to an array of all card objects in the scene. Unity offers us functions for getting sorted lists of objects by tag name. To create a tag for our cards, click the Tag drop-down list from the top-right corner of the interface (in the Object Inspector), and select the option Add Tag (see Figure 10-14).

Figure 10-14. Accessing the Tag Editor

Type in a name for the Tag (Card) and then assign that to all card objects in the scene. To do that, select all cards and then choose the Card tag from the Tag drop down list. This tags all the selected cards with the chosen tag (see Figure 10-15).

Figure 10-15. Assign the Card tag to the cards

> **Tip**   Give the Card colliders some depth in the Z axis to make collision detection easier.

Next I'll remove the Box Collider from the `Card Cover` object (we won't need it), and then I'll duplicate the object four more times so that each of the five card types has a card cover to match. Notice that I removed the Box Collider before duplicating so that I wouldn't have to remove it five times—once for each duplicate. See Figure 10-16.

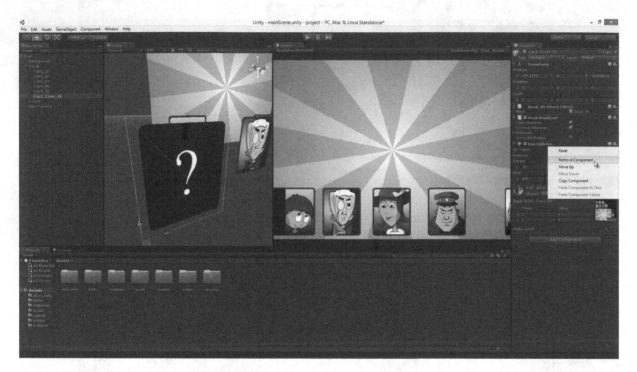

Figure 10-16. Remove unnecessary colliders from objects

> **Note**   While we're removing colliders from the card covers, let's also remove colliders from the cursor and the background objects, leaving only the colliders on the cards. We'll need the card colliders to detect mouse clicks. But otherwise, we won't need colliders at all. It's good practice to remove any components and functionality that you don't need.

Positioning and Arranging the Cards

Let's position all five cards in the scene to form the top row of the card grid, trying to keep the alignment and spacing we'll want for the final game. Ensure all cards are exactly level on the Z axis (depth) and Y axis—all cards should exist on the same plane. Take a look at Figure 10-17. For me, the Z value is –200, and the Y value is 407. You don't need to match these values exactly, as long as your arrangement looks like something close to Figure 10-17.

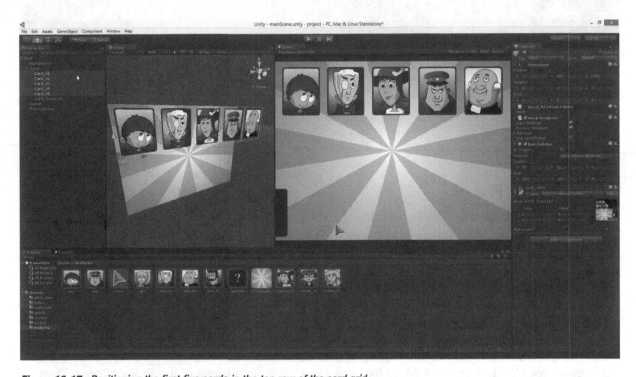

Figure 10-17. Positioning the first five cards in the top row of the card grid

Now position each of the cards covers in place, covering the cards. Make sure each card cover is covering exactly one card and is positioned further forward in the scene, toward the camera (in the Z axis), so it's drawn in front of the cards. The cards should match the same X and Y values of the cards they cover. Once you've configured this, make each cover object a child object of the card it's covering: use the scene hierarchy to parent the cover object to its card. You can always test to make sure you've gotten the relationship correct: when you transform (move) a card, the card cover will move with it. This is because child objects transform relative to parents. This grouping relationship between the card and cover will be useful later. Take a look at Figure 10-18.

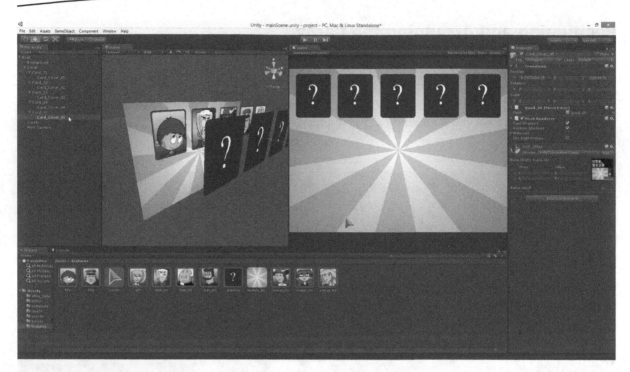

Figure 10-18. Positioning the card covers over the cards in the top row of the card grid

Positioning and Arranging the Cards—Starting

Before we duplicate the rows of cards downward, along with their covers, there's a script we should add to the cards to control their behavior during the game. Again, it's good practice to add the script before the duplication to ensure duplicates retain the script component. It is possible to copy and paste components from one object to another after duplication, but getting it right first time makes our lives easier. Create a new C# Script file Card.cs in the Scripts folder of the Project Panel. Then open the file in MonoDevelop.

Each and every card during our game can be in one of three potential states (the ActiveState). These states are

- **Concealed:** The default state for a card. In this state, the card is present on the grid but is being hidden from the player by a covering card. The player hasn't picked this card yet during the selection process.

- **Revealed:** Here, the card is present on the grid and is currently being shown to the player. A card enters this state when it's selected by a player (who removes the covering card) and then continues to select other cards to find a match. If the player subsequently fails to find a match by making a mistake and selecting a nonmatching card, then a Revealed card reverts to the Concealed state, meaning the player must begin their turn over.

- **Hidden:** When the player matches three identical cards successfully in a turn, those cards are removed from the grid and hidden from view for the rest of the game. This state is the Hidden state.

To code this functionality, take a look at the complete code in Listing 10-1.

Listing 10-1. Card.cs

```
using UnityEngine;
using System.Collections;

public class Card : MonoBehaviour
{
    //Card States
    public enum CARD_STATE {CARD_CONCEALED = 0, CARD_REVEALED = 1, CARD_HIDDEN = 2};

    //Current State for Card - read only
    public CARD_STATE ActiveState = CARD_STATE.CARD_CONCEALED;

    //Z Position States for card and covers - (X = Card Z Pos, Y = Cover Z Pos)
    public Vector2[] ZPosStates = new Vector2[3];

    //Cached transform for card
    private Transform CardTransform = null;

    //Cache transform for card cover
    private Transform CoverTransform = null;

    void Awake()
    {
        //Cache Card Transform
        CardTransform = transform;

        //Cache cover transform
        CoverTransform = CardTransform.GetChild(0).transform;
    }

    //Function to set card state
    public void SetCardState(CARD_STATE State = CARD_STATE.CARD_CONCEALED)
    {
        //Update State
        ActiveState = State;

        //Set Positions
        CardTransform.localPosition = new Vector3(CardTransform.localPosition.x, CardTransform.
localPosition.y, ZposStates[(int)ActiveState].x);

        CoverTransform.localPosition = new Vector3(CoverTransform.localPosition.x, CoverTransform.
localPosition.y, ZPosStates[(int)ActiveState].y);
    }
}
```

You might initially think this class rather is strangely implemented. Sure, it features the ActiveState member to keep track of the current card state (Concealed, Revealed, and Hidden). These state values are defined by the CARD_STATE enumeration. This much is to be expected perhaps. But what's strange is the implementation of SetCardState. Specifically, it's the way this code goes about hiding the card and covers from view as it changes state. If the player picks a card on the grid, the cover must hide to reveal the card behind. If the player makes a successful match, then both the card and its cover must hide because they are removed from the game. Now, Unity offers us various methods for hiding objects in a scene: we can deactivate a game object with Monobehaviour.SetActive, and we can also disable MeshRenderers. Both of these can hide an object from view. But the code in Listing 10-1 uses neither of these "standard" methods. Instead, it hides a card (or a cover) from view by transforming it out of view of the camera, to a nonvisible part of the scene.

It achieves this by maintaining a public ZPosStates array variable. This is a three-element array of 2D Vectors. Each of these three vectors map to the three states for a card (Concealed, Revealed and Hidden). For each state, the vector X Component represents the Z position for a card, and the Y component represents the Z position for a card cover on the same state. When a card changes state, the SetCardState function updates the position of the card and cover based on the ZPosStates. So why have I implemented card visibility by manipulating a transform component, as opposed to using the other methods? The answer to this question will be revealed in the next chapter. For now it's enough to know that it works and how it works.

Positioning and Arranging the Cards—Completing

Be sure to assign the script file (Card.cs) to each card in the scene, and then fill in the ZPosStates in the Object Inspector. The array elements correspond to each state. ZPosStates[0] is Concealed, ZPosStates[1] is Revealed, and ZPosStates[2] is Hidden. The Z Values for the card and cover on the Concealed state will be their default positions: when the cover and card are in front of the camera, but the cover is concealing the card. You can fill in these values by simply copying and pasting their current Z values into ZPosStates[0]. For the Revealed state: the card maintains its Z value, but the cover does not. So move the card cover backward on the Z axis until it's out view of the camera, copy its position, undo the transform to return the cover back to its default position, and then paste the value into ZPosStates[1].y to set its off-screen position. Repeat this procedure for ZPosStates[2] where both the card and cover are off-screen (see Figure 10-19).

Remember   You only need to complete the ZPosStates array for one card, and not all five cards. You can copy and paste Component values between objects. To do this, click the cog icon of the component and choose Copy. Then select a different card object, click its cog icon and choose Paste Component Values. Figure 10-19 shows this menu at work.

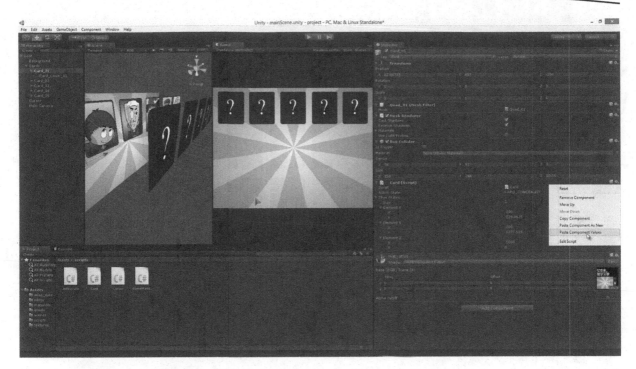

Figure 10-19. Configuring the Z values for the card and covers

Once you've applied the position settings to each card through the Card component, select all five cards in the top row and duplicate them twice (translating them in place) to create two additional rows below, as shown in Figure 10-20. This completes the card grid of 5×3. Be sure to rename any objects in the hierarchy to keep a consistent and meaningful naming system. Use the Batch Rename tool, as coded in Chapter 4, if required.

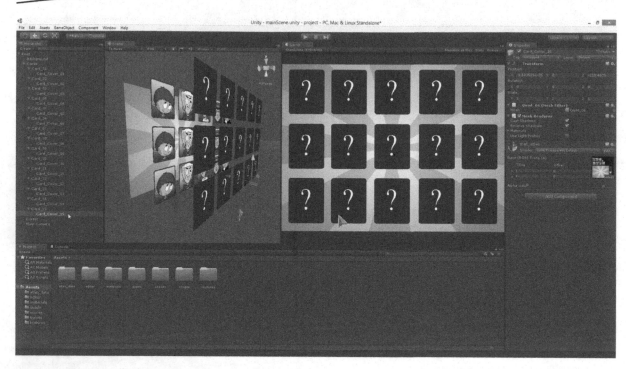

Figure 10-20. Duplicating the cards in place to create a card grid

The Game Manager

In terms of software design, the Game Manager class is prevalent in games: it's typically a singleton object that sits in the background and manages the game rules. The Game Manager does not correspond to something tangible in the level, like an enemy or vehicle or power-up. Rather, it codifies the unseen force that makes everything in the game hang together cohesively. Our card matching game will need a Game Manager class. Specifically, the role of this class will be to manage the player turns. This involves:

- Shuffling the cards in the grid at the start of game-play. This is to ensure the player gets a different arrangement of cards every time they play.

- Validating player input. Checking to see which card they selected and whether they matched three cards or made a mistake.

- Respond to player input. If the player matches three cards, the Game Manager is responsible for removing the matched cards from the grid. If the player makes a mistake, the manager will reset the turn and restore the covers to the cards.

To create the GameManager for our project, create a new C# file (GameManager.cs) in the scripts folder, and then assign this script to the root object in the scene. You can assign it to any active object in the scene—it doesn't have to be the root object. But (if you do choose a different object) it should be one that is created at the start of a scene, remains constantly active throughout the scene, and only terminates when the scene ends.

Shuffling the Cards

Shuffling refers to the process of creating randomization. In our case therefore, shuffling the cards is about reordering them in the grid behind the card covers so the player cannot predict which card will be where. In situations like this where randomness is required, the Unity Random class comes to the rescue. Take a look at Listing 10-2 to see the GameManager's Shuffle function. Note: this function is part of a larger class for which I have not given the complete source code. This is not an attempt on my part at obfuscation, but rather the reverse. The complete code for GameManager is too long to list here to be helpful. It is included in the chapter companion files, along with all source code for the project. Here, I list the highlights and key features of the class.

Listing 10-2. GameManager.cs—Shuffling the Cards

```
//Resets and Shuffles Cards
public void Shuffle()
{
//Reset all cards to starting states
//public member CardObjects is a list of all cards in scene
//This is is retrieved with:
//CardObjects = GameObject.FindGameObjectsWithTag("Card") as GameObject[];

foreach(GameObject CardObject in CardObjects)
    CardObject.SendMessage("SetCardState", Card.CARD_STATE.CARD_CONCEALED,
SendMessageOptions.DontRequireReceiver);

    //Cycle through all cards and exchange
    foreach(GameObject Card in CardObjects)
    {
        //Get Transform
        Transform CardTransform = Card.transform;

        //Get another random card to exchange position
        Transform ExchangeTransform = CardObjects[Mathf.FloorToInt(Random.Range(0,
CardObjects.Length-1))].transform;

        //Exchange positions
        Vector3 TmpPosition = CardTransform.localPosition;

        CardTransform.localPosition = ExchangeTransform.localPosition;
        ExchangeTransform.localPosition = TmpPosition;
    }
}
```

The Shuffle function iterates through all 15 cards in the scene and, for each card, exchanges its position with another randomly selected card in the grid. In this code it is possible for a card to randomly pick itself as a target for exchange, in which case the card will remain unmoved. To randomly select a card, it uses the Random.Range function, which is a method of the Random class. More information about Random can be found in the Unity documentation here: http://docs.unity3d.com/Documentation/ScriptReference/Random.html In short, the Range method picks a number at random between a minimum and maximum, inclusive.

One important feature of the code in Listing 10-2 is its use of the localPosition variable for setting the position of an object. An alternative is to use the position variable. So what is the difference between localPosition and position? In short, setting position moves an object to an absolute world position, as measured from the world origin. Setting localposition moves an object relative to its parent's position, which may or may not be at the world origin.

Note   The function Shuffle in Listing 10-2 is called internally by the GameManager at game play start to randomize the card grid.

Handling User Input

Another responsibility of the Game Manager is to handle and respond to user input. In our card selection game, user input consists only in picking cards from the grid. This input can be provided by mouse clicks or touch screen taps. Listing 10-3 shows you the input handler for the Game Manager.

Listing 10-3. GameManager.cs—Handling User Input

```
//Handle user input
public void HandleInput()
{
    //Ignore disabled input
    if(!InputEnabled) return;

    //Ignore if no input
    if(!Input.GetMouseButtonDown(0) && Input.touchCount <= 0) return;

    //Tap Position
    Vector3 TapPosition = Vector3.zero;

    //Handle desktop input
#if UNITY_STANDALONE || UNITY_WEBPLAYER
    TapPosition = Input.mousePosition;
#endif

    //Handle mobile input
#if UNITY_IPHONE || UNITY_ANDROID || UNITY_WP8
    Touch T = Input.GetTouch(0);

    if(T.phase == TouchPhase.Began)
        TapPosition = T.position;
    else
        return; //Not required touch type
#endif

    //Generate ray from touch position
    Ray R = Camera.main.ScreenPointToRay(TapPosition);
```

```
    //Get hits in scene to detect card selection
    RaycastHit[] Hits;

    Hits = Physics.RaycastAll(R);

    //Cycle through hits
    foreach(RaycastHit H in Hits)
    {
        //Play step
        PickCard (H.collider.gameObject);
        UpdateTurn(H.collider.gameObject);
        return;
    }
}
```

Much of this code has already been touched on in Chapter 9 when considering user input. When a user clicks a card in the grid, it selects that card and calls the UpdateTurn function to determine whether the selected card matches any previously selected cards. Notice how this code maps touch and mouse input together.

Turn Management

The game unfolds through turns. A *turn* is a moment when the player makes choices from among the cards in the grid to find a three-card match. Their first choice is given for free, meaning they are permitted to choose any card. And their second and third choices are regulated to see whether they match with the original choice. A Turn is complete when the player either fails to make a match, or when the player matches all three cards. The GameManager keeps track of turns through two main functions: StartTurn and UpdateTurn. See Listing 10-4.

> **Tip**   I recommend reading Listing 10-4 (and its explanation) with the card matching project open.

Listing 10-4. GameManager.cs—Handling Turns

```
//Function to start new turn for player
public void StartTurn()
{
    //Reset Step Counter
    TurnStep = 0;

    //Clear Selected Array
    for(int i = 0; i<SelectedCards.Length; i++)
        SelectedCards[i]=null;
}
```

```
//---------------------------------------
//Function to Update Turn
public void UpdateTurn(GameObject PickedCard)
{
    //Add card to selected array
    SelectedCards[TurnStep] = PickedCard;

    //Increment turn step
    ++TurnStep;

    //Should we exit now?
    if(TurnStep <= 1) return;

    //If picked more than one card in sequence, then check is the same
    if(SelectedCards[TurnStep-1].GetComponent<MeshFilter>().mesh.name != SelectedCards[TurnStep-2].
GetComponent<MeshFilter>().mesh.name)
    {
        //Is not same. Player made mistake. Reset turn.
        StartCoroutine(LoseTurn());
        return;
    }

    //Player made successful match. Is end of turn?
    if(TurnStep >= NumMatches)
    {
        //Player made all matches. Move to next turn
        StartCoroutine(WinTurn());
    }
}
```

The GameManager calls StartTurn at the beginning of each new turn to reset its internal variables that keep track of player progress. Specifically, it maintains two variables TurnStep and SelectedCards. Both these variables are reset and cleared inside StartTurn. TurnStep is an integer variable that ranges from 0–3. The 0 means the player is making their first choice of card from the grid; 1 means the first choice has been made and they are now making their second choice, and so on. The array SelectedCards is three elements in length and is a list of all cards selected by the player for this turn. This array is used on each call to UpdateTurn to see whether the player has matched cards. The last selected element in this variable is always expressed by TurnStep.

The UpdateTurn function is called on each TurnStep- after every card selection. Here, the SelectedCards array is queried for the latest card selected to see whether there is a match. The match detection works by testing whether any two selected cards are based on the same mesh asset. This works because all cards of the same type are instances of the same mesh.

Summary

Great work! You've reached this point and the card matching game is working. I recommend taking a careful look over the sample project for this chapter to see the game in action and give it a test run. See Figure 10-21. Together the GameManager and Card script file provide the core functionality for the game. They make it work, but, of course, the game is not without problems or limitations. One bug is that the player might click on the same card in the grid multiple times, and the GameManager recognizes these as separate selections. This makes it possible to cheat—you can fool the Game Manager into thinking you matched three cards when all you really did was click the same card three times. This bug can be fixed easily by temporarily disabling the Box Collider on the card while the player selects other cards, or by checking the card state before flipping, preventing Unity from detecting the click (make sure you restore the Box Collider again when the turn is over!).

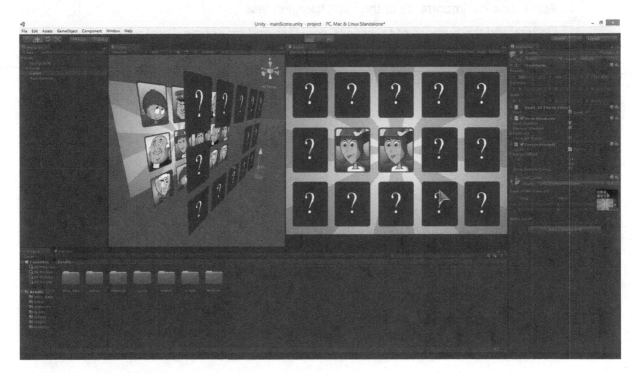

Figure 10-21. The card matching game in action

However I said also there'd be a twist to this chapter, and this points back to some coding decisions I made in Listing 10-1 in which I concealed objects by moving them off-screen with a Transform component, as opposed to using other methods or components. Specifically, we're now going to extend this game by adding networked multi-player functionality. This will allow two people to play the card matching game in turns across multiple computers, either through the same local network or via the Internet. In doing this, each player can see the actions of the other, allowing complete interactivity between the two computers. Before moving on to implement this however, let's recap what we've learned in this chapter. By now you should be able to:

- Confidently config and prepare 2D Game Projects
- Understand how to effectively asset manage your project
- Appreciate the need for naming conventions
- Copy and paste components from one object to another
- Create design documents for your game
- Break down the concepts of your game into modules or blocks that are amenable to code and object-oriented design
- Appreciate the importance of the Game Manager class
- Understand the purpose of transform.position and transform.localposition
- Make effective use of scene hierarchies
- Understand how to remove unnecessary components such as colliders from your projects

11

Completing the 2D Card Game

This chapter resumes from where the previous ended. It assumes you've been working through the card game project and that you now have a working version. This version is currently a single player game where the player must find three card matches within a grid of cards. If you don't have a project to work with, you can start from the project files I've created, found in the book companion files at Project_Files/Chapter11/Project. Figure 11-1 shows the project created so far. In this chapter we'll transform that single-player project into a networked multi-player version. In short, we'll adapt the project so two players across either a local network or the Internet can play the same game together, with each player participating in turns and being able to see the actions of the other player on their turn. To achieve this, we'll make use of the Unity API and its range of networking classes. Specifically, we'll examine a trio of classes: the Network class, the MasterServer class and the NetworkView class.

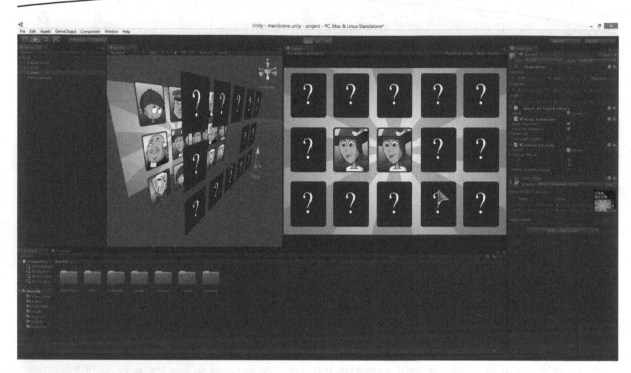

Figure 11-1. The 2D game project created so far. In this chapter, we'l make it a multi-player game

Networking in Unity — Getting Started

If you ever make a game where two or more players, on separate computers, must play and interact together in real-time as though they shared the same game world, you'll need to use the Unity Networking functionality. In short, the networking classes make it possible to distribute or share a virtual world across computers and locations. In the context of our card matching game, we'll want to share the card grid arrangement across computers, as well as the actions of each player as they go about their turn. This is to make sure both players are synchronized and know what their opponent is doing and when it's their time to take a turn. Here, each player will take their turn in selecting cards from the grid to make a three-card match. While one player selects cards, the opponent will watch and learn. If the player makes a mistake by selecting wrongly, control will switch over to the opponent, who makes their choices while the opponent watches on. For every successful three- card match, the player increases their score, and the winner is the player with highest score when all cards have been matched. So let's get started at making our game multi-player in this way.

To start, I'll open up the card-matching project we've created so far and add a new C# script file to the project named NetworkedGame.cs. See Figure 11-2. This class is responsible for establishing and maintaining a connection between all the computers involved in the game. For our purposes this will be only two computers (it's a two-player game), but Unity games are not limited to this number. Remember to attach your script file to an object in the scene—I've attached it to the Root object, which also features the GameManager script.

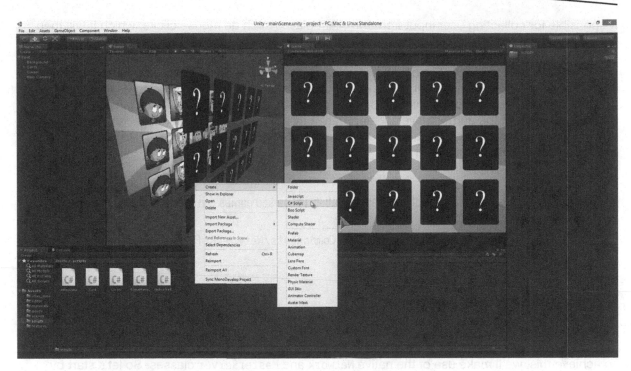

Figure 11-2. Adding a NetworkedGame.cs file for handling network connection functionality

Whenever two or more computers should connect for a game, a relationship needs to be established between the computers. This is so they can exchange data reliably, both about the players and about what's happening in the game. This relationship introduces two critical concepts to networking: *client* and *server*. These terms will be discussed briefly here and their function and purpose will become clearer as we progress in the chapter.

- **Server:** When two or more computers connect, one and only one is the server. This computer acts as the host for the game and is, in effect, the master of ceremonies. Just as the host of a dinner party picks and chooses their guests along with the entertainment for the evening. The server can also be a player in the game—it is not excluded from playing. But the chief role of the server is to be the authority or lifeline for the game.

- **Client:** Every player in a multi-player game is a client (except for the server). Players join a networked game by connecting to the server. The server validates and authenticates the clients, and allows them to join the game if they're authorized. This means that none of the clients in a networked game ever connect directly to each other—even though it may seem that way to the gamer. The clients interact with each other only through the server, which acts like a central switchboard for the game.

Given these terms and their definitions then, our card matching game (which is two-player) requires one machine to act as a server, and the other to act as a client. The server hosts the game, and the client connects to the server to join in and play. The server for our game is an *authoritative server*. This means the instance of the game running on the client machine is lightweight. It's really only responsible for collecting user input from the client player, such as mouse clicks, which it will then forward onto the server machine who processes that input as normal, updates the game world, and then sends the latest world information back to the client so both players have a synchronized game world and experience. The client system cannot update or change the game world in any autonomous or local way and so it will never be possible for any player's world to deviate from the server's version. This approach will work fine for our card matching game: but for larger games that transmit more data, the authoritative server model may not be the optimal choice, in which case you'll need to get more inventive about how to send data between computers. Here however, we'll focus on the authoritative server model.

Note More in-depth and technical information on Unity networked games can be found in the Unity API documentation here:

http://docs.unity3d.com/Documentation/Components/NetworkReferenceGuide.html

---

Establishing a Server

The NetworkGame.cs script file that we added to the project in the previous section contain all the networking code responsible for establishing a client–server relationship between the two players. To achieve this, we'll make use of the native Network and MasterServer classes. So let's start by adding a function to our NetworkedGame class called BeServer. This function, when called, will make the running instance of our game act as a server and host for the game: that means it'll be the kind of game that will listen for connecting clients and will accept them to join the game. Take a look at Listing 11-1 to see the full source code for this function.

Listing 11-1. NetworkedGame.cs—BeServer

```
public class NetworkedGame : MonoBehaviour
{
    //Be server
    public void BeServer()
    {
        Debug.Log("being server");
        //Create server
        Network.InitializeServer(2, 25000, !Network.HavePublicAddress());

        //Register as host for a game
        MasterServer.RegisterHost("UNITY2D_TILEMATCH_01", "TurnGame_01", "Test for Unity 2D Game
Book");
    }
}
```

Note that the BeServer function is not called during the class Start function (there's no Start function), which means (right now) that BeServer is never called. That's fine for now: it's intentional. Here, I just want to show you what the function looks like and how you can set-up a server quickly and easily. The BeServer function firstly calls Network.InitializeServer to configure the running instance as a server. Calling this function (on its own) in no way changes how the game behaves: the game continues to run much as it would have done had this function not been called. But now the game is classified (by the Network class) as a server, which means it listens for clients and can accept their connections.

The next line calls MasterServer.RegisterHost. This line is, in fact, optional; but it's useful nonetheless! The MasterServer class makes use of a server, hosted by Unity Technologies, which acts like a public registry or database of currently active servers for Unity games. The RegisterHost function publishes your server and game information into that database for as long as your server is active. This makes it easier for clients (ones who are seeking to join your game) to search for and find your servers. It saves you from having to host your own dedicated servers (in many cases) or from players having to manually type-in IP addresses. Thus, in just two lines of code the BeServer function establishes the game as a server and publishes this fact to the MasterServer where it can be found by clients.

Notice that RegisterHost in Listing 11-1 registered the game type under the ID of UNITY2D_TILEMATCH_01, and gave this running instance a Name of TurnGame_01. This means the currently running server instance is named TurnGame_01 and it's a game type UNITY2D_TILEMATCH_01. Thus, it's possible to register multiple hosts (of different names) under the same game type.

Establishing a Client

The NetworkGame.cs script file also features support for a BeClient function to make the running instance a client that connects to an established server. To become a client, however, a server must already exist: without servers there can be no clients. So in addition to a BeClient function (which will connect to a server), we'll also need a function to scan the MasterServer listings to find an appropriate server to connect with—namely a server of type UNITY2D_TILEMATCH_01. If such a server exists, we can establish a connection; otherwise there is no server to connect with. Thus, we'll also code a RefreshHostList function, to scan the MasterServer. This can be seen in Listing 11-2.

Listing 11-2. NetworkedGame.cs—RefreshHostList

```
//Function refresh to host list
public void RefreshHostList()
{
    //Clear any existing host list
    MasterServer.ClearHostList();

    //Populate new host list for game type
    MasterServer.RequestHostList("UNITY2D_TILEMATCH_01");
}
```

The RequestHostList function sends a request to the MasterServer to retrieve a list of all hosts registered with the specified game type. This function executes asynchronously, because it's polling a remote address, and thus it exits without returning a value and provides no host list. This means that, after calling RequestHostList, we have to wait until Unity "contacts us back" with the complete host list that we requested. It does this by calling the OnMasterServerEvent, and any class implementing this function will receive a call from the MasterServer when the host list has been retrieved. We can implement this event (along with the BeClient function) as follows in Listing 11-3, which is the complete listing for the NetworkedGame class.

Listing 11-3. NetworkedGame.cs—Complete Class Listing

```csharp
using UnityEngine;
using System.Collections;

public class NetworkedGame : MonoBehaviour
{
    //-------------------------------------------
    // Use this for initialization
    void Start ()
    {
        //Refresh host list
        RefreshHostList();
    }
    //-------------------------------------------
    //Function refresh to host list
    public void RefreshHostList()
    {
        //Clear any existing host list
        MasterServer.ClearHostList();

        //Populate new host list for game type
        MasterServer.RequestHostList("UNITY2D_TILEMATCH_01");
    }
    //-------------------------------------------
    //Called when object is destroyed
    void OnDestroy()
    {
        //Disconnect
        Network.Disconnect();

        //Unregister from Master Server
        if(Network.isServer)
            MasterServer.UnregisterHost();
    }
    //-------------------------------------------
    //Be server
    public void BeServer()
    {
        print ("being server");
        //Create server
        Network.InitializeServer(2, 25000, !Network.HavePublicAddress());

        //Register as host for a game
        MasterServer.RegisterHost("UNITY2D_TILEMATCH_01", "TurnGame_01", "Test for Unity 2D Game
Book");
    }
    //-------------------------------------------
    //Be client
    public void BeClient()
    {
        print ("being client");
```

```
    //Get Host data
    HostData[] HD = MasterServer.PollHostList();

    //Exit. No host found
    if(HD.Length <= 0) return;

    //Connect to first host
    Network.Connect(HD[0]);
}
//----------------------------------------
//Called on feedback from master server
void OnMasterServerEvent(MasterServerEvent msEvent)
{
    switch(msEvent)
    {
        //Called when host list is received from server
        case MasterServerEvent.HostListReceived:

        //If we are already a client or server, then ignore
        if(Network.isClient || Network.isServer) return;

        //We receive host list. Now Check for existing hosts

        //If no current hosts, then be server
        if(MasterServer.PollHostList().Length <= 0)
            BeServer(); //Act as a new host
        else
            BeClient(); //Connect to existing host

        break;
    }
}
//----------------------------------------

}
```

Let's discuss how this class works. By using this class and adding it to your project you will establish the running instance as either a client or server application. This allows you to create a connection between two players. The following points detail the core features of this class.

- The Start function calls the RefreshHostsLists function to retrieve a list of all hosts for the game type. It does this so that, if a host already exists, it will make the current instance a client and connect to the server. If no hosts for the game type exist, then it makes this running instance a server. This means that if you run two instances of this game, the first instance will become the server and the second will become the client.

- The function OnMasterServerEvent is called when a host list is retrieved from the MasterServer. By handling the MasterServerEvent.HostListReceived event, this class determines whether the running instance should be a client or server, depending on whether any hosts were found.

- The function `BeClient` is used to connect to the first host in the retrieved list. In your production code, it's unlikely you'll always want to connect to only the first host. You'll probably want to offer the player a choice of host to connect with. But for this card game we can use simply the first host.

- The function `OnDestroy` is the familiar destroy event, called when an object is removed from the scene. It's used here to disconnect from the server and the Unity Master Server. If you're connecting to a server, always be sure to include a corresponding disconnection call when it's time to disconnect.

Testing Networked Functionality

Let's now take our Unity game for a test run with the networked functionality we've created so far. To do this we don't even need to have a network or multiple computers—we can test on a single machine. However, that being said, testing networked behavior does work a little differently to the norm, because the Unity Editor only allows us to preview and run one instance of our game at a time. This is problematic because our testing requires two separate instances of the game to be running simultaneously—one to be the server and one to be the client. Essentially: we'll need to build the game as a standalone executable, and run that outside the Editor while running a separate instance from within the Editor. To get started with this, select Edit ➤ Project Settings ➤ Player from the application menu, and make sure a check mark is inserted into the Run In Background check box (in the Object Inspector). See Figure 11-3. This check mark is important because it allows Unity applications to continue executing (instead of pausing) when input focus is moved away from the application window. This is important for networked games because servers need to be active and responsive to client requests, even when the server player or users might not be active in the game.

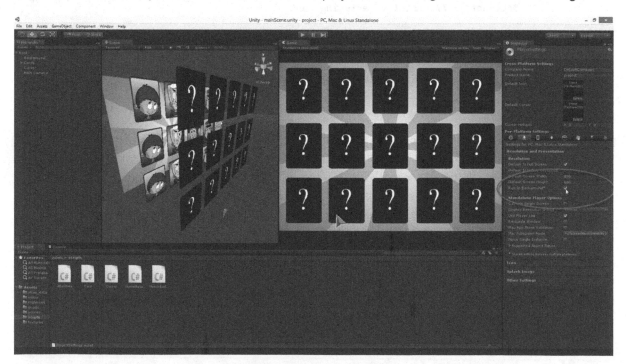

Figure 11-3. Enable Running In Background to prevent Unity applications from pausing when input focus is lost

Then select File ➤ Build Settings, and add the current scene to the Build List, and create a standalone build for your desktop platform (either Windows (exe) or Mac (app)). See Figure 11-4.

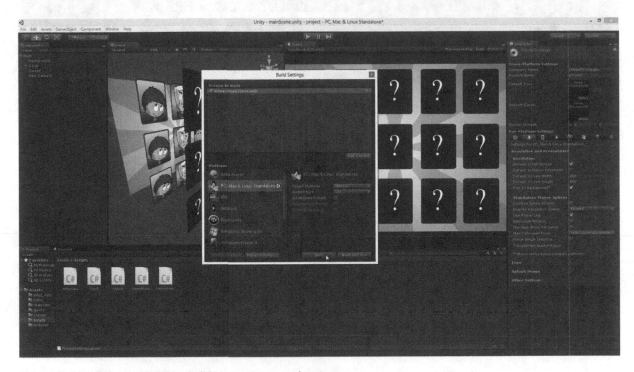

Figure 11-4. Creating a standalone build to run as a server instance

> **Note**   Linux is also a desktop build target, in addition to Windows and Mac, but currently there is no native Unity Editor available for Linux systems. Our network testing requires two instances to run on the same system, with one instance being in the Unity Editor to receive debug messages. However, if you want to use Linux as your development system, some users have managed to get the Unity Editor up and running with Ubuntu and Wine. You can find tutorials for this online; although take care when searching because, in the world of Ubuntu, "Unity" also refers to its GUI system!

Then finally to test networked functionality: run the standalone build (your server) in Windowed mode (not full-screen), and then run your (client) game from the Unity Editor. Remember, because of the way we coded the NetworkedGame class, the first instance you run acts as the server and the second acts as the client (see Figure 11-5). Of course, you don't have to run one instance of the game from the Editor—you can run two separate as standalone builds instead. But running one instance in the Editor allows you to easily benefit from debugging features and console logs while developing.

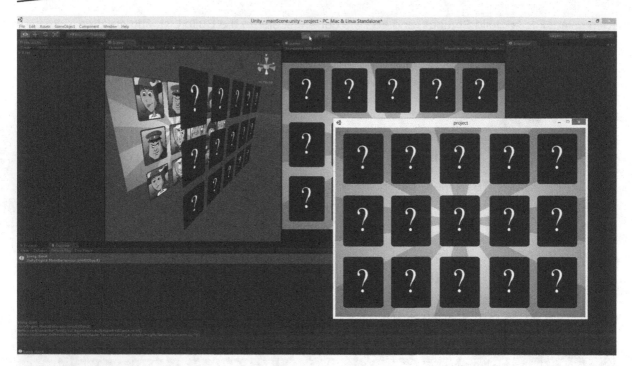

Figure 11-5. Testing networked functionality by running multiple instances on the same system. Notice the debug message printed in the console to confirm the server connection has been made

> **Note**   If you use a multi-monitor set-up, this is a great opportunity to put it to good use: running one instance in one monitor and another instance in the other.

When running the client from the editor you should see the appropriate debug messages printed to the console and also if you run the editor as the server. Seeing these messages confirms that the connection between client and server has been made, and it means we can continue developing the multi-player features for our game.

> **Note**   You may need to grant permission and exemption status to your game with your firewall and security software for networking to work correctly. Your gamers may also need to do this.

Network Views

Establishing a connection between the server and client is not the end of our work here, of course. The connection between the two is simply not enough to make our game multi-player and work as intended. In addition to making the connection, we still have to code exactly how the server and client should behave toward each other when connected. Because the server is to be authoritative, we must create a means whereby both computers (client and server) share a common reality. If the cards shuffle on the server system, for example, then they must not only shuffle on the client, but the shuffle must result in the same outcome on both computers; otherwise each player will use separate card grids! Additionally, we'll need each player to see what the other is doing: when one player reveals a card on the grid by removing its cover, the other player needs to see that. And finally, we'll need to synchronize player turns so each player can only pick a card during their own turn, and not during their opponent's turn. Creating this behavior will occupy us for the rest of this chapter: it'll be achieved using a combination of NetworkViews and RPCs (Remote Procedure Calls).

Let's start with Network Views. These allow Unity to automatically synch-up the cards so both players see the same thing and get the same card grid. To use Network Views, start by selecting all cards and card covers in the scene. Then, with them all selected, add a NetworkView component to them by choosing Component ➤ Miscellaneous ➤ Network View from the application menu (see Figure 11-6).

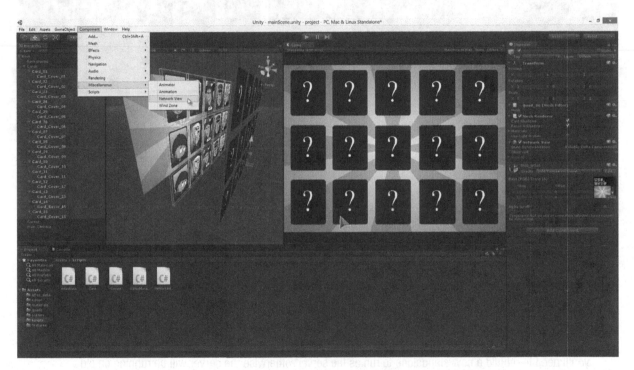

Figure 11-6. *Adding NetworkView components to the cards and card covers in the scene. This synchronizes or shares them between client and server*

> **Note** For more 'complex' games, with more players and objects to synchronize, you'll probably want to avoid using NetworkView for bandwith and performance reasons. Use this component sparingly. Instead, consider using alternative methods, such as Remote Procedure Calls (RPCs).

If you now select just one of the cards or card covers in the scene and examine its NetworkView component in the Object Inspector, you should see the value Reliable Data Compressed for the State Synchronization field, and a reference to the object's Transform component in the *Observed* field. If you don't, then change the values to reflect that. These two settings mean that the Transform component (and all its position, rotation, and scale values) will be shared between the server and client. You can prove this right now by running both the server and client instances side by side. By picking and revealing cards on the server, you'll see the change automatically reflected on the client (see Figure 11-7).

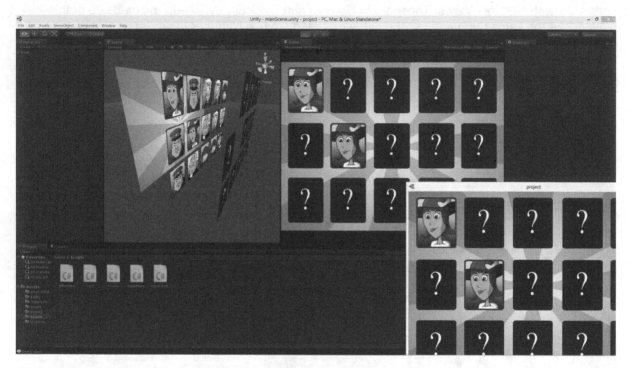

Figure 11-7. Synchronizing the card states from the server to the client

Tip   Because we've made a change to the project since the last standalone build in the previous section, you'll need to rebuild a new standalone to run as the server; otherwise the server will be running on old code. You'll need to apply this strategy every time you make a change to the project and want to test those changes.

Thanks to the NetworkView component we can now synchronize all the cards and card covers, from server to client. That means: when the state of the cards and covers change on the server, the client automatically updates to reflect the change. This behavior raises two issues that are worth noting here. First, the NetworkView components for the cards and covers are observing the Transform components of those objects: not any of the other components. This means that changes to the cards and covers on other components will not be synchronized between server and client.

Changes to other components happen only locally. You can, of course, add additional `NetworkView` components to fix this but doing so increases network bandwidth usage. This is why, in the previous chapter (see Listing 10-1), I coded the card hiding behavior by using the `Transform` component, to move the cards out of view from the camera, instead of disabling the `MeshRenderer` component. Updates to the `Transform` component are automatically shared, while updates to other components are not. Second, you'll notice that changes to the cards on the server will be reflected on the client, but the reverse is not true. Changes to the client cards do not affect the server: the synchronization is not bi-directional. That poses a problem for us because, right now, it's possible for the client player to reveal cards on the grid and so to bring their version of the game out of alignment with the server. So we'll fix that next.

Making an Authoritative Server

An authoritative server is one that has a monopoly on reality. It keeps track of what's happening in the game world and then tells the clients about it, and the clients have no choice but to accept what the server tells them because the server can never be wrong. The card game we've created does not (yet) conform to this set-up because clients can pick cards from the grid without the server ever knowing. What needs to happen to fix this problem is that all client requests to "do things" in the world must be routed through the server. The server will then do those things on behalf of the client, and then send back the result of the client's action so the client can update its version of the world to match the world of the server. Now, because the main game functionality happens inside the `GameManager` class, created in Chapter 10, we'll need to revisit that class and amend its code so that only the server can apply the game rules. To get started, open up the `GameManager.cs` source file in MonoDevelop: as shown in Figure 11-8.

Figure 11-8. Returning to the GameManager class

> **Note** Of course, when I say "the server can never be wrong" I don't mean errors and corruptions cannot happen because the server is truly infallible and everything it does is guaranteed to work just as you intended. I mean only: the server must be accepted by clients as infallible, as a matter of convention. This is what it means for a server to be authoritative.

First, when the game begins we'll want to disable all user input on both the server and the client. When the connection is established between the two players, and when play is ready to begin, we'll enable input for the server player only (to take their turn first), and then enable input on the client when the server grants permission after their turn is completed. From there, we'll repeatedly enable and disable input between the client and server, as the turn cycle requires. To create this kind of communication between server and client we'll need to use RPCs (Remote Procedure Calls).

An RPC is simply the ability for either the server or client to launch (run) a function on the other computer. To get started using RPCs, let's add a NetworkView Component to the root object of the scene, which also features a GameManager and NetworkedGame Component. To do that, select the Root object and choose Component ➤ Miscellaneous ➤ NetworkView from the application menu (see Figure 11-9). This time, however, we'll change the component's default settings. We'll do this because we don't need to observe the transform for the Root Object. The only reason we're adding a NetworkView in this case is because the component gives us a function we can easily call in script to run RPCs. So set the State Synchronization to Off, and choose None for the Observed field. In the next section we'll look at how to use RPCs.

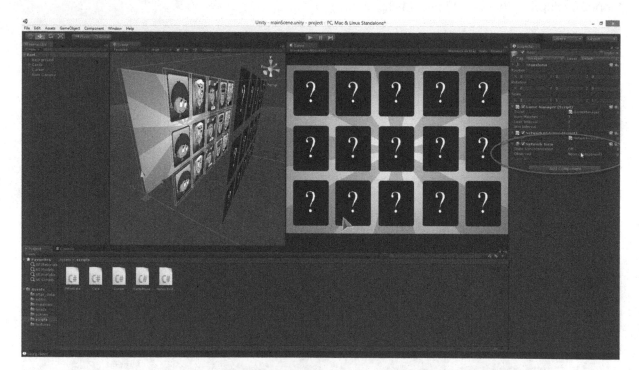

Figure 11-9. Adding a NetworkView Component to the Root object

Using RPCs

The aim of this section is to disable user input for both computers until a connection is established, after which the server needs control over when input is enabled and disabled on either system, to regulate turns. The GameManager class features an EnableInput function, given in Listing 11-4. This function does little more than set a Boolean flag and hides the mouse cursor. However, when the flag is false, this causes other functions in the class to ignore input.

Listing 11-4. GameManager.cs—EnableInput

```
//Function to enable/disable input
public void EnableInput(bool bEnabled = true)
{
    //Set input enabled flag and show/hide cursor graphic
    CursorRender.enabled = InputEnabled = bEnabled;
}
```

Let's amend our code so this function is called (and set to false) at application start to disable input for both client and server. Input should only be enabled (for the server) when a connection is established between both computers in the game. Listing 11-5 amends GameManager, and it achieves what we need.

Listing 11-5. GameManager.cs—Enabling Input for Server at Connection Time

```
//----------------------------------------
void Start()
{
    //Do all my other stuff here
    //[...]

    //Disable input
    EnableInput(false);
}
//----------------------------------------
//called when client successfully connects to server
void OnPlayerConnected()
{
    //If we are server, then Shuffle cards and enable input
    if(Network.isServer)
    {
        Shuffle();
        EnableInput(true);
    }
}
//----------------------------------------
```

Here the GameManager class now supports the OnPlayerConnected event, which is called automatically by Unity, on the server, whenever a client connects. There's also an equivalent MonoBehaviour.OnConnectedToServer event, which is called on the client when a connection is made to the server, but we don't need to use that. Here also, a check is made with Network.isClient to see whether we are the server. You can also use the Network.isServer flag too. In this sample the EnableInput function (in OnPlayerConnected) is called locally on the server and not on the client as an RPC.

> **Note**   Strictly speaking, we don't need to check Network.isServer or Network.isClient inside the function OnPlayerConnected. This is because OnPlayerConnected is only called on servers. But I like to include the check here: first, to show you that you can use the Network class to determine whether the running instance is a server or client. And second, because it's possible (through oversight) for a client to manually call the OnPlayerConnected event.

When the server player ends their turn however, we'll want to switch players—disabling input on the server and enabling input on the client. To do this, we'll use an RPC. To make any function an RPC, it should be prefixed with the [RPC] tag. Thus to make EnableInput an RPC, the function can be written as in Listing 11-6.

Listing 11-6. GameManager.cs—Creating an RPC Function

```
//Function to enable/disable input
[RPC]
public void EnableInput(bool bEnabled = true)
{
    //Set input enabled flag and show/hide cursor graphic
    CursorRender.enabled = InputEnabled = bEnabled;
}
```

Of course, marking a function with [RPC] does not implicitly call that function. We must call it manually using the NetworkView class. As a result, when the server player ends their turn, we can invoke the RPC EnableInput function on the client from the server using the code in Listing 11-7. This code is a ChangePlayer function, which switches between a client and server player.

Listing 11-7. GameManager.cs—Switching Players

```
//Change player
public void ChangePlayer(PLAYER_TYPE Type)
{
    //Make active
    ActivePlayer = Type;

    if(ActivePlayer == PLAYER_TYPE.SERVER_PLAYER)
    {
        EnableInput(true); //Called locally

        //Called on client
        networkView.RPC("EnableInput", RPCMode.OthersBuffered, false);
        return;
    }
```

```
    if(ActivePlayer == PLAYER_TYPE.CLIENT_PLAYER)
    {
        EnableInput(false); //Called locally

        //Called on client
        networkView.RPC("EnableInput", RPCMode.OthersBuffered, true);
        return;
    }
}
```

In Listing 11-7 the RPC is made on the client from the server using the RPC method. This method accepts a function name as an argument, plus a parameter list. It also accepts an RPCMode enumeration value, which is documented more fully at: http://docs.unity3d.com/Documentation/ScriptReference/RPCMode.html. In short, the RPC mode chooses who is to receive the function call. OthersBuffered means that all other players (except the sender, which is the server in this case) will receive the call; even clients who connect after the call was originally sent, because the call is buffered. For our game, being two-players, there will be no other players joining. But buffered calls could prove useful for your own games: try them out!

RPCs from Client to Server

The client can also invoke RPCs on the server—although a client can never invoke an RPC on another connected client unless it's indirectly through the server. For the card game, our clients should be lightweight. Their chief purpose is to receive input from the player, and then pass on that input to the server where it's processed and used to update the game world, and then passed back to the client through the NetworkView classes. However, this configuration means that the client must receive input and update the server—it must send as well as receive data. It can do this using RPCs, and it calls them on the server in exactly the same way a server calls them on the client, using the NetworkView.RPC method. See Listing 11-8 for the UpdateCardStatus function where a client calls a RPC on the server. This function is called from the GameManager.HandleInput method, which is a function that processes user input (when it's enabled) to see which card the player clicked on during their turn. The complete source code and project for this game can be found in the companion files associated with this chapter at: Project_Files/Chapter11/.

Listing 11-8. GameManager.cs—Sending RPCs to the Server

```
//Changes State of Selected Card (CardObject)
//Called when user picks a card from grid
public void UpdateCardStatus(GameObject CardObject, Card.CARD_STATE State)
{
    //If client then send data to server
    if(Network.isClient)
    {
        object[] Args = new object[2];
        Args[0]=CardObject.name;
        Args[1]=(int)State;

        networkView.RPC("UpdateCardStatus",RPCMode.OthersBuffered, Args);
    }
```

```
    else //Update Directly - no need for RPC; we are server
    CardObject.SendMessage("SetCardState", State, SendMessageOptions.DontRequireReceiver);
}
```

//--

Although the code listed here doesn't represent the full code for the associated project, it nonetheless presents everything you need to know about networking to get the turn-based functionality between client and server up and running. By using Network Views and RPCs alone, you can configure relationships between servers and clients that support more or less any kind of networked behavior you need.

Summary

Congratulations! In reaching this point, you've just coded a fully functional 2D multi-player game in Unity. If you haven't already, I recommend taking a look at my effort in the companion files for this chapter. Despite the semblance of simplicity, this project nonetheless relies on a wide range of Unity's features—even some of the more obscure and undocumented ones—and it makes use of practically everything we've covered so far in this book. In Chapter 12 we'll take a more in-depth look at a range of isolated topics, some of which we've touched on already, and see what more can be said about them in terms of optimization and configuration. For now, let's recap what we've seen here. By now, you should be able to:

- Understand the concepts *client* and *server*

- Understand how the Network, NetworkView, and MasterServer classes relate

- Establish a server

- Register a game with the MasterServer

- Poll the MasterServer for a list of hosted games

- Connect to a game as a client

- Understand how to use the NetworkView component to synch data between client and server

- Understand the authoritative server model

- Use remote procedure calls (RPCs)

Optimization

This chapter looks at optimization; specifically performance optimization. That is, we'll explore practical techniques you can use when making games in Unity to help them run well (or better) across different devices and hardware, including mobile devices. These techniques are presented in a list throughout this chapter, with sub-headings to organize them. They are presented in no particular order (least of all in order of importance), and some of them are related and some not. But regardless, all of them are typically important considerations for optimization—and they're likely to be things you'll consider at some point during development, regardless of whether they ultimately turn out to be the right solutions or approaches for you and your circumstances. Before getting started, however, it's worthwhile for me to say a little about optimization generally, as it applies to Unity games and also beyond. So let's start there.

Optimization—What Is It?

The term "optimization" has been around in the games industry as part of its jargon for longer than I've been a developer. It's not a new concept or idea at all, generally speaking. Its details and manifestations have changed over time and with hardware, but its basic principles remain: Optimization is about making your game perform as best as it can, with the resources it has, across all your target platforms. However, despite the concept's age and the acknowledged importance of its aim, it's frequently underestimated. Specifically, three issues commonly arise.

First, somehow, without clearly seeing why, it's tempting to think that optimization is something you do only when your game is reaching completion; as though it's a technical polish or surface gloss you apply to smooth out a rough core or foundation. Often, many developers create their game *first* without regard to optimization, complete with graphics and animation, and then finally ask the question: "How can I *now* make this game run better?" This approach is often a recipe for disaster and frustration, and many developers discover this the hard way. In short, if you want your game development experience to be as smooth and easy-going as possible, then I recommend making optimization a consideration *from the outset*. I recommend designing optimization into the foundation of your game: before you start coding and even before you start making art assets—especially 3D meshes. If you design with optimization in mind, you'll find that game development becomes easier.

Second, even when the importance of optimization is understood, it's tempting to see it as a "one size fits all" technique- as though all games can be optimized or enhanced using the same approach. This is not true, however. Optimization is game-specific. It can be thought of as a balancing act. The idea is to identify all the specific *areas* in your game where opportunities exist to reduce its computational expense so far as possible and economical, without fundamentally comprising *your* artistic vision. Sometimes optimizations require lots of hard work and planning; and sometimes quite amazing optimizations can be made by making only the simplest of adjustments. But this all depends on the details of your game. This means that I cannot tell you how *you* should optimize *your* game. All I can realistically do in a chapter such as this is highlight a number of general techniques and principles that many find helpful for optimization, as well as explain why they are supposed to be helpful, so that you can apply that knowledge to reach judgements for tailoring optimizations in your own projects.

Third, a relatively new view is that optimization is something that only applies to mobile devices. Now while it's true that mobile devices, often more limited in power than desktop and console counterparts, are especially sensitive to optimizations, and it's also true that optimization need not end here. All computer hardware is finite in its capacities and resources (mobile or not), while imagination and creative vision is not in the same way limited or restricted. This means that whenever you try to put your imagination into a game that must run on a computer, there's always the danger that it will exceed or stress the hardware if optimization is not kept in mind. Therefore, I recommend thinking of optimization as something that applies to all games on all computers. Think of optimization as something that all games need.

It's my view that the three attitudes or views listed here are actually the greatest obstacles to optimization—more so than any of the technical specifics given in the rest of this chapter. Once you avoid the three preceding traps and respect the importance of optimization (once you see development through the eyes of an optimizer), then you're already well on your way to creating optimized games. So with that said, I'll now present you with my list of optimization tips. Many of these tips are already discussed in more depth in the Unity Documentation (see the following note for a link). However, in this chapter I'll discuss the subject in more general and explanatory terms.

> **Note**   More information on optimization techniques can be found at:
> `http://docs.unity3d.com/Documentation/Manual/iphone-PracticalGuide.html`

Tip #1—Minimize Vertex Count

The famous adage "less is more" frequently applies to optimization for Unity games, especially when it comes to meshes. Each and every mesh in your scene—whether 2D or 3D—is composed from vertices. These are control objects that help a mesh maintain its shape and form. In theory, the more vertices a mesh has the more detail it has. But more detailed meshes are computationally more expensive than less detailed meshes, because the CPU and GPU have more information to process. If your game has very few meshes or very few vertices in total then it's likely you'll never experience a problem. But this is not the way most games work—most games feature lots of meshes, and sometimes very detailed meshes. The Unity renderer has lots of techniques and optimizations built in to draw meshes quickly and efficiently across different devices, but you can really help that renderer do its work even more efficiently if you reduce the vertices in your meshes so far as possible, ensuring (as always) that you don't compromise on your artistic vision. Figure 12-1 shows how you can read the current vertex and triangle count for the active camera on the Stats panel. Note that the Stats panel displays the number of triangles and vertices *currently being rendered*—and not the *total* number of vertices and triangles actually in the scene, which will often be more because the camera usually does not see the entire scene at once.

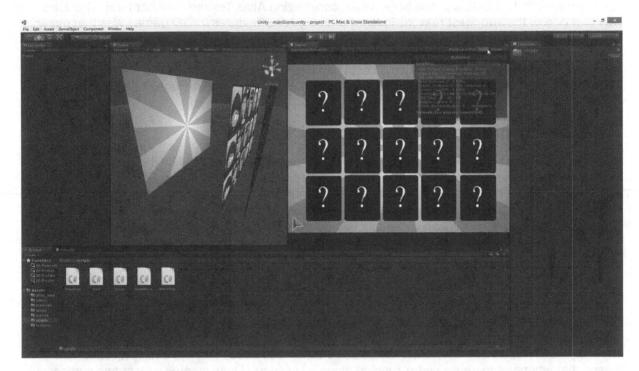

Figure 12-1. *The Stats Panel can be helpful in assessing run-time performance: measuring vertex and triangle count; as well as draw calls*

You might think that vertex and triangle count shouldn't be an issue for 2D games, because most of them use only "simple" quad planes to show billboard sprites. However, it can become an issue, typically for tile-based 2D games. That is, for games (such as top-down RPGs) that use layered, square-tiles to compose the terrain and geometry for an expansive level or map. Such games often use 1 quad for each tile—and some levels can even be 4000×4000 tiles. This means: always be on the look-out for reducing vertices in your meshes. So, how many vertices is too many? The answer is: however many prevent your game from working well. In combination with other confounding factors, such as complex shaders or textures or materials, this number could range from 3 vertices to even 300k. In practice: always test on the minimum-specification devices that you're aiming for. See how your game runs on them during debugging. If it runs poorly, and if you reasonably suspect it's due to the vertex count, then reduce mesh vertices and test again.

Note   More information on mesh optimization can be found here:
`http://docs.unity3d.com/Documentation/Manual/OptimizingGraphicsPerformance.html`

Tip #2—Minimize Materials

Unity allows you to create as many materials as you need for your meshes and objects and you can even assign multiple materials to the same mesh. Using materials comes at a performance cost, however, in terms of draw calls and draw calls are relatively expensive on any platform. This issue has been touched on before in this book, when considering Atlas Textures in Chapter 6. There we saw that one of the strongest reasons in favor of using Atlas Textures for 2D games was that many objects could share the same texture and material. Sharing materials in this way between objects allows the Unity renderer to internally batch those objects into the same draw call, and this typically improves on performance than if those objects had been drawn in separate calls. The upshot of this is that performance can be improved whenever two or more objects can share the same material.

Tip #3—Minimize UV Seams

Many 3D modelling programs, such as Maya and Blender, allow users to view the vertex count of their meshes when modelling. Unity users are often surprised to find that their meshes, when imported, are listed as having significantly higher counts than the ones listed in the modelling software. It seems that, after importing a mesh into Unity, its vertex count increases. Why is this? The answer lies primarily in Mesh UV seams (although other kinds of seams cause this too: such as sharp edges and smoothing groups). A UV seam marks one or more edges in the mesh where its texture mapping is split or broken intentionally by the artist. To encode where seams run in a mesh, the data is encoded into the vertices through UV mapping (see Figure 12-2). Practically every mesh must have three or more seams to allow its texture to tile and flow properly over its surface, avoiding distortion and artefacts. During the modelling and texturing of a mesh, the artist makes aesthetic and technical judgements about where the seams (or cuts) should be placed. Most 3D modelling programs take these seams into account when calculating the vertex count for a mesh, but Unity does not do this. Instead, Unity doubles-up on all vertices running a long a seam. This means that wherever there's a vertex running along a UV seam, Unity creates a least two vertices: one vertex to encode each side of the UV seam. The result is that UV seams increase the vertex count of the mesh. Now, because we've already established that minimizing mesh vertices is to be recommended, we can also establish that minimizing UV seams is to be recommended. Thus: when creating meshes, use as few seams as possible. There is, however, at least one exception to this rule regarding texture usage, which is discussed in the Note that follows.

Figure 12-2. UV mapping a cube in Blender, creating the seams for unwrapping

Note   When it comes to showing vertex counts between Unity and 3D modelling software, there's often a discrepancy. The reason is because 3D modelling software typically displays the number of vertices you actually see in the viewport to construct the model. But the Unity count includes the number of vertices used internally, in an Index Buffer, to render the model correctly when working with graphics hardware.

Tip #4—Recycle Texture Space by Overlapping UVs

One of the understated gems of optimization is the recycling of texture space through overlapping UVs in the mesh. Textures can be large and leave a heavy memory footprint, if not managed carefully. For this reason, it's advisable to keep textures as small as possible in terms of pixel dimensions. But doing this ultimately means you're reducing the resolution and detail of textures on meshes in the scene. However, by using this in combination with *increasing* UV seams in meshes, it becomes possible to overlap mesh UVs in texture space so that different parts of the same mesh map to the same group of pixels in the texture (see Figure 12-3).Here, a symmetrical corridor mesh has been cut directly through the center with a straight UV seam. This increases the mesh vertex count in Unity, true. But, it also means that both sides have their UVs mapped to the *same pixels* in the texture, effectively cutting the texture needs of this mesh in half. In this case, we no longer need space inside the texture to map each half separately. So optimization with regard to UVs frequently boils down to finding equilibrium, where the fewest UV seams are arranged to produce the greatest number of overlapping UVs. Again, this balance is (as always) supposed to be kept within reasonable limits: meaning that it's useful *to you* only as long as you're not compromising your artistic vision beyond what is acceptable *for you*; as long as your game is looking as it's supposed to look.

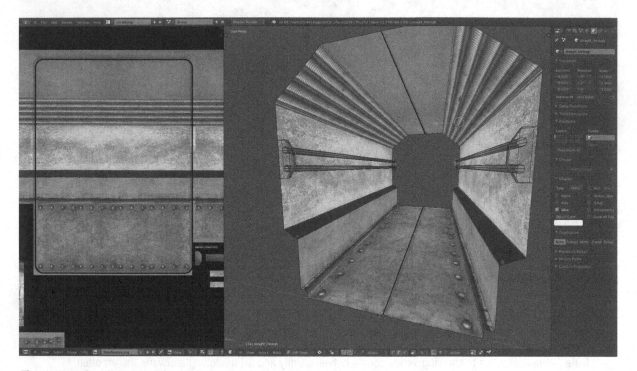

Figure 12-3. Creating overlapping UVs to economize on texture usage

Tip #5—Use Per-Platform Texture Settings

If you select a texture in the Unity Project Panel and examine its settings in the Object Inspector, you'll see its options regarding size and compression are customizable on a per-platform basis. This means you can adjust the size and compression of textures differently for each target platform: Windows, Mac, Android, iOS, and so on (see Figure 12-4).

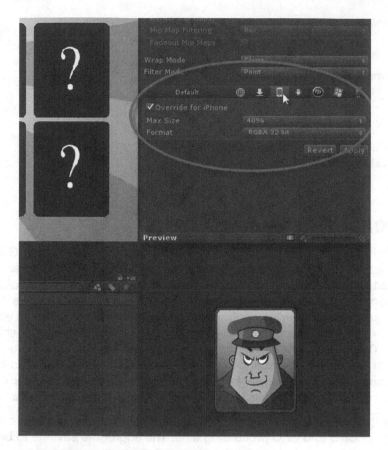

Figure 12-4. *Adjusting texture size and compression for each platform*

For texture compression on Android, the format *RGB* ETC is recommended, except for Alpha Textures. For iPhone, *PVRTC* is recommended. These settings can only be changed when the Texture *Type setting* is set to *Advanced*.

Tip #6—Cache Components and Objects

One of the most common C# scripted statements when working with the Unity API, is this.transform, or just transform. This statement (and others like it, such as audio) accesses a C# property, which returns a reference to the transform component of an object. From this, you can directly set the GameObject's position, orientation, and scale. However, accessing the transform component in this way indirectly calls on additional functionality that can have an accumulative impact on performance, if called enough times in events, such as Update or OnGUI. You can optimize such expressions from the outset, however, by using Object Caching. That is, by getting a reference to the component or object, and by storing it in a local variable. Listing 12-1 gives an example of object caching at work.

Listing 12-1. Object Caching

```
void Awake()
{
    //Cache Transform (MyTransform is a class variable)
    MyTransform = transform;
}

void Update(){
    //Update position using cached transform
    MyTransform.localPosition = MyPosition;
}
```

Tip #7—Avoid Using Update

The Update function is called once per frame on every component for every active GameObject in the scene. And this is not the only function called frequently—there's also LateUpdate and FixedUpdate. These functions are typically used to update game behavior and events that must change over time. However, the frequency of these functions has the potential to make them a source of performance nightmares. Consequently, use them sparingly. Begin to see them as places where you put code only if you really have no other sensible options. For example: if you have enemies that should die when their health reaches 0 or below, after taking damage from player weapons, then you don't need to use Update. It may at first sight seem necessary: to check enemy health, every frame, to initiate a death sequence when appropriate. But, because you already know that enemies take damage *only* when the player attacks them, you only need to check enemy health after the player performs an attack.

In short, by arranging your code to be *event-driven* insofar as possible, as opposed to *frame-driven*, you can free up lots of CPU and GPU processing time. The aggregate savings to be made here can be impressive.

Tip #8—Minimize Colliders

Some meshes come with Collider Components by default. But if a mesh has no collider, then one can be added from the main menu by choosing **GameObject ➤ Physics** (see Figure 12-5). Colliders are physics-based components that internally use a simplified mesh to approximate the volume of an object. The purpose is to facilitate fast and effective collision detection between objects so that you know when collisions happen and can prevent solids from passing through other solids, to simulate real-world behavior. Calculating this, as well as other physics based interactions, is performance intensive. To alleviate this problem, it's recommended to remove any and all collider components from the scene that are unnecessary—that is, colliders on objects for which you don't need collision detection or physics based reactions. This may include: GUI objects, particles, ceiling props, distant mountains, and other objects which the player never touches.

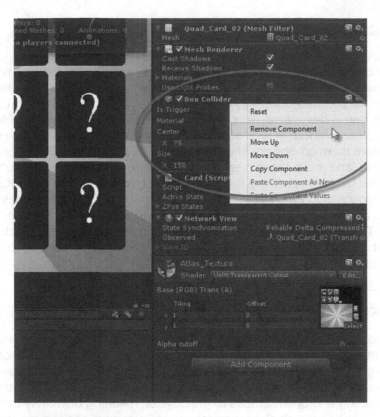

Figure 12-5. Removing a Collider Component from an object

However, even in cases where an object needs a collider, typically further optimizations can be made. For example: a mesh collider is more expensive than any other primitive collider, such as a box or sphere collider. This is because a mesh collider typically involves many more vertices and shapes. So, if you can adequately use a box collider instead of a mesh collider to approximate the volume of an object, then do it.

Tip #9—Avoid OnGUI and the GUI class

The OnGUI function and the GUI class can be two of the biggest drains on performance, especially for mobile games. OnGUI is expensive primarily because it's called multiple times *per frame*. This means you almost never use it to perform game-logic or core functionality—the purpose of OnGUI is exclusively for drawing GUI elements. The GUI class can work well for smaller and simpler interfaces, but should really be avoided for complex interfaces with many interactive elements, such as inventories, statistic panels, mini-maps, option screens, and type-in dialogs. I've almost never seen high-performance come from the default GUI class when implementing more feature-filled GUIs. To implement these, Unity offers very little native support. At the time of writing there are two main and popular solutions to this: either a custom solution is developed, using Atlas Textures and Quads (as we've seen throughout this book), or a third-party add-on must be purchased, such as NGUI or EZGUI.

Tip #10—Use Object Pooling

Imagine this: the player character is firing a fast-reload weapon (such as a chain gun) and each shot spawns a new bullet into the level. The fire-rate for this weapon means that two bullets are generated per second. Assuming the bullet object is created in the project as a prefab, how should the bullet generation be scripted? One way to handle this is to call the Instantiate function for each bullet, whenever the gun is being fired. This method might be called "Dynamic Object Creation." However, there's another method: at level start-up you could generate a large batch of bullets (perhaps 30), and store them off-screen. Then, whenever the player fires a weapon, you would continually show, hide, and move these pregenerated bullets, as required, to *simulate* bullets being spawned, as opposed to really spawning them. This latter method is known as Object Pooling. In general, Object Pooling is to be preferred over Dynamic Object Creation because it avoids the performance issues that sometimes comes from dynamic memory allocation, especially on mobile operating systems. The upshot of this is: avoid instantiating and destroying objects dynamically. Instead: generate objects at level start-up, and then show and hide as required to simulate object destruction and creation.

Tip #11—Use Static Batching

If you have Unity Pro, and if you know that one or more game objects never moves during game play, then mark them as Static using the Static check box at the top-right corner of the Object Inspector (see Figure 12-6). This typically applies to scene terrain, architecture, and other material props, such as walls and windows, and tables, and lamp posts. Enabling the Static check box forces Unity to perform batching and optimizations to the objects, meaning ultimately that it can render them in fewer draw calls and thereby boost performance. In summary, ticking a check box on a GUI is a really easy thing to do. So, if you're experiencing performance problems pertaining to rendering overhead, then make sure you've ticked that box for all static objects.

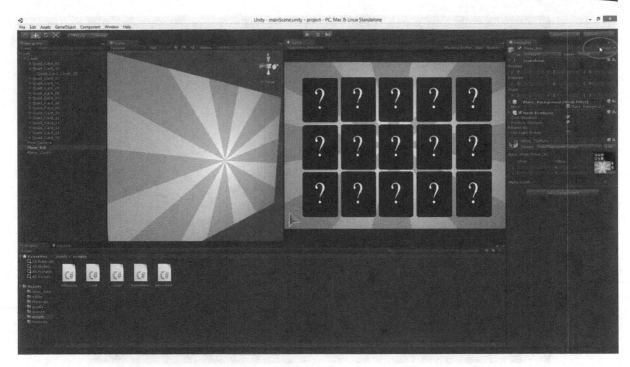

Figure 12-6. Enable static batching for non-moving scene objects

Tip #12—Utilize Skyboxes

A Skybox is a light-immune cube with inverted normals that is always positioned and aligned so the camera is at its center. This means the camera will always render the interior faces of the Skybox. Because of this, cubic panoramas may be textured onto it to simulate a surrounding and distant environment. Consequently, Skyboxes give you the power to simulate distant and unreachable details in the world without having to use meshes, shaders, or complex materials. Some people only ever use Skyboxes to create a sky. Sometimes this is concerted and artistic decision, but sometimes it's because the designer sees no other way to use them. But with Skyboxes you can simulate space environments with many stars and planets, or distant mountain landscapes. And you can even layer and animate them to create parallax effects, as well as project videos onto them. For readers who are interested, my game Baron Wittard (http://www.wittardgame.com/) makes extensive use of Skyboxes (see Figure 12-7). In any case, the benefit offered by Skyboxes is that they really can save you from making lots of distant details and from using extra meshes and complexity. If you get creative with Skyboxes, you can make some amazing performance savings.

Figure 12-7.   Baron Wittard by Wax Lyrical Games. This scene is around 60% Skybox!

Tip #13—Avoid Dynamic Lights and Shadows

Dynamic lighting refers to any light that is calculated in real-time, as opposed to being baked into the level through light-mapping or light-probes. Dynamic lights are computationally expensive, and shadows cast from dynamic lights are even more expensive- perhaps one of the most expensive real-time computations. Consequently, if you're experiencing performance issues pertaining to rendering, then I recommend disabling real-time lighting and shadows as a first-step, even if it is only to ascertain what the performance might otherwise be so as to make an informed judgement about where optimizations can be made. Unity 4 Pro does offer some support for real-time shadows on mobile devices, but I strongly recommend using them sparingly.

Tip   If you're experiencing performance problems while using real-time lights, trying switching the Light Type (in the Object Inspector) from *Important* to *Non-Important*. I appreciate that all lights are probably important to you, but this is simply the name Unity uses to mark the distinction between Pixel-based and Vertex-based lighting respectively.

Tip #14—Bake It; Don't Simulate It

In video games, the word "bake" refers to precalculation. That is, bake refers to generating something in advance to make it look as though it's happening or exists in real-time. Light-mapping, for example, is about baking a set of textures with lighting information at *design-time* to make your level appear illuminated by lights at *run-time*. However, light-mapping is not the only area where baking is used. Depending on your game and requirements it's possible to bake path-finding data, collision data, artificial intelligence, animations, and more. Baking data ahead of time in this way can save a lot of real-time processing, though typically at the expense of a larger memory footprint. More often than not, however, this is a price worth paying.

Summary

This chapter is structured differently from the others in that it reads more as a list of tips and tricks than as a structured course or tutorial. This is intentional and necessary because there is no right or wrong path to optimization. There is no one-size-fits-all solution for optimizing games. Optimization is game-specific and this chapter has highlighted some of the core elements involved in improving the performance of your games with Unity. You may notice that one word, above all others, repeats itself throughout this chapter (apart from the word 'optimization'). That word is "minimize." Minimize stands for reduction, for slimming-down and cutting-off excess and wastage. It means simplification and making things lighter. These are the primary characteristics of optimization. By now you should:

- Understand what optimization is and its importance
- Understand the importance of finding a balance between optimization and achieving your creative vision
- Be able to see development with the eyes of an optimizer
- Understand that optimization is a design consideration
- Appreciate that optimization is game-specific
- Understand some general principles regarding optimization
- Appreciate that optimization applies across devices
- Be able to make informed decisions on optimization

Chapter 13

Wrapping Things Up

Congratulations on reaching this chapter—you should now be in a strong position to create 2D games in Unity (even if you're using the free version). The techniques I've demonstrated here work both with Unity Free and Unity Pro. Of course, what's been presented in this book, however, should not be seen as the end of the line for 2D game development. It should be seen less as an ending point and more as a starting point. No book, no matter how large, could say everything there ever was to know about 2D game development. The subject of 2D games is simply too large to encompass and discuss in its entirety. For this reason, there's inevitably a lot this book leaves unsaid or untouched. The purpose of this book has not been to cover all aspects of 2D development, but rather to examine a foundation or core that underpins all 2D games. By learning and understanding this core, and a general 2D work-flow, you're now in a position of greater power and independence. This is because, whatever kind of 2D game you want to make and whatever kind of challenges it throws at you, you now know the fundamentals of how to draw, process and handle 2D graphics with Unity in a way that's optimal.

What I want to do here, in this closing chapter, is discuss briefly some aspects about 2D games that this book didn't cover. In doing this, I'll offer some advice as to how you may approach those tasks, or at least how to find out more about them.

GUIs and Resolution

2D games are often rendered using orthographic cameras, as we've seen. Doing this means our graphics can look in-game as they do in Photoshop or GIMP. The graphics are drawn in 2D screen space and are measured in terms of pixels. This applies both to our game graphics and our GUI graphics. This however presents an interesting problem to which, even today, there's no single or agreed solution. The problem is this: if your graphics are fixed in terms of pixel positions and dimensions, then they are *resolution dependent*. So, if you create an interface with buttons and widgets positioned within an 800×600 pixel region, how will that interface look at a different resolution, such as 1920×1080? How should an 800×600 interface be shown at different resolutions?

These questions highlight a problem that is especially felt today when games are developed for an increasing variety of devices, including mobile devices, some of which don't even allow you to change screen resolution. This means your games must "look correct" across a wider range of resolutions if they are to successfully reach wider audiences.

One solution to this problem is simply to scale your original graphics to fit whatever resolution is active or specified on the system. Although this solution works, and is sometimes used, it can never really be a satisfactory solution for someone who genuinely wants to support the widest resolutions possible and also have their graphics displayed at the highest quality. This is because it neglects to consider the potential differences in aspect ratio between resolutions. If an 800×600 interface is scaled non-uniformly to fit an 1920×1080 resolution, then not only will your graphics up-scale but they'll be stretched out of proportion to appear wider than they are tall.

Another solution is simply to create different versions of your graphics for different resolutions: one version for each resolution. This is, in many respects, the "ideal" solution insofar as it gives you the greatest control over how your graphics will look at every resolution. But it's not without its limitations: it involves at lot of extra asset-creation work! True, you can mitigate some of this by using vector art applications (which creates graphics that infinitely scale to different sizes) to create your original art work. But even so, this solution inevitably increases the resource footprint of your game.

An alternative solution, and one that is common, is to develop a relative-positioning and anchoring system—the kind that has been used in web development for a long time. In short, with this method, you design perhaps two or three versions of your interface (a smaller version for mobile phones, a medium version for tablets and notebooks, and a larger version for desktop PCs, consoles, and TVs), and then you position all GUI components, not in terms of absolute screen pixels but in relative and normalized terms (where 0.5 represents screen center). By specifying positions in relation to screen size (width and height), you create elements that auto-position and adjust to fit the display at any size.

If you're interested in creating resolution independent GUIs, I recommend taking a look at the NGUI add-on for Unity, which can be found here at `http://www.tasharen.com/?page_id=140`.

Tiles and Tile-sets

Many 2D games feature tile-sets, including RTS games, RPG games, and even side-scrolling platform games. A tile-set refers to a texture filled with smaller square images, arranged in rows and columns. By selecting images and painting with images from the set, designers can create worlds. They do this by arranging the tiles into different configurations (see Figure 13-1). The possibilities are endless with tile-sets in terms of the environments and levels you can make.

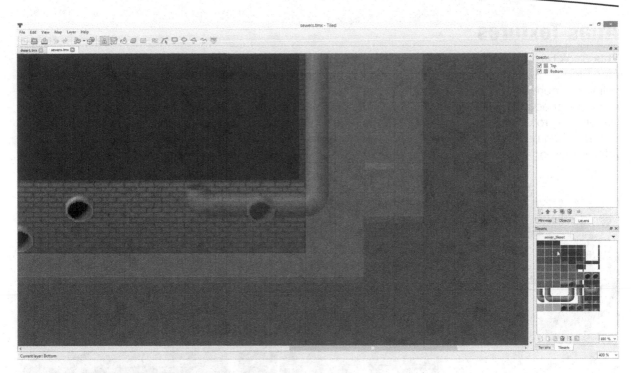

Figure 13-1. Creating levels from tile-sets using the Tiled tile editor

Unity, however, doesn't ship with any native tile editor. This means there's no out of the box support for creating 2D levels from tile-sets. Even so, there're ways to implement or support this functionality. In addition to creating your own solution, there're tools already out there, specifically:

- ■ **Tiled** is a free and cross-platform tile editor that is available on Windows, Linux, and Mac. Using this software (as shown in Figure 13-1) you can import and configure tile-sets, and also use the level editor to create environments from tile-sets. In addition, there are third-party scripts and tools available to import Tiled data into Unity. The Tiled editor can be downloaded from http://www.mapeditor.org/. More information on integrating Tiled with Unity can be found at https://github.com/bjorn/tiled/wiki/Support-for-TMX-maps.

- ■ **UniTile** is a commercial and built-in Unity tile editor system. It works similar to Tiled, except it's integrated into the Unity Editor. For more information, see http://www.mudloop.com/unitile.

- ■ **2D Toolkit** offers not only an integrated tile-set solution for Unity, but also a wider 2D toolset, including sprites and 2D collisions. More information can be found here at http://www.unikronsoftware.com/2dtoolkit/.

- ■ **RotorZ Tile System**, unlike the previous entries, is both a 2D and 3D tile system—you can create tiles in either dimension. More information can be found here at http://rotorz.com/tilesystem/.

- ■ **Tidy Tile Mapper** is a 2D and 3D tile mapping system that allows for runtime edits and level streaming. See http://u3d.as/content/doppler-interactive/tidy-tile-mapper/2AF for more information.

Atlas Textures

This book has covered the process of generating Atlas Textures from code via an editor plugin (see Figure 13-2). While this atlas generator is functional and suitable for most purposes, some users will want more control over the positioning, alignment, and arranging of textures within the atlas to optimize space usage. In addition, it's also useful to be able to tweak and edit the atlas after it is generated. To achieve this you could further expand on and refine the code presented in this book, or you could use the TexturePacker software, which is designed for creating Texture Atlases. More information on this software can be found here at `http://www.codeandweb.com/texturepacker`.

Figure 13-2. Generating Atlas Textures using the custom atlas generator created in this book

Fonts

If your game needs to render text for showing scores, names, and other alphabetical or numerical data, then you *can* use the native `GUI.Label` function. But, typically this function is performance prohibitive and doesn't always offer the flexibility developers need for text. In these cases, you'll probably need to use bitmap-based fonts. These are Atlas Textures featuring every alphanumeric character needed, arranged in rows and columns. Your game shows its text by simply UV mapping quads with the appropriate parts of the texture sheet. You can generate the font texture atlases manually like any regular Atlas Texture, but there are tools available for automating and simplifying the process. These are listed here:

- **BMFont**—http://www.angelcode.com/products/bmfont/
- **BMGlyph**—http://www.bmglyph.com/

Unity Alternatives

If you've reached this far in the book and concluded that Unity 2D game development isn't for you, or if you simply want to know the options available to you, then you may be interested in some alternative engines or APIs you can use for 2D games instead of Unity. Here is a list of some popular tools and frameworks in the contemporary games industry. Some are complete integrated engines, which include level editors and scripting environments, and others are programming libraries and interfaces intended to work with your existing tool sets.

Engines

Below is a list of game engine alternatives including links to their home pages:

- **Gamemaker Studio**—http://www.yoyogames.com/studio
- **RPG Maker**—http://www.rpgmakerweb.com/
- **Stencyl**—http://www.stencyl.com/
- **Construct2**—https://www.scirra.com/construct2
- **Torque2D**—http://www.garagegames.com/products/torque-2d
- **GameSalad**—http://gamesalad.com/
- **Novashell**—http://www.rtsoft.com/novashell/
- **Starling**—http://gamua.com/starling/

Libraries and APIs

Below is a list of game libraries that can be used for building a 2D game engine:

- **Love2D**—https://love2d.org/
- **Cocos2D**—http://cocos2d.org/
- **Pygame**—http://www.pygame.org/
- **SDL**—http://www.libsdl.org/
- **Clanlib**—http://www.clanlib.org/
- **Gosu**—http://www.libgosu.org/

Asset Creation

Creating graphics, animations, and sounds for your games is the largest part of the asset creation process, whether you're making 2D or 3D games. It can be time consuming and hard work. There are however a range of content-creation software and tools available to make the asset-creation process smoother and easier than it would otherwise be. There are simply too many content creation tools to list them all here, but here are some of the most popular, along with their web links.

Image Editing Software

Below is a list of software packages that can be used for image editing:

- **Adobe Photoshop**—http://www.adobe.com/uk/products/photoshop.html
- **GIMP**—http://www.gimp.org/
- **Corel Painter**—http://goo.gl/4UUOyl
- **Krita**—http://krita.org/
- **MyPaint**—http://mypaint.intilinux.com/
- **PaintShop Pro**—http://goo.gl/HzyGhm

Vector Graphic Software

Below is a list of software packages that can be used for creating vector graphics:

- **Adobe Illustrator**—http://www.adobe.com/products/illustrator.html
- **Inkscape**—http://inkscape.org/

2D Animation Software

Below is a list of software packages that can be used for creating 2D animations:

- **Toon Boom Studio**—https://www.toonboom.com/
- **Anime Studio Pro**—http://anime.smithmicro.com/
- **Blender**—http://www.blender.org/
- **3DS Max**—http://www.autodesk.com/products/autodesk-3ds-max/
- **Maya**—http://www.autodesk.com/products/autodesk-maya/
- **Strata**—http://www.strata.com/

> **Note**   Blender, 3DS Max, Maya, and Strata are traditionally regarded as 3D modelling and animation software. However, using orthographic cameras, they can be used to create 2D graphics and animation.

Summary

In closing, I'd like to thank you for your time and attention throughout this book. I hope it has proved useful in many ways and has oriented you on the path toward 2D games. There are many routes to that destination even within the Unity software. This book highlights primarily just one route, but it's one that's tried and tested and known to work well for a range of games across a range of devices. This chapter has however emphasised possible routes to improvement as well as advice and tips on alternative methods, and also on some of the available content creation tools available for creating 2D assets. So, whatever you choose to create in 2D, I wish you every success in your projects.

Alan Thorn.

Index